T0305857

Macroeconomic Performance in a Globalising Economy

The process of globalisation has been ongoing for centuries, but few would doubt that it has accelerated and intensified in recent decades. This acceleration is evidenced as much by the strong synchronicity in the rapid transmission of financial crises starting in late 2007, as it is by the decade of almost unprecedented growth in international trade and financial market liberalisation that preceded it. This book shows how the international economy has become more connected via increased production, trade, capital flows and financial linkages. Using a variety of methodologies, including both panel econometrics and DSGE modelling, a team of experts from academia, central banks, the OECD and the IMF examine how this increased globalisation has affected competitiveness, productivity, inflation and the labour market.

This timely contribution to the globalisation literature provides a longer-term perspective while also evaluating some of the potential implications for policy makers, particularly from a European perspective.

ROBERT ANDERTON is Adviser in the External Developments Division of the European Central Bank and Professor in the School of Economics at the University of Nottingham. His current work involves analysing the external dimension of the euro area, the global economy and the impacts of globalisation on the macroeconomy.

GEOFF KENNY is Deputy Head of the in Econometric Modelling Division at the European Central Bank. In this capacity he has responsibility for the Division's macro-modelling and forecasting activities. He has previously lectured in economics at the Smurfit Graduate School of Business, University College Dublin and the National University of Ireland, Maynooth.

Macroeconomic Performance in a Globalising Economy

Edited by
Robert Anderton
Geoff Kenny

CAMBRIDGE UNIVERSITY PRESS

CAMBRIDGE
UNIVERSITY PRESS

University Printing House, Cambridge CB2 8BS, United Kingdom

One Liberty Plaza, 20th Floor, New York, NY 10006, USA

477 Williamstown Road, Port Melbourne, VIC 3207, Australia

314-321, 3rd Floor, Plot 3, Splendor Forum, Jasola District Centre, New Delhi - 110025, India

103 Penang Road, #05-06/07, Visioncrest Commercial, Singapore 238467

Cambridge University Press is part of the University of Cambridge.

It furthers the University's mission by disseminating knowledge in the pursuit of education, learning and research at the highest international levels of excellence.

www.cambridge.org
Information on this title: www.cambridge.org/9780521116695

First published 2011
First paperback edition 2016

A catalogue record for this publication is available from the British Library

Library of Congress Cataloging in Publication data
  Macroeconomic performance in a globalising economy / [edited by]
  Robert Anderton, Geoff Kenny.
    p. cm.
  ISBN 978-0-521-11669-5 (hardback)
  1. International trade.   2. International economic relations.
  3. International finance.   4. Monetary policy.   5. Globalization–
  Economic aspects.   6. Macroeconomics.   I. Anderton, Bob.
  II. Kenny, Geoff.   III. Title.
  HF1379.M337 2010
  382–dc22
  2010043681

ISBN   978-0-521-11669-5   Hardback
ISBN   978-1-316-60194-5   Paperback

Contents

Figures

x   List of figures

Tables

Contributors

ROBERT ANDERTON, Adviser in the External Developments Division, European Central Bank and Professor, School of Economics, University of Nottingham, UK.

CHRISTOPHER GUST, Federal Reserve Board, Washington, DC, USA.

PAUL HIEBERT, Principal Economist in the Euro Area Macroeconomic Developments Division, European Central Bank.

GEOFF KENNY, Deputy Head of Division, Econometric Modelling Division, European Central Bank.

ISABELL KOSKE, Structural Surveillance Division, OECD, Paris.

MICHAEL KUMHOF, International Monetary Fund, Washington, DC, USA.

DOUGLAS LAXTON, International Monetary Fund, Washington, DC, USA.

SYLVAIN LEDUC, Federal Reserve Bank, San Francisco, USA.

JAMES R. MARKUSEN, Professor, University of Colorado at Boulder, USA and Visiting Professor at University College Dublin, Ireland.

PHILIPPE MOUTOT, Deputy Director General, Directorate General Economics, European Central Bank.

KANDA NAKNOI, Purdue University, West Lafayette, USA.

NIGEL PAIN, Macroeconomic Policy Division, OECD, Paris.

GABOR PULA, Senior Economist in the International Policy Analysis Division, European Central Bank.

FRAUKE SKUDELNY, Senior Economist in the Euro Area Macroeconomic Developments Division, European Central Bank.

MARTE SOLLIE, Economics Department, OECD.

JÜRGEN STARK, Member of the Executive Board of the European Central Bank.

JOHN B. TAYLOR, Mary and Robert Raymond Professor of Economics at Stanford University and George P. Shultz, Senior Fellow at the Hoover Institution, Stanford, CA, USA.

ROBERT J. VIGFUSSON, Federal Reserve Board, Washington, DC, USA.

GIOVANNI VITALE, Senior Economist in the Monetary Policy Strategy Division, European Central Bank.

Foreword

Globalisation has been one of the most pervasive and important economic trends shaping the world economy over the last two and a half decades or so, leading to greater international economic interdependence across the globe on both the real and financial sides. This has affected a wide range of economic variables as well as providing significant challenges for policy makers. There is no doubt that globalisation has long-run benefits for both advanced and emerging economies through a more efficient resource allocation, along with welfare gains from deepening specialisation, increased competition, lower prices, greater product choice and ultimately higher living standards. Nevertheless, more recently, the increased interconnectedness of economies across the globe has also been associated with global financial turmoil and a highly synchronised global economic downturn.

This book is therefore a timely, as well as highly comprehensive, contribution to the globalisation literature, providing mostly a longer-term perspective while also touching on some of the elements and events associated with the financial crisis that began in mid 2007. The inspiration for this book was the ECB 2007 conference on Globalisation and the Macroeconomy. Hence this volume consists of papers presented at that conference as well as other research papers on this topic. Overall, the book tells us how the international economy has become more connected via increased production, trade, capital flows and financial linkages and how this has possibly affected competitiveness, productivity, inflation and labour markets, while also evaluating some of the potential implications for policy makers. In order to address these issues the papers in the book exploit a variety of methodologies, including both panel econometrics and DSGE modelling. The analysis covers globalisation's impacts in the service sector as well as the more traditional traded goods and manufacturing sectors. It therefore provides a detailed analysis of the major influences of globalisation on the euro area and other major economies. Some key questions investigated by the book are:

(1) How has the emergence of China as a global player in world export markets affected the competitiveness of the euro area?
(2) How might globalisation be affecting the labour market?
(3) Has globalisation changed the exchange-rate pass-through to import prices; and to what extent has globalisation influenced world commodity prices and inflation in advanced industrialised countries?
(4) How might developments in the exchange rate and other asset prices be considered as key variables for policy makers?
(5) How is monetary policy affected by an increasingly globalised economic environment?

The increased linkages due to globalisation seemed to be a major reason behind the strength of the global upturn of the 2000s, with exceptional growth in Asia – particularly China – helping to boost activity in the rest of the world. In particular, world trade grew strongly, partly because of the rapid growth in 'vertical specialisation' which created widespread global production chains. Meanwhile, international capital flows grew enormously, reflecting greater access to finance across the globe. By the same token, it seems that the increased international interconnectedness of financial and product markets contributed to the financial turmoil that began in mid 2007 as well as the mechanisms behind the subsequent highly synchronised downturn in global trade and activity.

In addition to documenting many of the above inter-linkages, a number of the associated policy implications are also addressed. In terms of monetary policy, there has been much debate about the possible increased role of global factors in the determination of inflation, and whether globalisation may have weakened the ability of central banks to control their domestic rate of inflation. Overall, the conclusion seems to be that globalisation has had effects on inflation in the shorter term, largely arising from relative price impacts and increased competition. Accordingly, it is necessary to actively monitor possible ongoing changes in the inflationary process resulting from globalisation. However, the bottom line continues to be that monetary policy ultimately determines the inflation rate over longer horizons. At the same time, the recent financial turmoil has also shown that globalisation has increased the degree of international financial interconnectedness, which has important implications for cross-border propagation of systemic risk, and thereby gives rise to an urgent need for greater international cooperation in the supervision and regulation of financial markets. In particular, macro-prudential financial supervision needs to be strengthened considerably to monitor and help prevent the propagation of systemic risk.

Another key policy message of this book relates to the continued need for structural reforms in the economies of the euro area countries. Flexible product and labour markets are increasingly necessary in order to cope with the challenges arising from globalisation and to speed up the adjustment process, thereby enhancing the ability of euro area firms to adjust efficiently to shocks and allow resources to move flexibly towards expanding sectors, as well as helping to improve competitiveness. At the same time, an efficient adjustment in response to the forces of globalisation will also be facilitated by focusing on price stability and continuing to anchor inflation expectations in the face of relative price shocks. Finally, against the background of the recent global downturn, protectionist pressures are rising in certain regions of the world. Given the large welfare loss that a rise in protectionism would cause, this calls for additional vigilance in resisting such pressures worldwide.

JÜRGEN STARK
Member of the Executive Board, European Central Bank

Acknowledgements

This volume takes much of its inspiration from a conference entitled 'Globalisation and the Macroeconomy' held at the European Central Bank in Frankfurt in the course of July 2007. The aim of the conference was to bring together researchers from central banks, the academic community and international organisations in a two-day meeting to present papers and discuss globalisation and its impacts on economic activity and inflation. The discussions were aimed at improving our understanding of the pace and changing characteristics of globalisation and at identifying the various channels through which it affects the macroeconomy as well as the associated implications for macroeconomic policy. Many of the insights gleaned from these exchanges are reflected in the various contributions to this volume. We would therefore like to thank the presenters of papers at the conference as well as their discussants and co-authors. We also offer a special thanks to our colleagues on the conference organising committee and other ECB colleagues who provided strong support for the project, in particular Luca Dedola, Filippo di Mauro, Katrin Foster, Paul Hiebert, Hans-Joachim Klöckers, Lucas Papademous, Gabor Pula, Jürgen Stark and Daria Taglioni. The conference also benefited greatly from outstanding administrative support from Joanna Steele and Anja Tonn, while Britta Bertram, Stephanie Brown and Claudia Sullivan-Sepúlveda have been very supportive in helping to put this volume together.

1 Globalisation and macroeconomic performance

Robert Anderton and Geoff Kenny

1.1 Introduction

The term 'globalisation' is generally accepted to refer to the process of steadily increasing interdependence of national economies via trade, production and financial market linkages. While this process has been ongoing for many centuries, few would doubt that it has accelerated and intensified in the last decades. This acceleration is evidenced as much by the strong synchronicity in the rapid transmission of financial crises starting in late 2007, and the subsequent global economic downturn, as by the decade of almost unprecedented growth in international trade and financial market liberalisation that preceded it.

Two key elements stand out as the driving forces behind this increased interdependence. First, the barriers to trade as well as the costs of transporting goods, services – including financial services – and information across the globe have been reduced considerably. This development has been inextricably linked to rapid advances in information and communication technology. Second, there has been a significant expansion in global economic activity linked to the opening up of emerging economies to international trade and production, notably the greater involvement of emerging Asia in world trade, as well as Central and Eastern Europe following the collapse of the Soviet Union. The economic globalisation brought about by these changes has been one of the major trends shaping the world economy over recent years. On the real side, international trade has expanded substantially, with the emerging Asian economies in general – and China in particular – taking a prominent role. Global trade openness – measured as world imports and exports of goods and services as a share of world GDP – has practically doubled over the last two decades, from 33.9 per cent of world GDP in 1986 to 60 per cent of world GDP in 2006. On the financial

The views expressed in this chapter are those of the authors only and do not necessarily reflect those of the European Central Bank or the ESCB.

side, international capital flows have increased even more rapidly than trade in goods and services, leading to a remarkable rise in cross-border holdings of assets and liabilities. The share of gross international asset holdings in world GDP – which provides a measure of financial openness – has shown an eightfold increase over the last twenty-five years. This sharp increase in overall economic interconnectedness – in both real and financial terms – is the core of the concept of globalisation adopted throughout this volume. Such openness has precipitated many complex changes with implications for all economic agents including firms and households as well as governments and other policy makers, including central banks.

When considering the impact of globalisation on the production process for firms, Baldwin (2006) has suggested that this can be thought of as having taken place in two steps. First, a decreasing necessity to make goods close to the point of consumption in view of rapidly falling transportation costs – a process which has been ongoing for many decades now – can be termed the 'first unbundling'. More recently, a 'second unbundling' has greatly extended this first unbundling, whereby rapidly falling communication and coordination costs have led to a declining necessity to perform different stages of the production process geographically close to one another. In turn, this has implied an increase in offshoring, first in manufacturing tasks and, more recently, in services and, associated with this, a perceived negative impact on labour demand and the employment situation of households in many advanced economies. In the long run, such adjustments would be expected to benefit both advanced and emerging economies through a more efficient allocation of resources coupled with welfare gains associated with deepening specialisation, higher productivity, lower prices, greater product choice and, ultimately, higher living standards. In the short run, however, this process is likely to embed significant adjustment costs for both firms and households, giving rise to potentially important and contentious effects on the distribution of income. Such forces are likely to be associated with an increase in the risk of protectionist policies which, as witnessed by international economic developments in 2008 and 2009, may tend to be strengthened in a context of economic or cyclical downswing.

In the remainder of this chapter, we provide an introduction to the debate on the macroeconomic and policy consequences of this increased international economic interdependence by highlighting the key questions addressed in the book's subsequent chapters. It is our hope that the chapter will help guide the reader through the volume and identify the main cross-linkages between the different contributions. Although much of the debate on globalisation is ongoing and empirical evidence continues to be gathered, the chapter also serves to summarise the current state of our knowledge on the macroeconomic effects of globalisation as well as its associated policy challenges.

1.2 European perspectives on globalisation's key stylised facts

In Chapter 2 of this volume, Bob Anderton and Paul Hiebert provide an introduction to the key issues associated with the globalisation debate from a European perspective and, in particular, they highlight the main stylised facts that can be identified. Regarding the international dimension to economic activity, they highlight the significant increases in the trade openness of the euro area over the past decade as well as the strong rise in euro area stocks of foreign assets and liabilities as a percentage of GDP. They also note the fall in export market shares for the euro area and other major developed economies over recent years. In addition, the authors analyse the structure of euro area trade specialisation and show euro area exporters to be specialised in medium-tech and higher-productivity sectors. Moreover, they show that, in general, specialisation has not changed much over time – possibly signalling the influence of structural rigidities which impair domestic adjustment in response to the changing international environment. In line with the trade-enhancing effects of the single market and the introduction of the euro, Anderton and Hiebert also highlight the strength of growth in intra-euro area trade over recent decades. However, they note that euro area imports from China and other emerging economies, such as the Central and Eastern European countries (CEECs), are growing even more rapidly – a development which has put significant downward pressure on euro area import prices of manufactured goods over the past ten years.

In their overview of key stylised facts, Anderton and Hiebert also attempt to synthesise what we know about the euro area domestic adjustment in response to this shifting structure of international trade. Whilst recognising that globalisation is not the only factor playing a role (other factors such as technological change, macroeconomic policies and structural reform in product and labour markets may be equally or even more important), they highlight several broad areas of domestic adjustment on which the globalisation debate should focus. First, productivity growth has been weak over the last decade in the euro area, contrary to the boost which would have been expected to accompany increasing globalisation. This weakness in productivity appears to be concentrated to some extent in services. Second, employment gains have mainly been in services while manufacturing has contributed negatively to overall employment growth. More recently, there are some indications that the recent composition of employment growth has been biased toward medium- to high-skilled workers in line with the view that globalisation may have resulted in a relative shift in labour demand away from lower-skilled workers in advanced economies. Third, there has been significant wage moderation over the last decade, with a falling wage share but overall quite limited evidence of widening income disparity in the euro area.

Anderton and Hiebert also highlight the sizeable relative price movements that have been observed during the most recent phase of intensified globalisation. At the same time, there has been little compression of profits – at least on a structural basis – evident in the euro area aggregate statistics. This development runs counter to the view that stronger competition associated with globalisation would result in lower domestic mark-ups. Part of the explanation for this may link to the above-mentioned impact on the labour markets, and wage-setting outcomes in particular, where real wage increases have been overall quite subdued. A final important issue highlighted in this chapter is the flattening of the Phillips-curve relationship that is apparent in the euro area over the last decades. This has happened in conjunction with a more general trend of declining inflation in advanced economies, a phenomenon often attributed to downward pressure on prices due to the stronger competition linked to increased openness. The empirical evidence on the role of globalisation per se in driving these developments is much debated with several contributors to the debate arguing that such benign inflation outcomes derive from other sources such as better policy – in particular monetary policy – or, more simply, good luck. The evidence on the role of globalisation in driving down inflation is discussed further in Section 1.4 below, while in Section 1.5 the implications for monetary policy are considered – in particular the extent to which such developments may be associated with a weakening of a central bank's ability to control its primary objective, i.e. the domestic rate of inflation in its economy.

1.3   Globalisation of production and new trade paradigms

Given the dramatically shifting economic landscape described in Section 1.2, it is not surprising that much recent theoretical research has focused on trying to assess both the transition (short-run) and long-run (steady state) implications of greater openness and stronger trade liberalisation. The key issue at the heart of such analysis is to identify what determines a firm's ability to compete – and survive – in increasingly competitive world markets where technological change permits the type of unbundling or 'delocalisation' of the production processes highlighted by Baldwin (2006). Much of the most insightful theoretical work in this area integrates elements of the new trade theory of Helpman and Krugman (1985), which emphasises the role of imperfect competition and industrial structure, with the work of Melitz (2003), which emphasises the importance of firm heterogeneity.

Sutton (2007), for example, has analysed how differences in productivity and quality – the two dimensions of firm 'capability' – affect the survival of firms in different phases of the globalisation process. Distinguishing between the impact effects of trade liberalisation in advanced countries (the 'North') and the emerging countries ('South'), he argues in favour of a three-stage adjustment process. First, globalisation leads to a shake-out of low-capability firms in the North ('impact' phase), with a compression in the distribution of capability across firms. Wage and capability differentials across countries subsequently create strong profit incentives for firms in low-wage countries to build up capabilities as well as for capability transfers from North to South ('catch-up' phase). Subsequently, a third phase takes place, whereby the general increase in access to foreign markets will provide a further shake-out in the market.

In another relevant study, Ottaviano, Taglioni and di Mauro (2009) study the effects of trade liberalisation from a European perspective. Drawing on the work of Melitz and Ottaviano (2008), they propose a general equilibrium model to analyse the issue in a context where a country's aggregate competitiveness is driven by both country fundamentals – in particular market accessibility – and the effective positioning of domestic enterprises in the overall productivity distribution of firms operating in a given industry. The model shows that the change in the set of firms that trade and invest abroad together with the changing sets of goods traded and destinations served is a source of important gains from trade liberalisation in terms of productivity and efficiency that more aggregate analyses will tend to overlook. With the reallocation of resources primarily taking place within sectors, the least productive firms are likely to terminate production, with their market share to be reallocated to more productive foreign and domestic firms, thus raising aggregate industry-level productivity and competition. Furthermore, a country whose share of exporting firms increases over time will experience a rise in aggregate productivity as well as in aggregate competitiveness in international markets.

A key feature of the most recent phase of globalisation has been the role of technology in exposing traditionally non-traded sectors to strong international competition. In Chapter 3 of this volume, Jim Markusen studies some of the adjustment implications of trade and foreign direct investment for the business services sector. This topic has been getting increasing attention, reflecting the concern among high-income countries about the loss of medium- to high-skilled, white-collar jobs as a result of offshoring of key service activities. Markusen argues that for business services there is a need for a different approach than that used for trade in goods, since other characteristics, apart from skill requirements, seem to be of greater importance for services activities that can be considered as 'offshorable'. Such service-specific characteristics include, for example, the degree of codifiability and routinisation of certain tasks and the lack of a need for face-to-face interaction among the parties involved. Furthermore, the nature of trade barriers may be different, with barriers often being the fixed costs of establishing foreign commercial presence, e.g. as a result of legal and taxation regulations, rather than border barriers and trade costs.

To address the issues specific to the service sector, Markusen proposes a two-country model that is able to capture some of these features. He allows for two different types of fragmentation. Firstly, services production (the input) is modelled as being geographically fragmented and separated from goods production (the output). Secondly, services themselves are modelled as being fragmented into an upstream headquarters activity (e.g. R&D or management) and a downstream production activity. Although the model is not calibrated with real data, numerical simulations under different trade liberalisation scenarios point to significant potential welfare gains. For example, trade and investment in services tends to benefit relatively small economies that are abundant in skilled labour. Markusen identifies several sources of these gains. Firstly, offshoring allows service firms to source from abroad the downstream part of service production that is costly at home. This improves their competitiveness in both markets. Second, access to foreign service providers through trade or investment increases the range of services available to domestic manufacturing producers and this has a positive impact on overall productivity. Finally, access to foreign markets allows domestic service providers to spread their fixed costs over a larger output. Markusen's analysis also highlights the potential redistributive impacts of trade in services via its impact on the real wage of both skilled and unskilled workers. One important finding is that, for plausible parameter settings, the real wage of both skilled and unskilled workers may increase, reflecting the idea that the real productivity gains across the economy accrue to both sets of workers, i.e. a 'lift all' impact. This result echoes the overall limited evidence of changes in the income distribution highlighted in Section 1.2 above.

1.4   Pass-through and the role of the exchange rate

Another key issue concerning the macroeconomic adjustment associated with more intense international competition is whether it has affected the degree of exchange-rate pass-through to prices. The extent of the exchange-rate pass-through into import prices is clearly important for policy makers as it crucially affects, among other things, trade balance dynamics and the impact of exchange-rate fluctuations on domestic prices. In Chapter 4 of this volume, Christopher Gust, Sylvain Leduc and Robert Vigfusson take this issue up from the perspective of the US economy. They aim at explaining how closer trade integration with low-cost countries may have affected how import prices respond to exchange-rate movements. Key elements in their model are adjustment to the extensive margin, whereby foreign firms decide whether to export to the USA or not, and variable mark-ups in imperfectly competitive markets.

In their chapter, the authors document an increasing disconnect between the US exchange rate and the prices of imported finished goods in the last two decades, as the elasticity of the latter to the former seems to have fallen significantly. In other words, a 10.0 per cent depreciation in the US dollar is reflected in a much smaller increase in import prices compared to the 1980s. The paper then shows that this fall in the elasticity could be explained by greater trade liberalisation reflecting lower tariff and transportation costs and the lower costs of foreign exporters (associated with the emergence of low-cost economies). Their analysis is based on a general equilibrium model which features a variable demand elasticity and endogenous exporter entry and exit decisions. Entry of new exporters tends to erode price mark-ups and leads to greater co-movement of the exchange rate with import prices. This is consistent with the view that trade integration induces more competition and that this reflected in lower mark-ups for domestic producers. However, since the demand elasticity is declining in its own price, low-cost exporters will take advantage of favourable marginal costs and choose a higher and more variable mark-up. This effect dominates the effect of entry, decoupling import prices from exchange rates.

Related to the discussion on possible changes in exchange-rate pass-through, in Chapter 5 Michael Kumhof, Doug Laxton and Kanda

Naknoi take a fresh look at the issue of the weight to be attributed to the exchange rate in the optimal design of monetary policy. In their chapter, the authors argue that various factors may play a key role in determining whether the exchange rate should enter monetary policy rules, namely the endogenous determination of the range of goods that a country exports and imports, together with real rigidities in both exporting and importing. The authors develop a two-region DSGE model that integrates the theory of comparative advantage or endogenous tradability into a monetary model with nominal and real rigidities. The model highlights the role of trade frictions at the core of the latest advances in trade theory – for example, the fixed costs of becoming an exporter and also the 'iceberg' trading cost which implies that a certain fraction of traded goods is lost during the shipping process. The main result is that the real exchange rate belongs in an optimal simple monetary rule when these features are taken into account. The endogeneity of the trade pattern amplifies the real effects of the exchange rate in the short run so that not reacting to exchange-rate fluctuations leads to a sub-optimal stance of monetary policy and a significant undershooting of inflation from the target.

In the final chapter of this volume, John Taylor also stresses the need for macroeconomic researchers to possibly rethink current monetary policy rules to take into account the implications of globalisation.[1] He points out that the evidence of reduced exchange-rate pass-through could indicate the need for central banks to pay more attention to exchange-rate developments. While recognising that the answers from research on this question remain mixed, a stronger role for the exchange rate – as suggested by Michael Kumhof and his co-authors – could also argue in favour of more international policy coordination. Taylor also argues in favour of a heightened importance for exchange-rate 'diplomacy'. He cites the G7 dialogue with China aimed at an appreciation of China's exchange rate as a recent success of such diplomacy and argues that such strategies must necessarily be multilateral and involve all the interested parties. The concept of exchange-rate diplomacy also raises the 'assignment' problem of deciding whether the finance ministry or the central bank should be ultimately in charge of the currency. Despite the fact that a case in favour of the latter could be made given the close link between the exchange rate and the interest rate, Taylor argues that the close interrelationship between exchange rate policy and other non-monetary policies (e.g. trade or fiscal policy) argues in favour of assigning exchange-rate policy to finance ministries.

[1] See also Taylor (2007).

1.5   Globalisation's effects on product and labour markets

In Chapter 6, Isabell Koske, Nigel Pain and Marte Sollie take up the issue of globalisation's impact on domestic product markets in advanced economies. In particular, they aim to quantify the impact on inflation in OECD economies due to the opening up to trade with emerging low-cost countries. Their analysis is conducted in three main steps. First an accounting framework is used to decompose the change in the domestic demand deflator into an import penetration effect, a relative inflation effect and the change in prices of domestically produced goods. The main finding of this exercise is that the combined impact of lower-cost imports from China and other dynamic Asian economies has reduced domestic US inflation by 0.1 percentage point (pp) per annum in the period 1996–2005 and by 0.3 pp per annum in the euro area in the period 2000–2005.

Such estimates must be considered as clearly partial in nature given that they fail to account for the stimulus to OECD inflation rates linked to increased costs of raw materials and commodities. In a second step, the authors therefore aim to quantify the impact of increased domestic demand in low-cost countries on oil and commodity prices (e.g. of metals and minerals, agricultural raw materials, food and tropical beverages). They conduct a scenario analysis in which the growth rate of non-OECD economies is set equal to the lower growth rate of the OECD economies from 2000 onwards and this reveals a significant upward impact on commodity prices linked to the emergence of these economies. The chapter then quantifies the net effect of commodity plus non-commodity import prices on domestic consumer prices in OECD countries and cites a downward net effect for the euro area that is in the range of 0.0 to 0.25 pp. Lastly, the OECD study estimates the impact of import prices on domestic consumer prices and finds a declining long-run impact since the mid 1990s. The cyclical sensitivity of inflation to domestic economic conditions is also estimated to have declined over the last two decades although the authors do not find any robust significant additional impact from the global output gap in explaining domestic inflation rates.

While the analysis of Koske and co-authors focuses on all advanced economies in the OECD, in Chapter 7 Gabor Pula and Frauke Skudelny focus exclusively on the euro area economy and provide quantification of the impact of increasing import penetration on euro area prices and labour markets. The analysis is conducted using a variety of different methods, thus helping to assess the robustness of the available evidence.

Overall the authors also suggest some downward impact from global-isation on inflation with stronger effects on producer output prices than for prices at the consumer level.

A key area which has thus far received only limited attention is the effects of globalisation on labour markets. In their chapter Pula and Skudelny try to shed light on this aspect by estimating sectoral labour demand equations aimed at quantifying the impact of increased import penetration on employment and wages. For low-skilled sectors, their estimates suggest a direct negative impact of import penetration on employment and also a positive impact on the real wage elasticity of labour demand for low-skilled workers. Such increased sensitiv-ity of labour demand, coupled with overall lower bargaining power of employee organisations, may help explain some of the period of wage moderation that has been observed in the euro area over the last dec-ade. Nonetheless, given that technology and the capital stock are not included in their specification (mainly due to data problems), this evi-dence must be interpreted with some caution. Moreover, given the complexity of the globalisation effect and the presence of a number of simultaneous shocks (e.g. technology, structural reforms, etc.) the actual magnitude of the impact is subject to wide uncertainty.

1.6   Globalisation, asset prices and monetary policy

In considering the macroeconomic consequences of strengthened inter-national economic integration, including the possibility of an enhanced international transmission of economic shocks, a number of import-ant policy questions arise. As highlighted by the global economic tur-bulence of 2007–2009, monetary policy makers and financial sector supervisory authorities have in particular been confronted with many challenges.[2]

Regarding monetary policy, as highlighted also in the earlier chapter by Kumhof *et al.*, a fundamental question that arises is whether – and, if so, to what extent – policy makers must adapt their strategies and decision-making processes in a context of greater openness and deeper international economic interdependence. One important aspect on which this debate has focused is whether globalisation may have weak-ened the ability of independent central banks to control their domestic rate of inflation relative to the past. In Chapter 8 of this volume Philippe

---

[2] Trichet (2009) discusses a number of key monetary policy issues drawing on the experience of the financial crisis. Papademos (2009) draws some lessons from the cri-sis for financial supervisory policy.

Moutot and Giovanni Vitale also take up these important issues. They argue, in line with the analysis in Woodford (2007), that the monetary nature of inflation implies that higher openness per se does not impair the ability of central banks to control their domestic inflation rates. Arguing along similar lines, Mishkin (2007) has largely attributed the observed changes in US inflation dynamics to the success of monetary policy in better anchoring inflation expectations and not to structural changes, e.g. changes which could be linked to globalisation. Such conclusions are also very much in line with the analysis in Chapters 6 and 7 of this volume discussed above. In particular, these studies at most assign only a moderate role for globalisation in reducing inflation in many advanced economies over the last two decades whilst at the same time highlighting the strong countervailing upward pressures on inflation due to higher commodity prices.

While there is broad consensus that globalisation has not fundamentally impaired the ability of central banks to achieve their primary mandates, at the same time many lessons need to be drawn from the 2007–2009 crisis in global finance and its rapid global transmission. In this context, Moutot and Vitale argue that central banks need to place a renewed emphasis on the development and use of new tools – in particular tools which integrate better real and financial sector transmission channels. Another key lesson they draw from the recent experience is that central banks cannot afford a policy of benignly neglecting asset price bubbles. Instead, given that such bubbles can often signal economic risks that are likely to be inconsistent with the maintenance of domestic price stability, there is a stronger case for a countervailing policy of leaning against – often turbulent – asset price 'winds'. Taking account of the inherent difficulties in identifying asset price bubbles *ex ante*, such an approach would also call for an increased focus on risk and scenario analysis when assessing the stance of monetary policy. In line with this, Trichet (2009) also notes that both experience and developments in the literature support the adoption of some form of leaning against the wind, although he cautions against any mechanical implementation of such a strategy.

The appropriate policy response to large asset price misalignments cannot, however, be assessed from a purely domestic perspective. Reflecting on the experience with the turbulent global events of 2007–2009, Moutot and Vitale also stress that globalisation may be associated with a stronger international synchronisation of asset-price booms and busts and more widespread propagation of financial crisis around the globe. This calls for a greater emphasis on international cooperation among monetary policy makers and supervisory authorities, including the multilateral surveillance of asset-price misalignments. Very much in line with these conclusions, Papademos (2009) calls for a strengthening of the pan-European character of supervision.

1.7   Other policy challenges

Focusing on other (non-monetary) policy domains, Buti (2007) examines the question of the implications of globalisation for macroeconomic adjustment mechanisms in the euro area and the euro area countries. His analysis is centred on the idea that globalisation has implied an increase in structural (or 'supply') shocks relative to cyclical (or 'demand') shocks. Moreover, although such shocks may be more 'common' to the major economies, there will continue to be differences in country responses reflecting country-specific adjustment characteristics. In such a context, Buti argues that there is an enhanced importance for structural policies. Policy adjustments could include product market reforms such as the removal of barriers to competition and measures aimed at encouraging R&D spending as well as the reform of taxation and benefit systems. In the area of labour market adjustment, he argues that unemployment benefits should provide a high initial replacement rate whilst limiting the duration of benefits so as not to contribute to increased structural unemployment. Structural policies in labour markets also need to make a greater allowance for the increased migration flows associated with globalisation. Buti argues that well-functioning financial markets also strengthen the adjustment capacity and stability of the euro area by offering portfolio diversification possibilities. However, he notes that integrated financial markets can be a source of instability if regulation and supervision fail to keep pace with them.

REFERENCES

Baldwin, R. (2006). 'Globalisation: the great unbundling(s)', in *Globalisation Challenges for Europe*, Secretariat of the Economic Council, Helsinki: Finnish Prime Minister's Office, Chapter 1.

Buti, M. (2007). 'How globalisation affects euro area adjustment', contribution to the policy panel discussion at the ECB conference *Globalisation and the Macroeconomy*, Frankfurt, July 2007.

Helpman, E., and P. Krugman (1985). *Market Structure and Foreign Trade*, Cambridge: MIT Press.

Melitz, Mark J. (2003). 'The impact of trade on aggregate industry productivity and intra industry reallocation', *Econometrica*, 71(6), 1695–1725.

Melitz, Marc J., and Giancarlo I. P. Ottaviano (2008). 'Market size, trade, and productivity', *Review of Economic Studies*, 75(1), 295–316.

Mishkin, Frederic S. (2007). 'Inflation dynamics', speech at the Annual Macro Conference, Federal Reserve Bank of San Francisco, San Francisco, California, 23 March 2007.

Ottaviano, G., D. Taglioni, and F. di Mauro (2009). 'The euro and the competitiveness of European firms', *Economic Policy*, 24(57), 5–53.

Papademos, Lucas (2009). 'After the storm: the future face of Europe's financial system', speech at the conference organised by Breugel, National Bank of Belgium and the IMF, Brussels, 24 March 2009.

Sutton, J. (2007). 'Quality, trade and the moving window: the globalisation process', *The Economic Journal*, 117(524), F469–F498.

Taylor, John B. (2007). 'Monetary policy in a global economy: past and future challenges', presentation at the European Central Bank Conference *Globalisation and the Macroeconomy*, Frankfurt, 24 July 2007.

Trichet, Jean Claude (2009). 'Credible alertness revisited', intervention at the *Symposium on Financial Stability and Macroeconomic Policy*, sponsored by the Federal Reserve Bank of Kansas City, Jackson Hole, 22 August 2009.

Woodford, M. (2007). *Globalisation and Monetary Control*, NBER working paper No. 13329.

2 The impact of globalisation on the euro area macroeconomy

Robert Anderton and Paul Hiebert

2.1 Introduction

With a growing interconnectedness of economies through trade, production and financial market channels, globalisation has become an increasingly important phenomenon over the last decade. Indeed, more recently, the increased integration of economies across the globe in both financial and product markets related to the rapid growth of globalisation has also been associated with global financial turmoil and the highly internationally synchronised nature of the most recent global economic downturn. However, taking a longer-term perspective, what distinguishes the rapid growth of globalisation over the past decade has not been falling transport costs or tariffs alone – a process which has been ongoing for decades now – but rather new production paradigms enabled by both an expansion of global productive capacity and major technological changes facilitating the access and transfer of goods, services, people and knowledge across borders. In this sense, this latest acceleration of globalisation has been inextricably linked to technological change (and, accordingly, distinguishing between the impact of these two phenomena in practice is very difficult).

The rapidly changing world implied by these forces seems to have influenced a range of developments in advanced and emerging economies alike. This chapter takes a narrow view and focuses exclusively on gauging the macroeconomic impacts for the euro area, although in practice, globalisation has undoubtedly also had several other equally important implications – notably for financial markets and

The views expressed in this chapter are those of the authors only and do not necessarily reflect those of the European Central Bank or the ESCB. We are greatly indebted to U. Baumann, S. Dees, K. Forster, G. Pula, A. Patarau, R. Pereira, F. Skudelny and D. Taglioni for their invaluable inputs and comments. Special thanks are also due to G. Kenny, F. di Mauro and H. J. Klockers for their invaluable advice and comments, as well as other members of the External Developments and Euro Area Macroeconomic Developments Divisions of the ECB. Any remaining errors are, of course, the sole responsibility of the authors.

macroeconomic policies. The chapter takes a long-term perspective over a period predominantly characterised by the rapid growth of globalisation, notwithstanding the more recent interruption to the growth of global trade and capital flows that emerged towards the end of 2008 associated with the global financial turmoil and the associated downturn in global economic activity. Following an overview of the salient aspects of globalisation, which highlights the increasing openness of the euro area in terms of both trade and capital flows as well as the global reduction in transportation and information costs and the rise in the effective global supply of labour, this chapter then assesses the external impacts of globalisation on the euro area, focusing on trade performance, export specialisation and import prices. It then moves to assess euro area domestic adjustment with a supply-side focus, analysing separately impacts on productivity, labour markets and prices.

2.2 Overview of key aspects of globalisation

Globalisation, if narrowly defined as growing trade openness in response to falling trade and transport costs, has been ongoing for decades and in this sense is not a novel phenomenon. Over most of the last decade, however, this process appears to have accelerated, with a rapid rise across the globe in import volumes (Figure 2.1), which more than doubled for the euro area since the early 1990s. But more precisely defined, globalisation is the rapidly growing interconnectedness of economies also through production and financial market linkages and channels, with two broad factors underlying such a development. First, falling costs of transporting not only goods, but also services and information across borders (Figure 2.2) has led to changes in the production processes, most notably

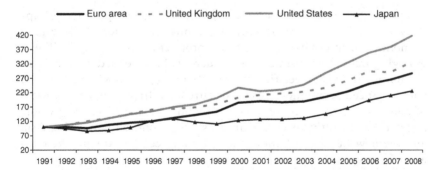

Figure 2.1 Imports in industrialised countries (volume index, 1991 = 100)
Source: IMF World Economic Outlook and ECB calculations.

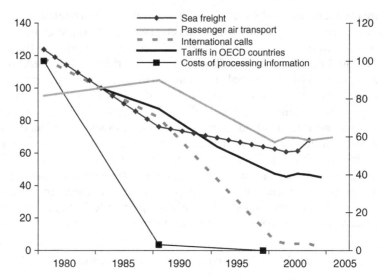

Figure 2.2 Costs of transport, information processing costs and tariffs
(Index, 1985 = 100)
Note: Tariffs are median of national mean bound tariffs for OECD countries; sea freight is average international freight charges per tonne; passenger air transport is average airline revenue per passenger mile/US import air passenger fares; international calls is cost of a three-minute call from New York to London; costs of processing information is cost of computing an average operation (sum and multiplication).
Source: Price and Cournède (2007).

related to the international fragmentation of production (see Baldwin, 2006).

Second, there has been a large expansion in global productive capacity on account of the rapidly increasing integration of emerging economies in international trade and production (Figure 2.3). These emerging market economies are frequently characterised as 'low-cost' economies given their relatively lower labour cost levels when compared with advanced economies such as the euro area. In particular, estimates of hourly compensation costs for the manufacturing sector as a whole suggest significantly lower labour costs of economies in emerging Asia and the new European Union member states compared with the euro area (Figure 2.4).[1]

[1] It should be noted that there are several important caveats regarding measurement, for example, the composition of manufacturing within each country obviously affects aggregate remuneration and therefore influences hourly labour costs.

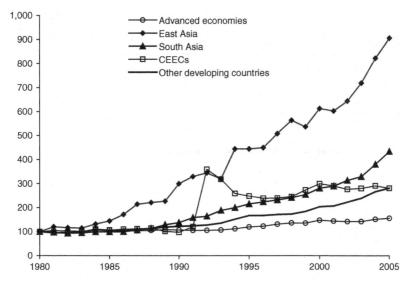

Figure 2.3 Export-weighted labour force by region
(Index, 1980 = 100)
Note: Export-weighted labour force computed as national labour force scaled
by export-to-GDP ratios.
Source: Jaumotte and Tytell (2007).

The economic globalisation brought about by these changes has been
one of the major trends shaping the world economy in recent years. On
the real side, international trade has expanded substantially, particularly with China and other emerging Asian economies as well as the
new EU member states.[2] Trade volumes have also increased strongly
for the euro area, with export and import volumes continually and rapidly outpacing the growth of GDP over the past quarter of a century
(Figure 2.5).

On the financial side, global international capital flows have increased
even more rapidly than trade in goods and services, resulting in substantial increases in holdings of international assets and liabilities across
the globe. A similar story holds for the euro area over the last decade,
where the ongoing strength of capital flows is particularly reflected in
the stock of outward and inward foreign direct investment (FDI), which
has virtually doubled as a percentage of GDP since 1999 (Figure 2.6).
One summary index of economic globalisation, produced by the KOF

[2] For a comprehensive assessment of the euro area's international performance, see
Anderton *et al.* (2004), ESCB (2005), Baumann and di Mauro (2006) and di Mauro
and Anderton (2007).

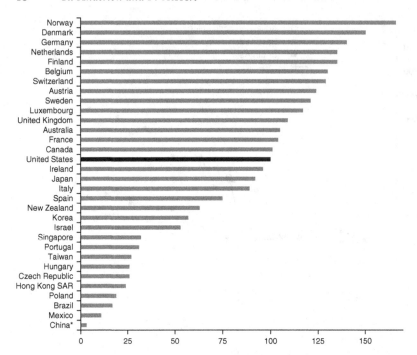

Figure 2.4 Hourly compensation costs for production workers
(2004 data; Index, United States = 100)
Note: Data for China refer to costs for all employees (data for other countries
only refer to production workers); coverage may also differ.
Source: US Bureau of Labor Statistics.

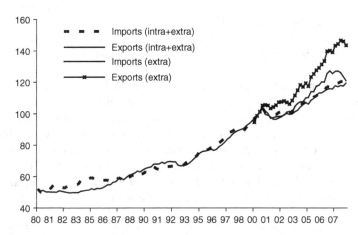

Figure 2.5 Total and extra-euro area imports and exports as
percentage of GDP
(Index: 2000 = 100; quarterly data; volume terms)
Note: The last observation refers to the third quarter of 2008.

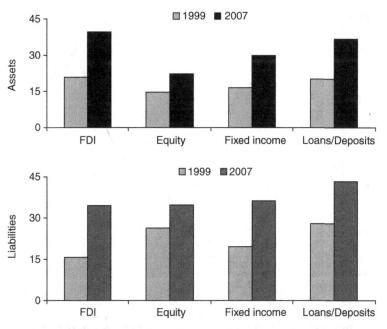

Figure 2.6 Euro area foreign assets and liabilities (as percentage of GDP)
Source: ECB calculations based on Balance of Payments data.

Swiss Economic Institute, increased substantially in the euro area in the years leading up to 2000 and has continued to stand considerably above the level of a comparable measure for the USA through recent years (see Figure 2.7).

The chapter takes a long-term perspective over a period characterised by the rapid growth of globalisation, although there has been a more recent reversal of the growth of global trade and capital flows that started towards the end of 2008 associated with the global financial turmoil and global downturn. This chapter therefore outlines the longer-term general impacts of the growth in trade globalisation on the euro area macroeconomy in four areas: on trade developments and competitiveness, productivity and the supply side of the economy, labour market effects, and implications for price determination. In general, the above changes in the global economic landscape would be expected to have wide-ranging impacts on macroeconomic developments across the globe. In the long run, increased trade openness along with other associated factors such as technological gains would be expected to benefit advanced as well as emerging economies through more efficient resource allocation, lower prices, more product choice, welfare gains

20   *R. Anderton and P. Hiebert*

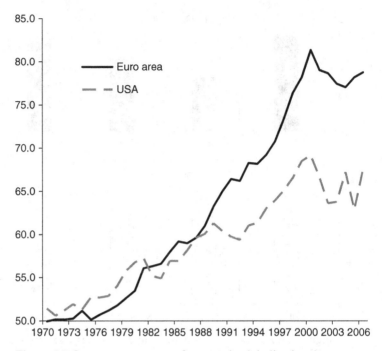

Figure 2.7 Summary measure of economic globalisation: euro area versus the USA
(Index)

Note: Euro area 16 obtained using 2007 GDP weights. Summary economic globalisation measure obtained on the basis of a weighted measure constructed using actual flows (trade flows, foreign direct investment flows and stocks, portfolio investment and income payments to foreign nationals) as well as hidden import barriers (mean tariff rate, taxes on international trade and capital account restrictions).

Source: KOF Swiss Economic Institute.

from deepening specialisation and, ultimately, higher living standards. In the short run, however, this process probably embeds some adjustment costs and distributional effects associated with sectoral reallocation of production and associated inputs. Indeed, globalisation – as with any other profound structural change – entails distributional aspects which may imply significant costs for some at the same time as considerable benefits for others. But such distributional aspects are only one part of the macroeconomic implications as economies refocus on areas of higher comparative advantage and, ultimately, lead to aggregate welfare gains. In this context, globalisation has implied domestic macroeconomic adjustment for advanced economies in several areas.

This chapter complements existing work on the topic of trade globalisation and its impacts on advanced economies,[3] focusing specifically on providing an overall assessment of the recent euro area macroeconomic experience. To this end, this chapter provides an examination of several stylised facts and empirical evidence to assess the role of globalisation in shaping euro area macroeconomic developments to date, drawing conclusions where possible. Indeed, drawing firm conclusions on the basis of observed outcomes is difficult in that the recent wave of globalisation has come in the context of several (not totally independent) other structural changes, such as European Monetary Union (EMU) and the ongoing impacts of the launch of the euro; the worldwide rapid pace of technological change, and several policy changes.

2.3 Globalisation and euro area trade and competitiveness

The emergence of global trade players such as China, other than causing an increase in world trade and boosting euro area exports, has brought about a reduction in export market shares of advanced industrialised economies such as the euro area. Such losses in share are to a certain extent automatic and may not be problematic if they reflect the ongoing reorganisation of world production in line with comparative advantage. However, the extent of the loss in share may be connected to the export product specialisation of the euro area and how it compares to these new competitors and whether it is changing appropriately over time. On the imports side, globalisation has implied a drastic shift towards imports from low-cost countries. This has involved imports of consumer goods, as well as intermediate imports – the latter related to the internationalisation of production – which has impacts on real domestic variables as well as prices.

2.3.1 Exports and competitiveness

In examining euro area exports, it would appear that major economies are losing export market share, while China has been gaining share. Against the background of the emergence of low-income countries as major players in world trade, export volume market shares of advanced industrialised countries – such as the euro area, USA, UK

---

[3] Several studies, such as European Commission (2006), the Federal Reserve Bank of Kansas City (2006), Helbling et al. (2006), Mishkin (2007), Price and Cournède (2007) and Dreher et al. (2008) have all analysed various aspects of globalisation and macroeconomic developments in advanced economies.

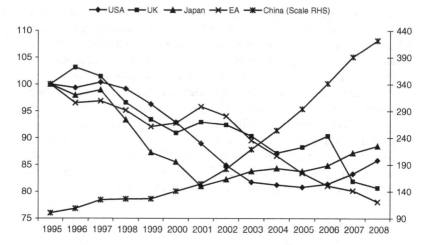

Figure 2.8 Export market shares
(In volumes; index 1995 = 100; annual data)
Note: Export market share is calculated as an index of export volumes
divided by an index of foreign demand (where foreign demand is defined as
a country-specific export-weighted sum of foreign import volumes of goods
and services).
Source: IMF, Eurostat and ECB calculations.

and Japan – have fallen in recent years, while the shares of countries such as China have dramatically increased (Figure 2.8). Given these developments, it may not be surprising that the losses in export shares occurring across a variety of advanced industrialised countries cannot be fully explained by changes in price competitiveness (in particular, export share equations for the euro area need a negative time trend in addition to the usual competitiveness term in order to capture movements in extra-euro area export volumes).[4] Nevertheless, despite the declines in export market share, extra-export volumes of the euro area were growing rapidly as a percentage of GDP due to the persistently robust growth in foreign demand until the end of 2008. Given that these favourable global demand conditions also seem to be at least partly driven by globalisation forces, this positive impact on exports has more than offset the dampening effect on exports of the loss in share.

As the rise in China's export market share seems to be the main counterpart to the loss in the euro area's export market share, we can provide further insights into the mechanisms behind this loss by examining Chinese exports in terms of their sectoral composition and how

[4] For further details, see ESCB (2005) and ECB Monthly Bulletin (2006b).

Table 2.1 *Revealed comparative advantage by factor intensity* *

Exports are predominantly	EA	USA	Japan	China	CEECs
Raw-materials intensive	0.5	0.7	0.1	0.5	1.7
Labour intensive	1.1	0.8	0.5	2.3	1.1
Capital intensive	1.2	0.9	1.6	0.3	1.2
Research intensive	1.1	1.4	1.5	1.0	0.5

* Balassa index of revealed comparative advantage; average for the period 1993–
2006. An index greater than one indicates that a country specialises in that product.
EA is the euro area; CEECs are the Central and Eastern European countries.
Source: Chelem and ECB calculations; di Mauro and Forster (2008).

they compare with the export specialisation of the euro area, and how
euro area exporters are adjusting their export structure over time in
order to respond to this competitive challenge. However, as discussed
in more detail below, these measures of trade specialisation are subject
to various caveats and should be interpreted with caution.

Over the period 1993–2006, euro area exporters have been largely
specialising in capital- and research-intensive products as well as labour-
intensive goods (Table 2.1). By contrast, the other advanced competitor
countries – i.e. the USA and Japan – do not have a revealed comparative
advantage in labour-intensive products but are relatively more specialised in exports of research-intensive goods (with Japan also specialising
in capital goods exports). Meanwhile, China is specialised in exporting
labour-intensive goods. Although the euro area seems somewhat over-
weight in labour-intensive sectors, the sectoral export specialisation by
factor intensity generally seems to broadly reflect the countries' relative
factor endowments, with higher-skilled workers being relatively abundant in the euro area and Japan and the USA, while lower-skilled workers are prevalent in China.

Figure 2.9 shows that the euro area's export specialisation is not
changing much over time in research- and labour-intensive products,
which seems surprising given that one might expect the euro area to
show signs of moving away from labour-intensive products following the large increase in the effective global labour supply available at
cheap wage rates. On the one hand, this lack of movement in specialisation might reflect structural rigidities in the euro area countries,
where product and labour market regulations may constrain the ability
of firms to adjust in a rapid and optimal fashion to the forces of globalisation. On the other hand, it might also be the case that the euro
area is not under significant competitive pressures to move away from
some labour-intensive products where they may not be in direct price

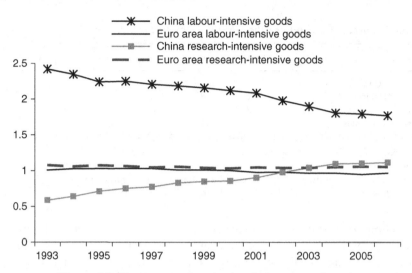

Figure 2.9 Change over time in revealed comparative advantage by factor intensity
Note: Balassa index of revealed comparative advantage
Source: Chelem and ECB calculations.

competition with emerging countries as the euro area exports may be superior in terms of quality.[5]

However, Figure 2.9 also clearly shows that China is rapidly moving away from labour-intensive products and increasing its specialisation in research-intensive products, and eventually becoming similar to the euro area at the end of the sample period in terms of its degree of specialisation in research-intensive products. Overall, these results should be viewed with some caution as there are several caveats regarding these measures of revealed comparative advantage. First, the measures may be somewhat subjective as some products are difficult to classify

[5] A major question concerning the competitiveness of Chinese exports is whether the lower price of Chinese exports indicates a lower quality of Chinese exports in comparison to major advanced country exporters such as the USA or UK. On the one hand, Fontagne, Gaulier and Zignago (2007) look at the export specialisation of North–South countries and claim that although the export specialisation of the two sets of countries is quite similar when considered across broadly defined sectors, they are quite different when the differentiation of products – reflected in unit value indices – is taken into account. Overall, their analysis shows that advanced economies are maintaining their advantage in the upper segment of product markets and that North–South countries are not competing directly with each other. By contrast, Jarvis (2006) matches products according to quality criteria and shows that China and other low-cost countries can export products of the same quality – but at significantly lower prices – as high-cost countries.

Table 2.2 *Revealed comparative advantage by sector**

	EA	USA	China
High-technology industries (HT)	0.8	1.4	1.0
Aircraft and spacecraft	0.8	3.5	0.1
Pharmaceuticals	1.5	0.9	0.3
Office, accounting and computing machinery	0.7	1.0	1.6
Medical, precision and optical instruments	0.9	1.7	0.9
Medium-high-technology industries (MHT)	1.2	1.1	0.6
Electrical machinery and apparatus, n.e.s.	0.9	1.0	1.5
Motor vehicles, transport equipment, n.e.s.	1.3	0.9	0.1
Chemicals, excluding pharmaceuticals	1.2	1.2	0.5
Machinery and equipment, n.e.s.	1.2	1.2	0.7
Low-technology industries (LT)	1.0	0.8	1.6
Wood	1.2	1.0	0.4
Textiles, clothing, footwear	0.9	0.4	3.5

* Balassa index of comparative advantage (average 1993–2006).
Source: Chelem and ECB calculations.

by factor intensity because they use several factors of production to a similar extent. Second, the classification by factor intensity may be misleading if a country focuses primarily on the labour-intensive production stages of a predominantly research-intensive good (this may particularly apply to China where foreign firms may be outsourcing the labour-intensive parts of production for a variety of research- or capital-intensive products and then using China as an export base).

Turning to Balassa indices of export specialisation by technological content, we distinguish between high-, medium- and low-tech sectors (Table 2.2). The euro area as a whole is relatively specialised in medium-high-tech exports and appears to be less open to direct competition in these sectors from China, which is specialising primarily in low-tech sectors, particularly textiles, clothing and footwear.[6] This is not true, however, for all euro area countries. In particular, Greece, Portugal and, to a lesser extent, Italy appear to be rather strongly specialised in

[6] One further criticism of measures of revealed comparative advantage is that the internationalisation of production may render measures of export specialisation less meaningful nowadays as exported goods now embody substantial international outsourcing of production inputs. This issue is addressed in detail in Baumann and di Mauro (2006) who compute an index of trade specialisation which nets out intermediate imports of exports and compares it with the export specialisation results reported above. This modified version of the Lafay index of revealed comparative advantage by industry generally gives similar results to the traditional Balassa indices of export specialisation reported in this paper, confirming that the euro area is highly specialised in medium-high-tech sectors and has not changed its specialisation much over time.

low- and medium-low technology sectors (particularly textiles, etc.),[7] where China is gaining predominance largely due to its substantially lower labour costs.

This seems to be consistent with the fact that the loss in export market share of the euro area is the result of a relatively diverse performance across euro area countries, with the export share losses of some euro area countries weighing rather heavily on the euro area aggregate. This suggests that some individual euro area countries who have lost export market share over the past decade or so – such as Italy, Spain and Portugal – may have been more strongly affected than others by globalisation, possibly as a result of their lower-tech export specialisation which may expose them more directly to competition from China. The analysis by Esteves and Reis (2006), who extend traditional weights used in effective exchange rates to cover not only competition in third markets but also product specialisation, comes to similar conclusions. Their approach significantly increases the weight of competition with non-Japan Asia for Italy, Spain and especially Portugal, reflecting the fact that these countries have a product specialisation more concentrated in sectors such as textiles, clothing and footwear which are particularly vulnerable to competition from Asian economies, particularly China.

2.3.2   Imports and the rising share of low-cost countries

Intra-euro area imports have been growing strongly, but euro area imports from low-cost countries such as China and the EU New Member States (NMS) have been growing even more rapidly. Over the last decade, both intra- and extra-euro area imports of manufactured goods showed robust growth, but the ratio of intra to extra-euro area trade volumes has steadily declined which – again – may not be fully explained by movements in relative prices (Figure 2.10).[8] Globalisation forces have been driving the relatively stronger growth of extra-euro area imports – which has displaced some intra-euro area trade – with outsourcing to low-cost countries and the internationalisation of production playing an important role. During the past ten years, the shares of low-cost countries in extra-euro area imports of manufactures – particularly those from China and the new EU member states – have increased considerably, accompanied by a loss in the import shares of higher-cost extra-euro area importers such as the United States,

---

[7] See Box 3 in Baumann and di Mauro (2006) and ECB (2006a).
[8] The relative price of the two sources of imports in 2008 is very similar to what it was in 1995, perhaps implying that a structural trend decline is taking place in the ratio of intra- to extra-import volumes that is not explained by relative prices.

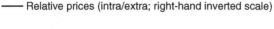

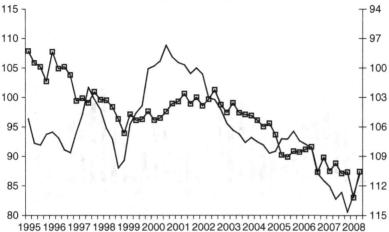

Figure 2.10 Euro area imports of manufactured goods
(Index; 2002 QI = 100; monthly data)
Note: Last observation refers to December 2008.
Sources: Eurostat.

Japan and the United Kingdom (Figure 2.11).[9] These developments, while admittedly boosting the welfare of euro area consumers, have on the other hand probably affected the transmission of foreign demand shocks to euro area domestic demand by weakening some of the potential positive intra-trade spillovers on domestic demand.[10]

One possible implication of the internationalisation of production is that the increasing trend in outsourcing may have had a negative spillover on economic activity as it might have reduced the value added of export activities by increasing the reliance of euro area exporters on imported intermediate inputs. ESCB (2005) shows that the import content of exports (which is the inverse of the value added per unit of export), measured as the long-run elasticity of imports with respect to a one unit increase in exports, has risen for the euro area from 38 per cent in 1995 to around 44 per cent in 2000. Furthermore, this rise in the import intensity of exports is almost entirely due to trade external to the EU, as the import intensity of internal EU trade did not change

[9] Of course, this is also simply reflecting the flip side of the loss in export market share of the major advanced industrialised countries associated with the rapidly rising export share of China described earlier.

[10] See Anderton and di Mauro (2008) for a comprehensive description of these linkages.

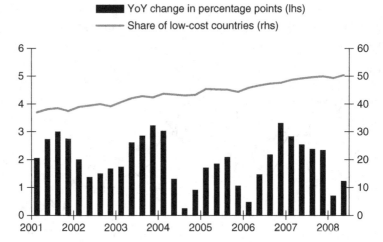

Figure 2.11 Share of extra-euro area manufacturing imports from low-cost countries
(LHS: Y-o-Y change in percentage points; RHS: in %, quarterly data)
Note: Last observation August 2008.
Source: Eurostat and ECB calculations.

much over this period.[11] However, globalisation and the international-isation of production has also boosted exports as well. As a result, given that the share of exports in GDP is now much larger (Figure 2.5), the net impact of a 1 per cent increase in exports on GDP growth may have remained roughly constant for the euro area.[12]

Rising imports from low-cost countries are also putting downward pressure on extra-euro area manufacturing import prices. This is mostly a result of the increasing share of low-cost countries in euro area imports combined with the relatively cheaper prices of imports from low-cost countries. Since the start of the 2000s, the share of low-cost countries in extra-euro area manufacturing imports has increased from just over one-third to almost a half (Figure 2.11). Among the low-cost countries, China and the EU NMS were the main contributors to this

---

[11] As the data relate to 1995–2000, the EU excludes the new EU Member States who joined the European Union in 2004.

[12] Another aspect of this globalisation-related phenomenon is its possible effects on the trade impacts of exchange-rate movements. Given that the import content of exports is rising over time, one would expect import prices to become an increasingly import-ant component of exporters' costs, which may lead to smaller losses in export price competitiveness in response to an appreciation of the exchange rate compared to the past, which in turn may mitigate the negative impact of a euro appreciation on export volumes (as an appreciation will reduce the cost of imported inputs and exporters can reduce their prices to partly offset the loss in competitiveness from the appreciation). See Anderton (2007), as well as the later section on the terms of trade.

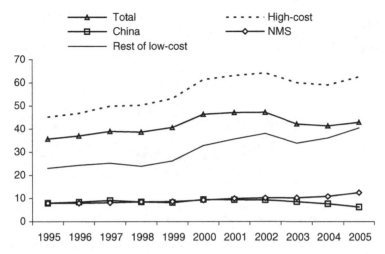

Figure 2.12 Extra-euro area manufacturing import price levels
(Euros per kilogram of manufacturing imports)
Sources: Eurostat Comext data and ECB staff calculations.

increase with both of their shares roughly doubling since the mid 1990s
to stand at around 12 per cent each in 2008. Based on highly detailed
data disaggregated both by sectors and countries over the period 1995–
2004, Figure 2.12 shows that the level of import prices (proxied by
absolute unit value indices) from China and the NMS are estimated
to be approximately one-quarter the import price of total euro area
import prices, and about one-fifth the price of imports from high-cost
countries.

Overall, it is estimated that the increase in import penetration from
low-cost countries over this period may have dampened euro area
import price inflation by an average of around 2 percentage points (pp)
each year, mostly accounted for by China and the NMS. The impact is
decomposed into two components: the first is the 'share effect', which
captures the downward impact on import prices of the rising import
share of low-cost countries combined with the relatively lower price
level of low-cost import suppliers; and the second is due to differentials
in the growth of import prices (the 'price effect'), which captures the
impact of lower import price inflation from the low-cost countries relative to the high-cost ones over the sample period.

During the course of 2007–2008, there was speculation that this disinflationary impact of low-cost countries on euro area import prices
might be coming to an end due to increasing inflationary pressures
in those countries. At face value, the robust increases during 2008 in

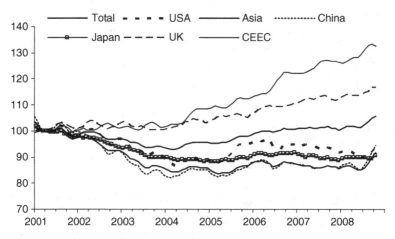

Figure 2.13 Prices of euro area manufacturing imports from selected countries and regions
Source: Eurostat and ECB calculations.

import prices by low-cost country import suppliers might be inter-preted as a sign that the downward impact from low-cost countries was waning (Figure 2.13). However, these import price increases primarily reflected the lagged impact of higher energy and raw materials prices up to the first half of 2008 which have pushed up the prices of virtually all euro area import suppliers (Figure 2.14).[13] Nevertheless, economic development, robust wage increases and terms of trade deterioration in low-cost countries, as well as increasing sophistication, variety and technological content of exports would suggest that low-cost countries are making a leap up in the value chain and that their export bundles are becoming increasingly similar to the more advanced western econ-omies, which will ultimately lead in the long run to a convergence of their export prices to higher international levels.

So far, we have referred only to the downward impact of low-cost countries on manufacturing import prices. However, there have also been globalisation-related effects on euro area import prices working in the opposite direction, as the strong growth in the non-OECD econ-omies in recent years seems to partly explain the significant rise in the prices of oil and non-energy commodities since 1999 up to the first half of 2008 (Figure 2.14). For example, Pain *et al.* (2006) calculate that if the GDP of the non-OECD countries during the period 2000–2005

---

[13] Amiti and Davis (2009) show that the significant rise in prices of US imports from China between 2006 and 2008 was mostly due to rising commodity prices.

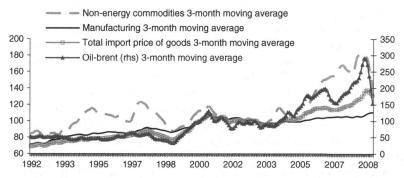

Figure 2.14 Extra-euro area import prices by commodity
(Indices: 2003 Q1 = 100; seasonally adjusted; 3 month moving average)
Note: Last observation refers to January 2009.
(Unit value indices; euro; 2001 Q1=100)
Source: ECB.

had grown at the slower pace of the OECD countries then the world
real oil price would have been up to 40 per cent lower by the end of
2005. Overall, Figure 2.14 shows how globalisation has helped to keep
extra-euro area manufacturing import prices fairly flat since the start
of the 2000s, while the rising price of oil and other commodities (particularly metals and foods) are reflected in the stronger growth of total
extra-euro area import prices over the same period. Meanwhile, from
the second half of 2008 onwards the downward pressure on euro area
import prices from the large fall in oil prices is reinforced by the continuing downward pressure on manufacturing import prices due to the
continually rising import shares from low-cost countries.

2.3.3   *Exchange-rate pass-through to euro area import prices and domestic prices*

Exchange-rate pass-through (ERPT) is another factor which may
have been affected by globalisation. For example, there may have been
a decline in ERPT for import and consumer prices due to stronger
competitive pressures or the shift to a lower inflation regime (Taylor,
2000). At the same time there may also be reasons why estimates of
ERPT might increase over time, such as the aforementioned increase
in import penetration (Figures 2.1 and 2.5) which leads to a higher
share of imports in the harmonised index of consumer prices (HICP),
implying a larger impact on the HICP of a change in the exchange
rate. The main conclusion of the empirical literature is that during the
past two decades ERPT has declined for a number of countries, particularly for the United States (see Marazzi *et al.*, 2005; Ihrig *et al.*,

2006, etc.). Although the empirical evidence for the euro area is somewhat mixed, some results suggest that the ERPT has declined. For example, although estimates of the pass-through for extra-euro area import prices at the sectoral level seem stable, compositional effects may have reduced ERPT to the aggregate import price because the sectoral composition of imports in recent years has moved towards lower ERPT products (such as chemicals and motor vehicles) and the share of imports accounted for by high ERPT products has fallen.[14] In addition, Anderton (2007) argues that the changing country composition of import suppliers may have reduced ERPT for euro area manufacturing import prices. For example, the ERPT of euro area manufacturing imports from the United States is around 90 per cent compared to an average ERPT of around 50–70 per cent, hence this higher ERPT combined with the significant fall in the share of the United States in euro area imports over the past ten years will result in a lower ERPT. Meanwhile, di Mauro *et al.* (2008) show that evidence for a decline in the ERPT to domestic prices is far less conclusive for the euro area in comparison to the United States. However, they do find some evidence of a decline in ERPT to consumer prices for some euro area countries such as Germany and, to a lesser extent, France and Italy. Meanwhile, Hahn (2007) finds some small decline in the ERPT to producer prices in industry, as the weight in electricity, gas and water supply, which has a high ERPT, decreases.

2.3.4   Globalisation and the terms of trade

One of the mechanisms by which globalisation may benefit advanced industrialised countries is via improvements in the terms of trade. Globalisation seems to be leading to downward pressure on manufacturing import prices from increased imports from low-cost countries and should, *ceteris paribus*, lead to improvements in the terms of trade. Although there is considerable volatility over time, mostly due to movements in the exchange rate, Figures 2.15 and 2.16 suggest that there is no strong evidence of a long-run trend improvement in the terms of trade for the euro area.[15]

---

[14] See Campa *et al.* (2007) and Osbat and Wagner (2008).

[15] Although movements in the exchange rate affect the terms of trade, the long-run trends in the charts should still be informative as the depreciation of the effective exchange rate of the euro during 1999–2000 has been roughly offset by the appreciation from 2002 onwards.

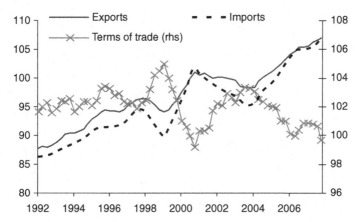

Figure 2.15 Euro area terms of trade for goods and services
(Unit value index; 2000 = 100; seasonally adjusted)
Note: The terms of trade are calculated by dividing the euro area export
price deflator of goods and services by the import deflator.
National accounts data are total trade (i.e. intra+extra).
Source: National accounts data (AWM database) and ECB calculations.

Figure 2.15 shows trade prices in total goods and services and depicts
a worsening of the terms of trade in recent years which is probably
driven by the rise in oil prices from 1999 onwards. Nevertheless, if we
exclude the direct impacts of oil prices by looking at import and export
prices for manufactured goods (Figure 2.16), there are still no signs of
a trend improvement in the terms of trade for the euro area. Although
this is a very preliminary and rough analysis and should be viewed with
caution,[16] there may be several reasons why the terms of trade have not
improved for euro area trade in manufactures. First, although low-cost
countries are putting downward pressure on euro area import prices,
high-cost countries might be upgrading the quality of their products
as a result of this increased competition and thereby increasing their
export prices to the euro area. Second, as mentioned earlier, the rising
import content of exports implies that imports are becoming an increasingly important cost component of exports which, in turn, means that
export and import prices may move more closely together than in the
past (thereby dampening the expected improvements in the terms of
trade resulting from globalisation). Third, increased competition from

---

[16] ESCB (2005) Box 2 investigates developments in the terms of trade in more detail
at the sectoral level but also finds little evidence of an improvement in the terms of
trade.

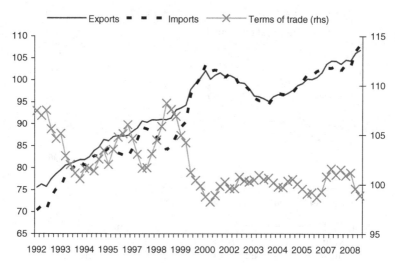

Figure 2.16 Euro area terms of trade for manufactured goods
(Unit value index; 2000 = 100; seasonally adjusted)
Note: The terms of trade are calculated by dividing extra-euro area export
price of manufactured goods by the import price of manufactured goods.
Source: Eurostat and ECB calculations.

China in world markets may have put downward pressure on euro area
export prices of manufactures.

2.4   Globalisation and euro area productivity

Globalisation is closely linked to the process of technological advance-
ment, and accordingly would be expected to boost productivity as trade
and capital flows lead to increased technical efficiency across economic
areas over time in the absence of frictions. Three channels may be of
particular importance in this process. First, globalisation may constitute a form of technology transfer both through input flows (i.e.
imports of capital goods and labour mobility) and the transfer of multifactor productivity (including, notably, the enhancement of management techniques to best-practice standards). Though often associated
with trade between developing and developed economies, technological
convergence nonetheless can occur for trade between developed economies (particularly in terms of multifactor productivity). Moreover, the
growth of offshoring may indicate that changing production paradigms
could also be considered in the context of technology transfer. Second,
globalisation may result in composition and scale effects, whereby
higher average productivity may result from both the composition of

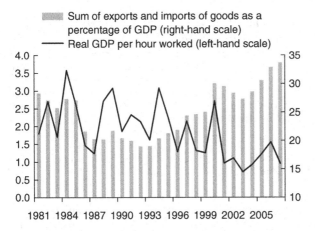

Figure 2.17 Output per hour growth and trade openness in the euro area
(Annual percentage changes)
Note: Trade openness is defined here as the sum of extra-euro area export values and import values expressed as a percentage of GDP.
Sources: ECB calculations based on Eurostat and AMECO data.

firms (given increased specialisation according to comparative advantage and competitive forces) and the possibility for firms to increase the scale of their operations (consistent with the notion of economies of scale and higher productivity in multinational firms). Third, globalisation may trigger defensive innovation, whereby firms are more innovative in response to stronger global competitive pressures (corroborated by the general finding that exporters tend to have higher productivity than firms producing solely for the domestic market). The second and third channels can be characterised as distributional channels to the extent that they imply gains for competitive firms as well as the potential demise of uncompetitive firms. To this end, maximum net benefits from globalisation would be expected where domestic labour and product markets are as competitive as those of key trading partners.

A review of the recent euro area experience would suggest that aggregate euro area productivity gains owing to globalisation were generally absent despite steadily increasing international openness in the period leading up to 2007, in apparent contrast to the above arguments (Figure 2.17). A closer look at the sectoral dimension underlying these aggregate productivity developments, however, yields a more nuanced picture, whereby the productivity shortfall can to a large extent be explained by developments in sectors with limited exposure to international competitive pressures or frictions which

Table 2.3 *Sectoral value added per hour, euro area versus the USA (annual average growth rate over 1995–2004, %)*

	euro area	USA	difference
Manufacturing	2.3	5.3	-3.0
Electrical and optical equipment	4.9	14.5	-9.6
Manufacturing excluding electrical	1.8	3.1	-1.3
Market services	0.4	2.8	-2.4
Distribution services	1.3	4.4	-3.1
of which: Wholesale trade*	2.1	4.7	-2.6
of which: Retail trade,* repair of household goods	0.7	5.1	-4.4
Finance and business services**	-0.6	2.6	-3.2
of which: Financial intermediation	1.7	4.9	-3.2
Personal services†	-0.4	1.0	-1.4

Note: Euro area excluding Greece, Ireland, Luxembourg, Portugal and Slovenia.
* Excludes motor vehicles and motorcycles.
** Excludes real estate.
† Personal services includes: hotels and restaurants; other community, social and personal services; and private households with employed persons.
Source: EU KLEMS database.

limit productivity gains. In particular, as shown in Table 2.3, the relative weakness in euro area hourly labour productivity relative to the USA has derived from weakness in sectors which can be thought of as more insulated from international competition. In particular, two salient features emerge from a sectoral analysis of productivity in the euro area and its relation to that of the USA. First, productivity growth remains considerably higher in manufacturing than services, with a particularly low outturn in the latter. Second, the main contributors to the productivity gap in the service sector with the USA remains concentrated in two areas: 'finance and business services', and 'distribution services' (including, notably, wholesale and retail trade), which can be thought of as Information & Communications Technology (ICT) using services.[17] This could suggest a role for competitive pressures – both domestic and international – though of course other factors such as capital intensity, technology, skill content, or the influence of terms of trade developments (for example,

[17] See Gomez-Salvador *et al.* (2006) for a more detailed exposition on this taxonomy. While there is also a significant gap in the 'electrical machinery' sector (containing such subsectors as office machinery and electronics), which can be thought of as 'ICT producing', a small weight of this sector in the economy implies a relatively minor contribution to the productivity shortfall.

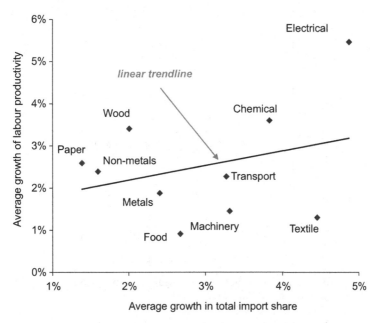

Figure 2.18 Changes in manufacturing openness and productivity in euro area sectors
(Average annual change between 1995 and 2004, %)
Note: Import share defined as imports divided by output by sector.
Source: COMEXT (trade data) and EU KLEMS (domestic), ECB calculations.

given their influence on international competitiveness) may also have contributed to this development.

Examining the traded goods sector in more detail, increasing productivity in relation to higher import openness is present within the manufacturing sector at a sectoral level. Indeed, trade openness appears to have a positive relationship with productivity within the manufacturing sector, though this derives to a large extent from impressive productivity gains in sectors generally characterised as having a high technology content, such as the electrical sector (see Figure 2.18). Moreover, the relationship of product market regulation with productivity has also been negative on average across euro area countries over the decade leading up to 2005, with a strong contribution from some more pronounced cases such as Ireland (see Figure 2.19). Such a negative relationship could result from rigidities inhibiting the positive reallocative and other benefits of structural changes to the economy such as globalisation and technological change.

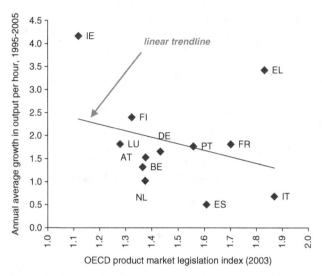

Figure 2.19 Product market regulation and labour productivity
growth across euro area countries
(Index and growth rate, %)
Note: The OECD index of product market regulation covers formal
regulations in state control of business enterprises, legal and administrative
barriers to entrepreneurship and barriers to international trade and
investment. For more detail, see Conway *et al.* (2005).
Source: OECD.

Available empirical evidence suggests a significant link between
openness and productivity through multiple channels, with stronger
positive impacts in more competitive markets. More specifically, it
would appear that, while globalisation has a strong role to play in boosting productivity, euro area productivity has been weak at the aggregate level over the last decade despite growing international openness.
More detailed sectoral analyses, based both on macro and firm-level
micro data, indicate that this weakness has derived to a large extent
from areas of the economy which are more sheltered from international
competition, thereby hinting at a role for policies aiming at enhancing
openness to such forces.

Empirical studies examining productivity developments across a wide
range of developed economies at a more aggregated level (generally on
the basis of cross-country and sectoral panels) suggest trade liberalisation contributes positively to economic performance. As reported in
Price and Cournède (2007), a one percentage point (pp) rise in trade
exposure is found to be associated with a rise in per capita income of 0.4
per cent. Helbling *et al.* (2006) find that a 1 per cent increase in relative

trade openness leads to a 0.12 per cent increase in relative productivity. Chen *et al.* (2007) find evidence of a productivity acceleration of EU manufacturing over past years through competitive effects induced by increased trade openness.

Empirical studies using firm-level data allow for a more detailed examination of the important channels through which globalisation enhances productivity – indicating that trade openness and capital flows foster technological spillovers and increased competition – leading to a higher scale of firm operations and more productive firm composition. On spillovers, Eaton and Kortum (2002) find that domestic productivity growth is mainly related to foreign rather than domestic innovation, while Baldwin *et al.* (2005) find bilateral spillovers are boosted by bilateral FDI. On scale effects, Geishecker *et al.* (2007) argue that multinational firms contribute more than domestic firms to enhanced productivity growth, with the finding that the small share of euro area firms which have affiliates abroad have higher survival rates and productivity growth. Melitz (2003) and Ottaviano *et al.* (2007) find that countries exhibiting technological advantage, freer entry and better accessibility to foreign firms develop a tougher competitive environment in which firms are more productive and operate at a larger scale. Concerning industry composition, Bernard *et al.* (2007), using plant-level data for the US manufacturing sector, find evidence of exit, growth and industry switching as a means of migrating from comparative-disadvantage to comparative-advantage activities, as well as changes in product portfolio.

In conjunction with the notion that globalisation boosts international competitive pressures, the general absence of aggregate euro area productivity gains over the last decade appear to derive from areas underexposed to international competition. In particular, relatively weak euro area productivity at an aggregate level can be linked to barriers to competition (both domestic and international), implying limited productivity-enhancing use of new technologies, multifactor productivity and regulatory impediments to adjustment. According to Gomez-Salvador *et al.* (2006), the euro area economy seems to have benefited much less from production and use of ICT, reflecting both lower investment in ICT compared with the USA and barriers to the diffusion or appropriate use of new technologies, in particular in the services sector (consistent with Table 2.3). Inklaar *et al.* (2008) find that for European Union countries, entry liberalisation has been beneficial for productivity growth in telecommunications, but not in other service industries. Van Ark (2007) argues that an institutional environment that slows down change may hold up the structural adjustment process in Europe and impede the reallocation of resources to their most productive uses. Kroszner (2006) argues that cross-country productivity differentials derive importantly from flexibility at the firm level and in labour markets, and competitive pressure throughout the economy.

2.5   Globalisation and the euro area labour market

Globalisation would be expected to influence euro area labour market conditions through two main channels. First, a redistributive channel would be expected as globalisation contributes to changes in the distribution of sectoral, occupational and skill composition in advanced economies. According to traditional paradigms, such a development in advanced economies would be expected to be biased predominantly against low-skilled workers in advanced economies (as increased offshoring possibilities lead to an increasing wage elasticity of labour demand with implications for worker bargaining power in this skill cohort) and in favour of high-skilled workers (given expanding export markets). This can be related to the notion of job losses with import competition and job gains from export demand, as posited in trade theories such as Heckscher-Ohlin, though this theory, like other prominent theories, would have mixed predictions regarding net changes in employment across and within industries, along with consequences for relative factor rewards (see Bernard *et al.*, 2007). Second, an aggregate scale channel would be expected in the long run, whereby labour demand is boosted by productivity gains accruing from international openness. Following from the analysis in the preceding section of this chapter, the scale effect is likely to have remained limited thus far in the euro area on aggregate given a weak overall productivity performance to date (though in the long term the balance could shift). In the long run, while the consequences for the labour market depend on the interplay of the scale effects with an aggregation of the redistributive aspects, in the short run, structural features of the labour market have a crucial role in adjustment mechanisms. As noted in Hoekman and Winters (2005), the effects of trade on wages and employment will depend on labour market institutions, the efficiency of capital markets and the mobility of factors across sectors (and borders).

As already alluded to in Section 2.2 of this chapter, one of the main features of the current wave of globalisation which distinguishes it from previous episodes is the possibility of production fragmentation and related offshoring as described in studies such as Baldwin (2006) and Feenstra (2007). While it is difficult to gauge its exact intensity, given a lack of direct information on which parts of production stages

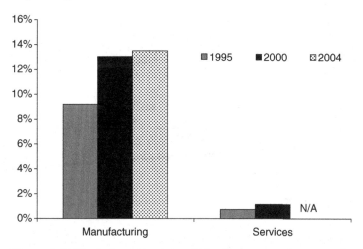

Figure 2.20 Trade-based narrow offshoring measure by sector for the euro area
(Share of industry's imported inputs in the industry's output)
Note: Offshoring defined 'narrowly', i.e. sectoral share of imported inputs of the given sector in its output; includes both intra and extra euro area trade; extrapolation for 2004 based on interpolated input-output table coefficients.
Source: ECB calculations based on COMEXT data and OECD input-output tables.

are contracted out, several methods may be applied to obtain information on international outsourcing, such as individual firm management information, anecdotal evidence and statistical evidence from various macroeconomic proxies (such as data on trade). Using the latter methodology, the macro proxy of trade content designed to capture a narrow measure of offshoring, it would appear that offshoring was growing in both manufacturing and services over the period 1995–2000, but nonetheless remained much higher in the former sector though growing less in recent years since that period (see Figure 2.20).[18] That said, anecdotal evidence, such as management studies, suggest that services outsourcing has been growing since 2000 in the euro area (see ECB, 2006a) – particularly in 'arm's length' service provision.[19]

[18] This measure is a proxy with several caveats, most notably that the import share, which could reflect domestic demand as well as domestic supply channels, plays a very important role in its dynamics. Computations made to obtain post-2000 outsourcing estimates using interpolated input–output table coefficients (unavailable for services).

[19] Bhagwati *et al.* (2004) note four ways in which services can be traded: (1) 'arm's length' service provision, whereby the supplier and buyer remain in their respective locations (e.g. call centres, back offices and software programmers); (2) services are provided by moving the service recipient to the location of the service provider

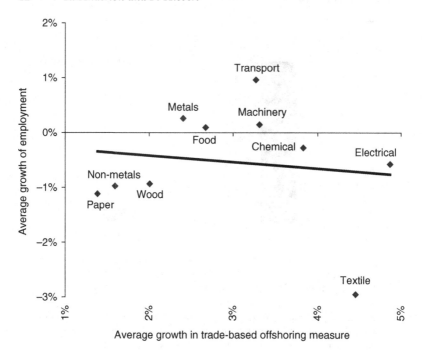

Figure 2.21 Employment and offshoring within euro area
manufacturing
(Average annual change between 1995 and 2004, %)
Note: Narrow offshoring refers to ratio of own imported inputs to
production.
Source: COMEXT (trade data) and EU KLEMS (domestic).

In analysing how offshoring relates to employment outcomes at the
industry level (within manufacturing, where data is available), it
appears that the relation to outsourcing across manufacturing industries is weak for employment in the manufacturing sector as a whole,
though there are significant impacts in some industries, such as textiles
(Figure 2.21).

Broadening the focus to also incorporate the service sector, survey
data also indicate a limited offshoring contribution to job losses. As
shown in Figure 2.22, survey data based on media reports indicates
that 'direct' job losses from offshoring are generally limited as a proportion of overall jobs lost – with an economy-wide average of 8 per cent of

(e.g. tourism and education); (3) the service provider establishes a commercial presence in another country (requiring an element of direct foreign investment); and
(4) the service seller moves to the location of the service buyer (e.g. construction and
consulting services, requiring temporary migration).

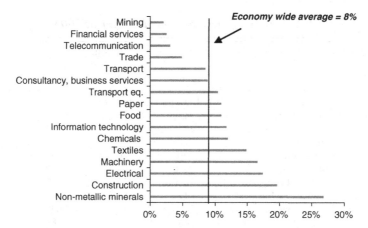

Figure 2.22 Survey data on euro area jobs directly lost due to offshoring
Note: Euro area excludes Greece, Luxembourg and Slovenia. Based on media survey on reported mass layoffs. Includes offshoring within the euro area as well as outside.
Source: European Restructuring Monitor.

total jobs lost.[20] The sectoral composition of such reported job losses is predominantly in manufacturing and is generally low in services, and to some extent can be seen as correlated with domestic productivity developments within the affected sectors.

Changing specialisation brought about by globalisation may, of course, imply that gross job losses are offset by gross gains on the aggregate. Indeed, there have been significant euro area employment gains since the mid 1990s, almost entirely in services, while manufacturing appears to have been in continued secular decline (see Table 2.4). In particular, business services employment has grown very strongly in the last decade, despite likely growing tradability of this component (see, for instance, Mann, 2003 and Markusen, 2007). Amiti and Wei (2005) argue that although service outsourcing has been steadily increasing it is still very low, and that in the United States and many other industrial countries insourcing of services (i.e. from foreign-located firms to domestic firms) is greater than outsourcing. Of course, factors other

[20] These findings are drawn from the 'European Restructuring Monitor', which records all industrial restructuring cases reported through a press review of daily newspapers and business press that (1) affect at least one EU country; (2) entail an announced or actual reduction of at least 100 jobs; (3) involve sites employing more than 250 people and affecting at least 10 per cent of workforce; or (4) create at least 100 jobs. For more, see www.eurofound.europa.eu/emcc/erm/info.htm.

Table 2.4 *Euro area employment, 1996 versus 2006*

	(millions)		
	1996	2006	change, 1996–2006
Total domestic	122.71	139.68	16.97
Total industry	34.53	35.02	0.48
Industry excluding construction	25.42	24.48	-0.94
Construction	9.11	10.54	1.42
Total services	81.49	98.87	17.38
Trade and transport	30.34	35.11	4.77
Finance and business	14.99	21.65	6.66
Other services	36.17	42.11	5.95
Agriculture	6.69	5.80	-0.89

Source: Eurostat data and ECB calculations.

than (though not necessarily totally independent of) globalisation may explain a significant amount of labour market adjustment over the last decade, such as technological and structural changes and their effects on permanent shifts in the distribution of workers throughout the economy in the labour market (for more on the latter argument, see Groshen and Potter, 2003).

These survey findings appear prima facie consistent with available empirical evidence on the aggregate employment effects of globalisation, which suggest a small negative estimated impact of import penetration and offshoring on euro area employment within the manufacturing sector. That said, little evidence is available on globalisation's impacts for employment in the economy as a whole. The analysis of Pula and Skudelny in Chapter 7 of this book suggests that a one percentage point increase in openness reduces manufacturing employment growth by 0–0.2 percentage point (depending on the industry composition). Mankiw and Swagel (2006) argue that trade-related losses are a small portion of overall job flows, a fact that is also empirically borne out by the analysis of Hiebert and Vansteenkiste (2008) for the US manufacturing sector. At the same time, Hiebert and Vansteenkiste (2009) find evidence for US manufacturing that other factors such as technological change tend to engender greater labour market impacts than changes in openness.

In examining factors governing offshoring decisions, survey data for the services sector suggest both a distance and cost component to such offshoring, with offshoring relatively higher to geographically close neighbours, and concentrated in industries characterised by a higher

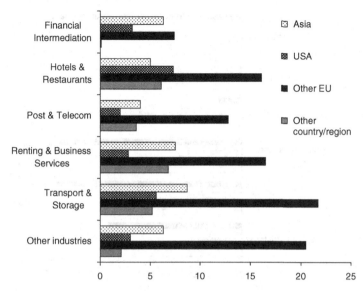

Figure 2.23 Survey data on current locations of outsourcing in euro area service sector
(Percentage of respondents)
Source: NTC Economics (2007).

degree tradability (see Figures 2.23 and 2.24). The geographic destination of service sector offshoring for euro area firms shows that the majority remains with geographically close firms such as non-euro area EU countries. On average 20 per cent of the firms claimed to outsource to foreign developed countries (EU + USA) and only 10 per cent to emerging economies (Asia + Others). As for factors cited in electing to outsource (i.e. domestically and internationally), reduction of staff costs is claimed to be a major factor in at least three of the services sectors, i.e. transportation and storage, business services and financial intermediation. These sectors, which are not normally broadly classified as lower-skilled areas, raise the issue that so-called 'white-collar' offshoring may have been on the increase, in contrast to the predictions of traditional trade theory that low-skilled jobs are primarily affected by trade competition. Unfortunately, little data exists to validate this notion statistically. Ultimately, though, the above survey data appears broadly consistent with chapter 3 of this book by Markusen, where it is argued that characteristics such as codifiability, routinisation, and the lack of need for face-to-face interaction are of great importance in the outsourcing decision for service industries, while costs and market penetration determine the geographical decision on where to outsource.

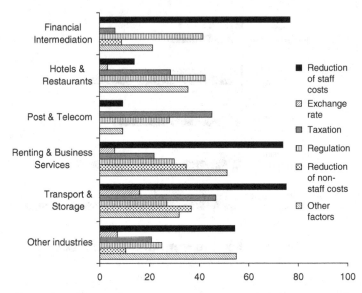

Figure 2.24 Survey data on current factors underlying outsourcing
in euro area service sector
(Percentage of respondents)
Source: NTC Economics (2007).

Indeed, while ICT accelerates the codification of knowledge and modifies the balance between codified and tacit knowledge, there may still be continued benefits from human interaction based on the latter (see Morgan, 2004). An alternative perspective comes from a European Sourcing survey by Eurostat (see Alajääskö, 2009), where it is found that manufacturing enterprises source far more than enterprises active in other sectors, while among the support business functions, the international sourcing of 'distribution and logistics' as well as 'marketing and (after-)sales' is most widespread.

Part of the growth in euro area employment over the last years, despite growing outsourcing, may relate to immigration developments. Migration flows may be related to outsourcing trends, insofar as they obviate the need for firms to go outside borders to have access to inexpensive low-skilled labour as part of cost cutting through production fragmentation – though the extent to which migration inflows limit cost-saving offshoring depends, of course, on the extent to which labour regulations oblige employers to pay immigrants at prevailing host-country rates (given, for instance, minimum wage legislation). There has been a steadily increasing inflow of migrants to the euro area, with a heterogeneous skill mix depending on geographic origin. Eurostat

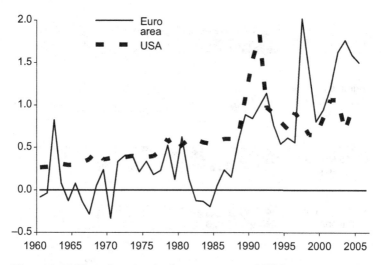

Figure 2.25 Net migration in the euro area and USA
(Millions of persons)
Note: Net migration is measured as the difference between the total
population on 1 January and 31 December for a given calendar year minus
the difference between births and deaths (or natural increase). Includes
Metropolitan France until 1997.
Source: Eurostat, US Census/Office of Immigration Statistics.

data indicate a steady growth in net inward migration in the euro area
over the last decade, bringing such flows recently to a level above the
USA (Figure 2.25). In examining the skill distribution of migrant versus native populations within the EU-15 (where data is available), it
would appear that migrant flows have involved both a relatively large
proportion of unskilled labour (from outside the EU) as well as a relatively higher medium- to high-skill content from migration within the
EU (Figure 2.26). Broadbent and Zsoldos (2007) indicate that of the
net total number of migrants flowing into the EU-15, almost two-thirds
have gone to Spain while the next two most important destination countries (in terms of absolute numbers) are Italy and the UK. At the same
time, they indicate that France and Germany have seen relatively few
migrants and the Netherlands has actually seen a small net outflow.
Heinz and Ward-Warmedinger (2006) find for the European Union
that the economic impacts of increased cross-border labour mobility
are likely to be positive, although potentially unequally distributed
across countries and sectors.

Turning to recent euro area wage developments, globalisation may
have been one contributing factor to an extended period of wage

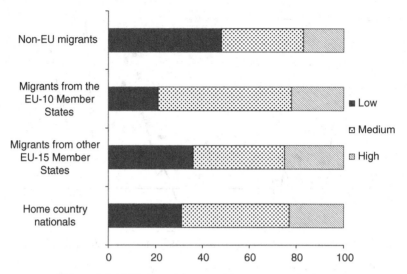

Figure 2.26 EU-15 resident working-age population by nationality and education level
(Percentage share, 2005)
Note: Educational level: low (lower secondary), medium (upper secondary), high (tertiary).
Source: European Commission (2006), based on Eurostat Labour Force Survey, Q1 2005, France and Austria Q2 2005.

moderation within the euro area (for instance, if offshoring or the threat of offshoring reduces the wage demands of workers). As indicated in Figure 2.27, real wages have been weaker than productivity both on aggregate and also within the manufacturing and services sectors – which can be considered as one of the central factors permitting the strong aggregate employment growth in the euro area in the decade leading up to 2006 indicated in Table 2.4. At the same time, there has been an ongoing weakening of the wage share of income over a longer period, which has been more severe than the corresponding fall in the USA since the mid 80s, bringing this measure in both regions to historical lows (Figure 2.28). While such a development might be taken to indicate that the bargaining power of workers may have declined in the context of globalisation, extreme caution should be made in drawing such conclusions given several caveats related to measurement issues[21] and the fact that much of this decline took place well before the recent

---

[21] It should be noted in this respect that several measurement problems limit the reliability of the wage share, including a growing importance of non-wage remuneration (particularly the growing number of self employed), which implies that this measure cannot be interpreted reliably as the share of income accruing to capital or labour.

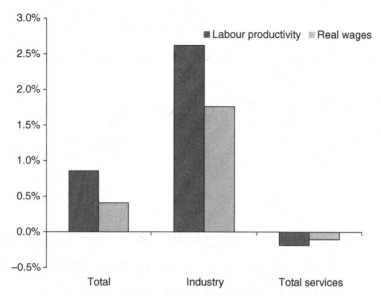

Figure 2.27 Real wages and productivity in the euro area
(Average annual change between 1996 and 2007)
Note: Real wages computed as nominal compensation per employee less the
respective value added deflator. Services sum of (1) trade, repairs, hotels,
restaurants, transport and communications, (2) financial, real estate, renting
and business activities, and (3) other service activities.
Source: Eurostat (ESA95).

phase of globalisation. Moreover, globalisation's contribution to an
extended period of wage moderation within the euro area may very well
have contributed to the strong job creation witnessed over the last decade as reported in Table 2.4.

Empirical evidence on the aggregate wage effects of globalisation
suggest that an increase in the real wage elasticity of labour demand
appears to have occurred in the last years, particularly for low-skilled
workers, which may indicate a decline in the bargaining power of these
groups (see, for instance, Chapter 7 of this book by Pula and Skudelny,
as well as Molnar *et al.* (2006) and Price and Cournède (2007)). The
OECD finds that jobs and wages have become more vulnerable to
external shocks – thereby possibly reducing the bargaining power of
workers, especially low-skilled ones, which may therefore contribute
to explaining the falling share of wages in national income. Jaumotte
et al. (2008) as well as Jaumotte and Tytell (2007) point to globalisation
playing only a minor role in reducing the wage share compared with
other factors such as technological change and labour market policies.

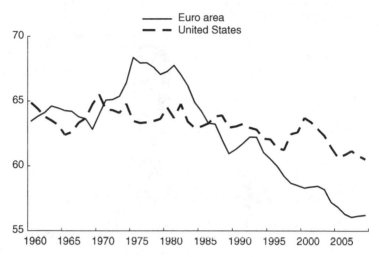

Figure 2.28 Long-term developments in labour shares in the euro area and USA
(In percentage of gross national income)
Note: Self-employment adjusted labour shares; total domestic economy. The labour share is defined as the ratio of total compensation of employees to gross national income at current market prices.
Source: AMECO database and ECB calculations.

They also find that countries that have enacted reforms to lower the cost of labour to business and improve labour market flexibility have generally experienced a smaller decline in the wage share. Concerning the question of whether the observed drop in the wage share of several advanced economies is structural or transitory, it would appear that there is not yet a consensus in the literature. On the one hand, the findings of Guscina (2006), based on a panel of OECD countries (over the period 1960–2000), suggest that the decline in labour's share during the past few decades may have been largely an equilibrium, rather than a cyclical, phenomenon, with technological progress having been capital-augmenting during the recent globalisation phase. On the other hand, other studies suggest that the observed fall in the wage share may be temporary (though possibly quite persistent), as while the wage share in income might match productivity over longer periods, a falling wage share might be evident at shorter horizons in the case of a relative decline in the return to labour, given relatively more important frictions in adjusting the capital stock.[22] In addition to observable factors,

---

[22] As argued by Schumacher *et al.* (2007), while wages would be expected to adjust in response to any changes in productivity shocks in the short run, employment would

an unobservable 'threat effect' –whereby workers in industrialised economies perceive themselves to have a weaker bargaining position and thereby moderate wage claims given a fear of production relocation to lower-cost economies – may have contributed to the fall in the wage share.[23]

Leaving aside aggregate developments and looking more closely at uneven developments in employment and wages across skill groups, it would appear growing skill bias in labour demand in the euro area has manifested itself predominantly in hours (and not in hourly compensation). A review of the evolution of real wages and hours in the manufacturing sector by skill (proxied by level of educational attainment) yields two noteworthy findings.[24] First, a wedge has developed in euro area manufacturing hours, with a sustained rise in the hours of high-skilled workers contrasting with falling hours of low-skilled workers. Second, real wage developments have remained similar across all skill groups (Figure 2.29), thereby the skill bias in euro area labour demand has fallen predominantly on 'quantities' (i.e. employment) and not 'prices' (i.e. wages) – in contrast to the USA, where wages appear to have exhibited more flexibility according to this skill classification.[25] At face value, this could suggest that labour market rigidities, for instance those preventing differentiated wage growth according to worker productivity, may imply a disproportionate adjustment in employment for a given shift in the wage elasticity of demand for lower-skilled groups.

Indeed, trade theory would suggest that enhanced trade between developed and developing countries places downward pressure on the relative returns to unskilled workers – whereby the relative real return to the factor used intensively in the production of a good whose relative price falls/rises should also fall/rise according to the Stolper-Samuelson proposition. This would also be consistent with changing euro area economic specialisation, based on comparative advantage, discussed in Fontagne et al. (2007) and di Mauro and Anderton (2007). Epifani and

be expected to adjust over medium-term horizons and the capital stock only in the long run given time-to-build constraints. In this vein, Ellis and Smith (2007) argue that a fall in factor income accruing to labour would be expected to result as long as the increase in the effective global supply of labour is not matched by an equivalent rise in the stock of capital.

[23] This could also imply a change in the equilibrium unemployment, or NAWRU, and also possibly some disconnect between product and labour market slack.

[24] It should be borne in mind that education-based skill classifications have some limitations, notably that they may be affected not only by the skill content of work, but also by changes in educational attainment patterns.

[25] Consistent with this, Hiebert and Vansteenkiste (2009) find for the US manufacturing sector that openness shocks produce relatively strong wage and productivity impacts relative to very limited employment impacts.

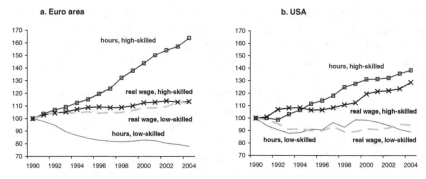

Figure 2.29 Hours and real hourly wages by educational attainment-based measure of skill level
(Index: 1990 = 100)
Note: Real wage index derived usng PPI as deflator; derived from wage and hour shares in total by skill multiplied with levels available in KLEMS. Skill data derived from national data on educational attainment, with high-skilled comprising those with university-level education and low-skilled comprising those with primary and/or secondary education (depending on the country). Hourly wages deflated using producer prices.
Source: ECB calculations based on EU Klems data.

Gancia (2008) present a model indicating that international trade, even between identical countries, can raise the relative demand for skilled labour. Moreover, they argue that the scale of an economy may be a key determinant of the skill premium. While globalisation may play a role in skill-biased labour demand, other factors such as skill-biased technological change or secular shifts of domestic production long present in advanced economies (from manufacturing to services) may still play an important, and even dominant, role in this process.

Examining prospective redistributive effects, there is empirical evidence of skill bias in labour demand (though the technology role is also of strong importance). As shown in Chapter 7 of this book by Pula and Skudelny, increased openness has a negative impact on labour demand for low-skilled sectors, which they attribute to factors such as increased competition and offshoring and a higher real wage elasticity of labour demand. Cuyvers *et al.* (2006) and Hijzen (2007) also indicate important differences in labour market developments for aggregate versus skill groups. In terms of the net effects across skill groups, Geishecker and Görg (2006) find on the basis of German micro data that the positive impact of outsourcing on high-skilled employment outweighs the negative impact on the low skilled. Anderton *et al.* (2006) also find that technology – in the form of skill-biased technical change – is the main factor explaining the decline in the relative demand for less-skilled

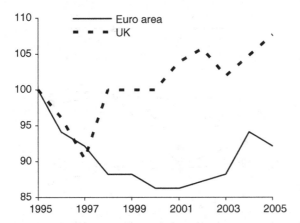

Figure 2.30 Income inequality in the euro area and the UK
(80/20 percentile ratio, index 1995 = 100)
Note: the ratio of total income received by the 20% of the population
with the highest income (top quintile) to that received by the 20% of the
population with the lowest income (lowest quintile).
Source: European Commission.

workers across a range of countries, but they also argue that the rapid
rise in technological change seems to be partly driven by the strong
growth in international trade and globalisation. Grossman and Rossi-
Hansberg (2006) argue that a productivity effect associated with offshoring can more than offset labour supply and relative price effects,
thereby leading to high wages for even low-skilled workers following a
rise in offshoring (though Olsen (2006) finds little empirical evidence
on the productivity effects of offshoring to date).

While an important skill dimension appears to have been present in
euro area labour market developments, there have been few signs of
growing income inequality relative to a decade earlier on the basis of
analysing the top and bottom quintiles of the income distribution, particularly by international standards – though such a finding is to some
extent conditional on the specific measure of inequality used. As indicated in Figure 2.30, income inequality for the euro area had declined
by 2005 to less than 95 per cent of its 1995 level, when comparing
the highest and lowest income quintiles (the 80/20 percentile ratio). A
recent increase in inequality, however, appears to have occurred, which
Bräuninger (2007) argues may reflect a rise in unemployment that
occurred in the first half of the decade as part of an economic slowdown. On the basis of Gini coefficients, it would appear that in general
income inequality in large euro area countries has generally increased
since the early 1980s (though considerable country heterogeneity is

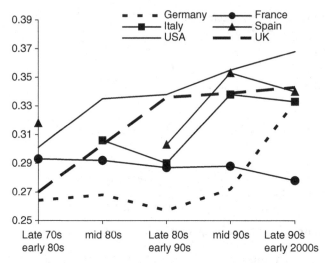

Figure 2.31 Gini coefficients from income distribution
Note: A high Gini coefficient indicates more unequal distribution, with
zero corresponding to perfect equality and one corresponding to perfect
inequality.
Source: Luxembourg Income Study.

present), though generally remaining below either the USA or the UK
(Figure 2.31). For the USA, Autor *et al.* (2007) suggest that the changing distribution of job task demands, spurred directly by advancing
information technology and indirectly by its impact on outsourcing,
goes some distance toward interpreting the recent polarisation of the
wage structure. Other factors may also be relevant, such as the possibility that wage earners are also capital owners, that government and private transfers mitigate the impact on overall inequality of a falling wage
share, and the emergence of non-wage components in wage bargaining
(see, for instance, Genre *et al.*, 2004). As for income inequality, Machin
and van Reenen (1998), Cuyvers *et al.* (2002) and Harjes (2007) find
only a modest contribution of international trade and immigration to
euro area income inequality developments.

All in all, globalisation's impacts on euro area labour markets have
been mainly visible in the form of a redistribution of employment across
sectoral, occupational and skill categories. Indeed, a review of available
empirical evidence indicates that the aggregate labour market impacts of
globalisation remain largely uncertain – with limited aggregate employment impacts contrasting with possibly more significant impacts on
the wage share and bargaining power. That said, there appear to have

been clear effects on certain sectors and skill groups, as the rise in off-shoring which characterises the recent phase of globalisation appears to have been associated with a clear skill bias in labour demand.[26] As real wages across skill categories have shown little differentiation in response to this, labour market adjustment associated with such a bias has been concentrated on employment. That said, there has been limited change in income inequality in the euro area when compared with other advanced economies, such as the UK or USA, thus far. Moreover, job losses associated with offshoring have been limited as a proportion of overall job losses in the euro area economy and, importantly, offset by employment gains elsewhere. In this vein, globalisation's contribution to an extended period of wage moderation within the euro area (for instance, through offshoring or the threat of offshoring) may very well have contributed to the strong job creation witnessed over the last decade. At the same time, the pronounced fall in the euro area wage share of income over the last decades appears to be linked not only to globalisation but to other possibly more relevant (though potentially related) factors such as technological and structural change.

2.6   Globalisation and euro area prices

Globalisation would be expected to have two main impacts on consumer price inflation in the short term – acknowledging that monetary policy determines inflation over the medium to long term – with the ultimate effect on prices remaining ambiguous as it depends on the interplay of various effects. First, a relative price effect implies that aggregate inflation can be simultaneously attenuated by developments in some prices through global supply channels (for example, from dampened prices of imports of manufactured goods or cheaper inputs into the production process) and accentuated by increases in other prices given global demand pressures (for example, related to strong emerging market economies' demand for energy and other commodities).[27] As relative price movements are a natural part of economic functioning and therefore

---

[26] More generally, the extent to which this can be attributed to globalisation (versus technology, for instance) in practice is uncertain – see the debate in the literature on the role of domestic versus global factors in producing labour market adjustment, for instance in Wood (1998).

[27] Concerning the supply channels, a mechanical change in price dynamics derives from both a static level effect (a level shift in prices through the increasing shares of emerging markets in the import basket of advanced economies) and dynamic price differential effect (a change in inflation dynamics given inflation differentials between emerging and advanced economies in conjunction with the change in import shares) – see ECB (2006b).

need not necessarily have any effect on aggregate inflation consistent with a central bank's inflation objective, such movements would only be expected to have short-term aggregate inflationary impacts insofar as the movements are sizeable and/or a combination of adjustment frictions and imperfect information imply prolonged impacts. Policy factors which could explain aggregate inflation impacts of relative price shocks could be monetary policy accommodation – either intentional, through an 'opportunistic' approach to disinflation,[28] or unintentional, given imperfect information and learning – or asset price misalignments resulting from globalisation. Second, increased competitive pressures associated with globalisation could constitute an indirect channel affecting prices as they contribute to change price elasticities by compressing firms' price–cost mark-ups or cost developments, and thereby exert a moderating influence on inflation as long as impediments to competition are not in place. In particular, increased competitive pressures would be expected to both dampen firm profit mark-up behaviour while also potentially altering developments in costs (such as the cost of capital and labour) which underlie price dynamics. While changing firms' mark-up behaviour, labour cost moderation and productivity enhancement may imply more muted price inflation, such pressures may take time to materialise given what could be a gradual process of adjustment in price setting for formerly protected industries along with frictions associated with the adjustment of production processes. In the context of a Phillips-curve framework, openness associated with globalisation may have contributed to changing the link between consumer price inflation and costs or standard domestic measures of macroeconomic slack, in particular through competitive impacts on changing price flexibility or through an increasing role for foreign conditions in the price formation process. Indeed, globalisation may influence the Phillips curve in two key ways.[29] First, it may have affected the wage and price-setting behaviour of households and firms, thereby affecting the responsiveness of inflation to standard measures of economic slack or production costs. On one hand, this could imply a decreased responsiveness of domestic

---

[28] For more on the opportunistic approach to disinflation, see Aksoy *et al.* (2006). As argued by Razin and Binyamini (2007), a flattening of the inflation–activity relationship induced by globalisation may induce the monetary authority guided in its policy by the welfare criterion of a representative household to put more emphasis on the reduction of inflation variability at the expense of an increase in the output gap variability.

[29] More generally concerning Phillips curve specifications, globalisation may have influenced the distribution and type of exogenous shocks to the inflation process (relating also to the relative price shocks described above), along with commensurate changes to observed inflation persistence and inflation expectations.

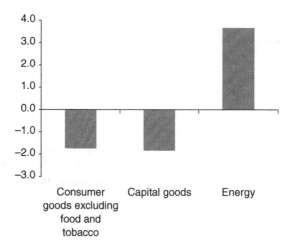

Figure 2.32 Producer prices: evolution of selected sub-indices
relative to overall index
(Change over 1996–2008 relative to overall index, %)
Source: ECB calculations based on Eurostat data.

inflation to the domestic output gap in favour of slack in the global economy, while on the other hand, heightened competition resulting from
globalisation may have made prices and wages more responsive to economic activity in the long run (see, for instance, Rogoff, 2006). Second,
globalisation might have changed the productive potential of the economy and therefore domestic slack itself, notably through productivity
effects given competitive pressures and associated innovation.

The recent euro area experience indicates that relative price impacts
have been strong over the last decade, with disinflation in manufactured
goods contrasting with a strong acceleration in prices for commodities.
As indicated in Figure 2.32, producer prices over the last decade have
been characterised by strong relative price effects, with muted development in consumer goods excluding food and tobacco along with
capital goods relative to average producer prices contrasting with relatively strong increases in the energy component (which also may have
affected prices further down the production chain). As indicated in
Figure 2.33, HICP subcomponents have also exhibited sizeable price
differentials, in particular with three energy-related items displaying
the highest increases over 1996–2006, while three ICT-intensive internationally traded goods exhibit the lowest increases over the period. In
particular, international trade dynamics may help to explain the extent
of disinflation in manufacturing resulting from openness, with price
impacts depending on the interplay between mechanical impacts from

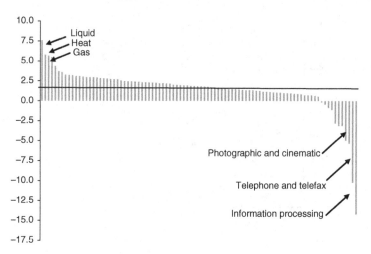

Figure 2.33 Consumer prices: average price changes in euro area HICP sub-components
(Average annual change over 1996–2006, %)
Note: Data for 92 HICP sub-components.
Source: ECB calculations based on Eurostat data.

relative inflation differentials for existing euro area import shares (possibly mitigated by pricing-to-market considerations) and price level differentials leading to the mechanical disinflationary impact owing to further penetration of low-cost countries into the euro area import basket. At the same time, commodity price volatility (in areas such as energy, minerals and food), in particular over 2008, may to some extent have been linked to globalisation forces.

Studies examining trade globalisation's aggregate impact on inflation tend to suggest a small net dampening impact of globalisation on prices until around 2005, deriving from subdued price developments in the manufacturing sector. The overall dampening impact on euro area inflation appears to lie in the range of 0.3 pp per annum over the five to ten years leading up to around 2005, taking into account the net impact of disinflationary effects of increased trade openness in the manufacturing sector and strong commodity price increases. On the basis of several methodologies, including aggregate and sectoral analysis, the calculations in Chapter 7 of this book by Pula and Skudelny indicate a direct dampening effect of import openness on euro area producer price inflation of 0.1–1.0 pp for the manufacturing sector over the period 1996 to 2004. The authors report a dampening impact on euro area consumer price inflation of 0.05–0.2 pp per year on average based on aggregate data over the same period. Pain *et al.* in chapter 6 of this book find a combined effect on consumer inflation from lower non-commodity import price inflation and higher commodity import price inflation of up to 0.3 per annum over the period 2000 to 2005. Using similar methodologies, Glatzer *et al.* (2006), Helbling *et al.* (2006) and Chen *et al.* (2007) report findings of a similar magnitude for other countries and regional groupings. More recent calculations for the USA suggest, however, that volatile commodity prices – and in particular leading up to the spike in mid 2008 – pushed up import prices from China (Amiti and Davis, 2008). In general, empirical evidence would lend support to the idea of a strong relative price shock associated with globalisation.

In contrast, evidence concerning the role of international competitive pressures in compressing firms' mark-ups is mixed. On the one hand, theoretical models would predict pro-competitive effects contributing to reduce mark-ups as domestic firms compete with international firms. On the other hand, generally high profitability of firms in the period leading up to 2006 would suggest that there was little compression of profit mark-ups over this period at the aggregate level. Though pro-competitive effects from increased international competition may have helped hold down firms' costs, on aggregate they appear to have had a more limited influence on firms' pricing power. In the euro area, available data suggest that firms' profit mark-ups have not been compressed on aggregate in recent years (Figure 2.34), though such indicators are a crude proxy of unit profits. While growth in the profit mark-up weakened over the last decade compared with a decade earlier, with a fall in the growth of both labour costs and the value-added deflator, a closer look at sectoral developments leads to a more nuanced picture. An estimated measure of sectoral profit mark-ups by Christopoulou and Vermeulen (2008) suggests that profit mark-ups in the euro area over the period 1993–2006 have been similar to or below those of the USA in manufacturing but systematically higher in services (see Figure 2.35). Moreover, the findings of Chen *et al.* (2007) support the notion that mark-ups have been compressed within the EU manufacturing sector, suggesting some compression of mark-ups for firms producing tradable goods subject to international competition. Such findings could support the notion that mark-ups have been compressed for tradable goods subject to international competition, but have moved little in service industries which tend to be more sheltered from such forces – though such a conclusion must be tempered by measurement issues related, in particular, to service sector mark-ups.

Empirical evidence suggests pro-competitive effects of trade have led to reduced mark-ups in European manufacturing, with Chen *et al.*

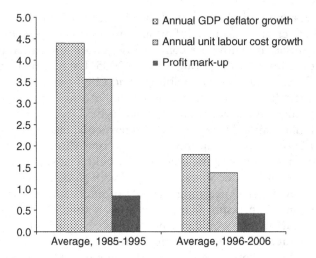

Figure 2.34 Evolution of euro area value-added deflator, ULC and profit mark-up
(Period average of year-on-year growth rate, %)
Note: Profit mark-up computed as annual growth rate of output price less annual growth rate of unit labour costs.
Source: ECB Area-wide model database (see Fagan *et al.* (2005)).

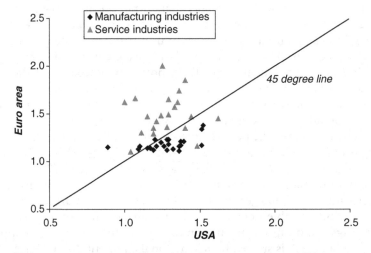

Figure 2.35 Estimated sectoral mark-ups: euro area vs. USA
(Mark-up ratios, average over 1993–2004)
Note: Data for 48 two-digit industries (28 in manufacturing, 22 in services). A ratio greater than one implies that prices are larger than marginal costs and can be interpreted as evidence of market power in an industry.
Source: Christopoulou and Vermeulen (2008).

(2007) reporting a fall of mark-ups in EU manufacturing by 1.6 per cent over period 1988–2000. All in all, it appears that the aggregate economy impact has been muted – indeed, on aggregate price–cost mark-ups have grown given the importance of other domestic factors. Abraham *et al.* (2006), relying on microeconomic data for Belgium, find that price–cost margins are typically lower in sectors that are subject to higher international competition (especially from low-wage countries).

Notwithstanding this finding of a limited compression of firms' mark-ups, a flattening in the Phillips curve appears to have occurred in the last decades, though it is not clear to what extent this reflects a growing influence of global or foreign measures of economic slack in the domestic inflation process (the monetary policy aspects of this are covered in Chapter 9). This development contrasts with theoretical arguments in favour of a steepening of the Phillips curve in response to globalisation, as competitive forces make prices more flexible in response to changing costs or measures of economic slack (see, for instance, Ball, 2006 or Rogoff, 2006). In the euro area, a flattening in the inflation–unemployment gap variant of the Phillips curve has been evident over the last decades (see Figure 2.36), though it should be kept in mind that changes in structural unemployment not captured by the simple measure of trend unemployment may have occurred over the period.[30] Notwithstanding this caveat, while this latest flattening coincides with the acceleration of globalisation over the last decade, its contribution must be considered in the context of other factors such as the more efficient conduct of monetary policy, 'good luck' (fewer negative macroeconomic or other shocks), fiscal discipline and structural reforms – though these policy factors themselves may very well have been affected by globalisation.

There is limited evidence that domestic inflation has become more sensitive to measures of foreign slack in addition to the standard import price channel.[31] On the one hand, Borio and Filardo (2007) find a significant role for global economic slack measures in Phillips curves of advanced economies (albeit with mixed results for the euro area). Specifically for the euro area, studies such as Paloviita (2007) and Rumler (2007) find euro area inflation dynamics are better captured by

[30] This flattening is consistent with the development in other advanced economies – see, for instance, Bean (2007) for a discussion of the UK inflation–unemployment relationship, as well as Chapter 6 and Anderton *et al.* (2009), who find a decline over time in the parameter for the output gap in Phillips curves for the OECD economies.

[31] Globalisation may have weakened the link of domestic liquidity on domestic prices or, alternatively, implied a higher role for foreign liquidity in domestic prices; Rüffer and Stracca (2006) find evidence of a significant spillover of global liquidity to the euro area economy.

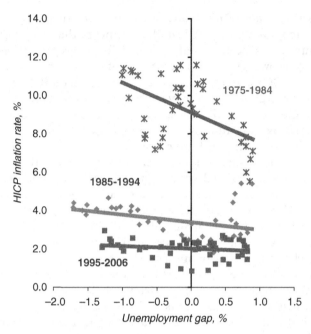

Figure 2.36 Euro area HICP inflation and the 'unemployment gap'
Note: Unemployment gap defined as the deviation of unemployment from trend unemployment measured by an HP filter with a smoothing parameter of 25,000.
Source: ECB Area-wide model database (see Fagan *et al.* (2005)), September 2007 version.

an open economy specification. In a similar vein, Ciccarelli and Mojon (2005) find that for several OECD countries, the global inflation rate moves largely in response to global real variables over short horizons and global monetary variables at longer horizons. In looking at inflation dynamics of highly disaggregated consumer price data, Monacelli and Sala (2007) find that a sizeable fraction of the variance of inflation can be explained by macroeconomic factors attributable to 'international' factors for both Germany and France, but that such factors are more relevant in the goods/manufacturing sector than in the service sector. For the UK, Batini *et al.* (2005) find external competitive pressures also seem to affect UK inflation via their impact on the equilibrium price mark-up of domestic firms. On the other hand, many other studies have failed to identify a significant role for global economic slack measures in Phillips curves of advanced economies. Calza (2008) finds limited evidence in support of the 'global output gap hypothesis' for the euro area. This appears consistent with the findings of Musso *et al.* (2007), who find that a flattening of the slope of the euro area Phillips curve occurred mainly in the 1980s, before the current globalisation phase. Broadening the studies to those looking at other economic regions, Ball (2006), Ihrig *et al.* (2007), Wynne and Kersting (2007) and Woodford (2007), argue for a negligible role for measures of global economic slack on inflation dynamics, while Pain *et al.* (2006) relate a rise in the sensitivity of domestic inflation in OECD economies to foreign economic conditions to an import price channel alone. On the basis of a new Keynesian Phillips-curve-based model, Sbordone (2008) finds it difficult to argue that an increase in trade would have generated a sufficiently large increase in US market competition to reduce the slope of the inflation–marginal cost relation.

All in all, globalisation appears to have had at best a small dampening effect on euro area prices on average over the five to ten years leading up to around 2005 as strong relative price shocks associated with low prices of imports of manufactured goods through global supply developments on balance offset strong increases in prices of hard commodities resulting from heightened global demand pressures over the period. In the period since that time, the balance of relative price shocks as characterised above could very well have been strongly inflationary at some stages. While a rise in international competitive pressures may have also contributed to wage moderation in the euro area, it appears to have led to little compression on overall profit mark-ups of firms. However, as in the case of productivity, exposure to international competition appears to have played an important role in sectoral mark-up developments. Beyond these effects, compelling evidence of a growing role for global measures of slack in the inflation process of the euro area and other advanced economies remains largely absent as a stand-alone factor – though, as argued by White (2008), it may be one of several factors which combined to produce the observed flattening in the Phillips-curve slope.

2.7   Conclusions

This chapter has taken a long-term perspective over a period predominantly characterised by the rapid growth of globalisation, notwithstanding the more recent interruption to the growth of global trade and capital flows that emerged towards the end of 2008 associated with the global financial turmoil and the downturn in global economic activity. Indeed, these recent events demonstrate how the increased international interconnectedness of financial and product markets exacerbated the financial turmoil that began in mid 2007, while the rapid growth in 'vertical specialisation' and widespread global production chains associated with globalisation contributed to the subsequent highly synchronised nature of the downturn in global trade.[32] However, the chapter focused on the longer-term trends and shows how globalisation has increased export competition in world markets over the past decade due to the emergence of new global trade players such as China, resulting in the shrinking of export market shares of advanced industrialised economies such as the euro area, while simultaneously stimulating world demand and euro area activity. The loss in share partly depends on how the export product specialisation of the euro area compares to these new competitors, with evidence showing that China is rapidly moving away from labour-intensive products and recently becoming similar to the euro area by increasing its specialisation in more research-intensive goods. On the imports side, globalisation has been accompanied in the euro area by a higher share of imports of manufactured goods from low-cost countries, which has resulted in stronger growth of extra-euro area imports relative to intra-euro area trade, while also putting downward pressure on import prices and inflationary pressures. Meanwhile, this downward pressure had been partly offset by higher demand for commodities from low-cost countries resulting in high commodity import prices – which had increased significantly up until the second half of 2008 prior to declining on average since that time in the context of the downturn in global economic activity.

This chapter then focused on globalisation and its prospective role in shaping three broad areas of the euro area macroeconomy: productivity, the labour market and prices. Notwithstanding difficulties in fully isolating globalisation from other important ongoing structural changes (such as changes in technology and policies), several key findings emerge. First, weak euro area productivity on aggregate over the last decade despite growing international openness has derived to a large extent from areas of the economy which are more sheltered from international competition, thereby hinting at a role for enhanced openness to such forces. Second, globalisation's impacts on euro area labour markets have been mainly visible in the form of a redistribution of employment across sectoral, occupational and skill categories. The associated skill bias in labour demand has been concentrated on hours worked rather than wages, while there has been limited growth in income inequality in the euro area to date compared with other

---

[32] For an analysis of how vertical specialisation amplified the global trade downturn associated with the financial crisis, that also explains the high degree of synchronisation of the downturn, see Anderton and Tewolde (2009).

advanced economies. Gross job losses associated with offshoring have been limited as a proportion of overall job losses in the euro area economy and, importantly, offset by employment gains elsewhere. Indeed, the strong net job creation witnessed over the last decade has benefited from the extended period of wage moderation to which globalisation has contributed. Third, increasing trade openness appears to have had a small dampening effect on euro area prices over the five to ten years leading up to around 2005, as strong relative price shocks deriving from low prices of imported manufactured goods have on balance offset strong increases in prices of hard commodities resulting from heightened global demand pressures over the period. Apart from this influence on relative prices, globalisation appears to have had limited observed impacts as yet on either aggregate profit mark-ups of firms or the role of domestic slack in the inflation process of the euro area over this period.

All in all, while the balance of empirical evidence suggests that globalisation alone may have had limited measurable direct aggregate impacts, its role in shaping domestic developments remains nonetheless significant for two reasons. First, globalisation appears to be having strong effects in certain areas/sectors of the economy and therefore can entail considerable relative adjustments – including in some cases considerable redistributional effects at the household and firm level. This, of course, implies significant benefits for some cohorts as well as significant costs for others. In this respect, the aggregate economic impacts (or, for that matter, public perceptions) of globalisation depend crucially on the weighting scheme – either explicit or implicit – used to sum all redistributive impacts. Second, the phenomenon of globalisation is intertwined with several other ongoing structural changes, such as technological change and diffusion. Synthesising the international and domestic impacts of globalisation for the euro area, it appears that there would be a key role for macroeconomic policies in facilitating adjustment to globalisation and in reaping its potential benefits. Appropriate structural policies remain particularly important in both reducing frictions associated with adjustment while boosting the euro area's productive potential. Three structural policy areas, in particular, are important. First and foremost, the prospective benefits of globalisation will only materialise insofar as policies foster global openness in goods, services and financial markets, and fight protectionism. Second, policies which facilitate smooth economic adjustment in a dynamic environment (e.g. an acceleration of structural reforms facilitating geographical and occupational mobility, wage flexibility, and competition and price flexibility in product markets) would help ease adjustment strains and associated distributional impacts, in particular those which have emerged in the euro area labour market. Third, policies which support an increase in the euro area's competitiveness (e.g. policies fostering innovation and the adoption of new technologies, modern education systems supporting the upskilling of labour in line with technological advancements, and initiatives to create a business-friendly environment and to enhance the effectiveness of the public administration) could help address the weak euro area aggregate productivity growth witnessed to date, and create widespread gains for all households and firms. Monetary policy, of course, also has a role to play as it provides the solid foundations for efficient and beneficial adjustment – as is argued in Chapter 9. In particular, a strong focus on domestic price stability facilitates efficient adjustment of the economy to relative price and other macroeconomic shocks associated with globalisation.

REFERENCES

Abraham, F., J. Konings, and S. Vanormelingen (2006). *Price and Wage Setting in an Integrating Europe: Firm Level Evidence*, National Bank of Belgium working paper No. 93 (October).

Aksoy, Y., A. Orphanides, D. Small, V. Wieland, and D. Wilcox (2006). 'A quantitative exploration of the opportunistic approach to disinflation', *Journal of Monetary Economics*, 53(8), 18877–93.

Alajääskö, P. (2009). *International Sourcing in Europe*, Eurostat Statistics in Focus, 4/2009.

Amiti, M., and D. Davis (2008). 'What's behind volatile import prices from China?', *Federal Reserve Bank of New York Current Issues in Economics and Finance*, 15(1).

Amiti, M., and S.-J. Wei (2005). 'Fear of service outsourcing: is it justified?', *Economic Policy* 20(42), 308–47.

Anderton, R. (2003). *Extra-Euro Area Manufacturing Import Prices and Exchange Rate Pass-Through*, European Central Bank working paper No. 219.

    (2007). 'Globalisation, exchange rate pass-through and trade impacts: a euro area perspective', paper presented at Banque de France Seminar on *Globalisation, Inflation and Financial Markets*, Paris, 11–12 June 2007.

Anderton, R., P. Brenton, and J. Whalley (eds.) (2006). *Globalisation and the Labour Market: Trade, Technology and Less-Skilled Workers in Europe and the United States*, London: Routledge.

Anderton, R., A. Galesi, M. Lombardi, and F. di Mauro (2009). 'Key elements of global inflation', in Reserve Bank of Australia Conference Volume Inflation in an Era of Relative Price Shocks, Chris Kent (ed.).

Anderton, R. and F. di Mauro (2008). 'Globalisation and the trade channel in the euro area', in *Globalisation, Regionalism and Economic Interdependence*, F. di Mauro, W. McKibbin and S. Dees (eds.), Cambridge University Press.

Anderton, R., F. di Mauro, and F. Moneta (2004). *Understanding the Impact of the External Dimension on the Euro Area: Trade, Capital Flows and Other International Macroeconomic Linkages*, European Central Bank occasional paper No. 12.

Anderton, R., and T. Tewolde (2009). 'Turmoil, global trade and the internationalisation of production', paper presented at University of Nottingham Conference, *The Global Financial Crisis*, Ningbo, China, 10–11 November 2009.

van Ark, B. (2007). 'Europe's productivity gap: catching up or getting stuck?', paper from the Conference Board Europe and Growth and Development Center of the University of Groningen June 2006 EPWP #06–02.

Autor, D., L. Katz, and M. Kearney (2007). 'The Polarization of the U.S. Labor Market', *American Economic Review*, 96(2), 189–94.

Baldwin, R. (2006). 'Globalisation: the great unbundling(s)', in *Globalisation Challenges for Europe*, Secretariat of the Economic Council, Helsinki: Finnish Prime Minister's Office, Chapter 1.

Baldwin, R., H. Braconier, and R. Forslid (2005). 'Multinationals, endogenous growth, and technological spillovers: theory and evidence', *Review of International Economics*, 13(5), 945–63.

Ball, L. (2006). *Has Globalisation Changed Inflation?*, NBER working paper No. 12687 (November).

Batini, N., B. Jackson, and S. Nickell (2005). 'An open economy New Keynesian Phillips curve for the UK', *Journal of Monetary Economics*, 52, 1061–71.

Baumann, U., and F. di Mauro (2006). *Globalisation and Euro Area Trade: Interactions and Challenges*, European Central Bank occasional paper No. 55.

Bean, C. (2007). *Globalisation and Inflation*, Bank of England Quarterly Bulletin 2006Q4.

Bernard, A., J. Jensen, S. Redding, and P. Schott (2007). 'Firms in international trade', *Journal of Economic Perspectives*, 21(3), 105–30.

Bhagwati, J., A. Panagariya, and T. Srinivasan (2004). 'The muddles over outsourcing', *Journal of Economic Perspectives*, 18(4), 93–114.

Borio, C., and A. Filardo (2007). *Globalisation and Inflation: New Cross-Country Evidence on the Global Determinants of Domestic Inflation*, Bank for International Settlements working paper No. 227 (May).

Bräuninger, D. (2007). *Globalisation and Distribution*, Deutsche Bank current issues (November).

Broadbent, B., and I. Zsoldos (2007). *Europe's Immigration Boom: Causes and Consequences*, Goldman Sachs global economics paper No. 159 (July).

Calza, A. (2008). *Globalisation, Domestic Inflation and Global Output Gaps: Evidence from the Euro Area*, ECB working paper No. 890.

Campa, J., L. Goldberg, and J. Gonzalez-Minguez (2007). 'Exchange rate pass-through to import prices in the euro area', in *The External Dimension of the Euro Area*, F. di Mauro and R. Anderton (eds.), Cambridge University Press.

Christopoulou, R., and P. Vermeulen (2008). *Markups in the Euro Area and the US Over the Period 1981–2004: a Comparison of 50 Sectors*, ECB working paper No. 856 (January).

Ciccarelli, M., and B. Mojon (2005): *Global Inflation*, ECB working paper series, No. 537.

Conway, P., V. Janod, and G. Nicoletti (2005). *Product Market Regulation in OECD Countries: 1998 to 2003*, OECD Economics Department working paper No. 419.

Cuyvers, L., M. Dumont, and S. Rayp (2006). 'International trade and the income position of low-skilled and high-skilled workers in the European Union', in *Globalisation and the Labour Market: Trade, Technology and Less-Skilled Workers in Europe and the United States*, R. Anderton, P. Brenton and J. Whalley (eds.), London: Routledge.

Cuyvers, L., M. Dumont, G. Rayp, and K. Stevens (2002). *Wage and Employment Effects in the EU of International Trade with the Emerging Economies*, University of Ghent working paper 2002/142.

Dreher, A., N. Gaston, and P. Martens (2008). *Measuring Globalization – Gauging its Consequences*, New York: Springer.

Eaton, J., and S. Kortum (2002). 'Technology, geography, and trade', *Econometrica*, 70(5), 1741–79.

ECB (2006a). *Competition, Productivity and Prices in the Euro Area Services Sector*, ECB occasional paper (April).

   (2006b). Effects of the Rising Integration of Low-Cost Countries on Euro Area Import Prices, *ECB Monthly Bulletin* (August).

   (2008). Globalisation, Trade and the Euro Area Macroeconomy, *ECB Monthly Bulletin* (January).

Ellis, L., and K. Smith (2007). *The Global Upward Trend in the Profit Share*, BIS working paper No. 231 (July).

Epifani, P., and G. Gancia (2008). 'The skill bias of world trade', *The Economic Journal*, 118 (July), 927–60.

ESCB (2005). *Competitiveness and the Export Performance of the Euro Area*, task force of the Monetary Policy Committee of the European System of Central Banks, European Central Bank occasional paper No. 30.

Esteves, P., and C. Reis, (2006). *Measuring Export Competitiveness: Revisiting the Effective Exchange Rate Weights for the Eruo Area Countries*, Banco de Portugal working paper No.11.

European Commission (2006). *The EU Economy: 2005 Review*, Brussels: European Commission.

Fagan, G., J. Henry, and R. Mestre (2005). 'An area-wide model (AWM) for the euro area', *Economic Modelling*, 22(1), 39–59.

Federal Reserve Bank of Kansas City (2006). *The New Economic Geography: Effects and Policy Implications*, Proceedings from Symposium held 24–26 August 2006 in Jackson Hole, Wyoming.

Feenstra, R. (2007). 'Globalisation and its impact on labor', Global Economy Lecture, Vienna Institute for International Economic Studies (February).

Fontagne, L., G. Gaulier, and S. Zignago (2007). 'Specialisation across varieties and North-South competition', *Economic Policy*, 23(53), 51–91.

Geishecker, I., and H. Görg (2006). 'Winners and losers: a micro-level analysis of international outsourcing and wages', unpublished ms., University of Nottingham (mimeo, August).

Geishecker, I., H. Görg, and D. Taglioni (2007). 'Survival, exit and entry: the contribution of multinationals to euro area aggregate productivity growth', paper presented at joint Banca d'Italia, CEPR, ECB and EUI Workshop on *Globalisation, EMU and the Re-shaping of European Economies*. Fiesole, 22–23.

Genre, V., R. Gómez-Salvador, N. Leiner-Killinger, and G. Mourre (2004). 'A widening scope for non-wage components in collective bargaining', in *Institutions and Wage Formation in the New Europe*, G. Fagan, F. Mongelli and J. Morgan (eds.), London: Edward Elgar.

Glatzer, E., E. Gnan, and M. Valderrama (2006). *Globalisation, Import Prices and Producer Prices in Austria*, Oesterreische Nationalbank Monetary Policy & the Economy Q3/06.

Gomez-Salvador, R., A. Musso, M. Stocker, and J. Turunen (2006). *Labour Productivity Developments in the Euro Area*, ECB occasional paper No. 53 (October).

Groshen, E., and S. Potter (2003). 'Has structural change contributed to a jobless recovery?', *Federal Reserve Bank of New York Current Issues in Economics and Finance* 9(8).

Grossman, G., and E. Rossi-Hansberg (2006). 'The rise of offshoring: it's not wine for cloth anymore', in *The New Economic Geography: Effects and Policy Implications*, Federal Reserve Bank of Kansas City.

Guscina, A. (2006). *Effects of Globalisation on Labor's Share in National Income*, IMF working paper No. 06/294.

Hahn, E. (2007). *The Impacts of Exchange Rate Shocks on Sectoral Activity and Prices in the Euro Area*, European Central Bank working paper no. 796.

Harjes, T. (2007). *Globalisation and Income Inequality: a European Perspective*, IMF working paper No. 07/169.

Heinz, F., and M. Ward-Warmedinger (2006). *Cross-Border Labour Mobility Within an Enlarged EU*, ECB occasional paper No. 52 (October).

Helbling, T., F. Jaumotte, and M. Sommer (2006). 'How has globalisation affected inflation?', *IMF World Economic Outlook*, Chapter 3 (April).

Hiebert, P., and I. Vansteenkiste (2008). 'Gauging the labour market effects of international trade openness: an application to the US manufacturing sector', in *Globalization, Regionalism and Economic Interdependence*, S. Dees, F. di Mauro and W. McKibbin (eds.), Cambridge University Press, pp. 126–59.

   (2009). 'International trade, technological shocks and spillovers in the labour market: a GVAR analysis of the US manufacturing sector', *Applied Economics*, 41(April).

Hijzen, A. (2007). 'International outsourcing, technological change and wage inequality', *Review of International Economics*, 15(1), 188–205.

Hoekman B., and L. Winters (2005). *Trade and Employment: Stylized Facts and Research Findings*, DESA working paper No. 7 (November).

Ihrig, J. E., S. Kamin, D. Lindner, and J. Marquez (2007). *Some Simple Tests of the Globalisation and Inflation Hypothesis*, Board of Governors of the

Federal Reserve System international finance discussion papers No. 891 (April).

Ihrig, J. E., M. Marazzi, and A. D. Rothenberg (2006). *Exchange Rate Pass-through in the G-7 Countries*, Board of Governors of the Federal Reserve System international finance discussion papers No. 851 (January).

Inklaar, R., M. Timmer, and B. van Ark (2008). 'Market services productivity across Europe and the US', *Economic Policy* (January), 139–94.

Jarvis, V. (2006). 'Outsourcing, outward processing and output quality: a case study of the ceramic tableware industry', in *Globalisation and the Labour Market: Trade, Technology and Less-Skilled Workers in Europe and the United States*, R. Anderton, P. Brenton and J. Whalley (eds.), London: Routledge, Chapter 8, pp. 126–42.

Jaumotte, F., S. Lall, and C. Papageorgiou (2008). *Rising Income Inequality: Technology, or Trade and Financial Globalization?*, IMF working paper No. 185 (July).

Jaumotte, F., and I. Tytell (2007). 'The globalisation of labor', *IMF World Economic Outlook*, Chapter 5 (April).

Kroszner, R. S. (2006). 'What drives productivity growth? Implications for the economy and prospects for the future', Board of Governors of the Federal Reserve System: speech at the Forecasters Club of New York, 27 September.

Machin, S., and J. van Reenen (1998). 'Technology and changes in skill structure: evidence from seven OECD countries', *The Quarterly Journal of Economics* 113(4), 1215–44.

Mankiw, G., and P. Swagel (2006). 'The politics and economics of offshore outsourcing', *Journal of Monetary Economics*, 53, 1027–56.

Mann, C. (2003). *Globalization of IT Services and White Collar Jobs: The Next Wave of Productivity Growth*, Institute for International Economics policy brief No. PB03–11 (December).

Marazzi, M., N. Sheets, and R. Vigfusson (2005). *Exchange Rate Pass-through to U.S. Import Prices: Some New Evidence*, Board of Governors of the Federal Reserve System, international finance discussion papers No. 833, April.

di Mauro, F., and R. Anderton (2007). *The External Dimension of the Euro Area*, Cambridge University Press.

di Mauro, F., and U. Baumann (2007). *Globalisation and Euro Area Trade: Interactions and Challenges*, ECB occasional paper No. 55.

di Mauro, F. L, and K. Forster (2008). *Globalisation and the Competitiveness of the Euro Area*, ECB occasional paper No. 97.

di Mauro, F., R. Rueffer, and I. Binda (2008). *The Changing Role of the Exchange Rate in a Globalised Economy*, ECB occasional paper No. 94.

Melitz, M. (2003). 'The impact of trade on intra-industry reallocations and aggregate industry productivity', *Econometrica*, 71(6), 1695–725.

Mishkin, F. (2007). 'Globalization, macroeconomic performance, and monetary policy', speech at the *Domestic Prices in an Integrated World Economy Conference*, Board of Governors of the Federal Reserve System Washington, DC (September).

Molnar, M., N. Pain, and D. Taglioni (2006). *The Internationalisation of Production, International Outsourcing and OECD Labour Markets*, OECD Economics Department working papers No. 561.

Monacelli, T., and N. Sala (2007). 'The international dimension of inflation: evidence from disaggregated consumer price data', prepared for the JMCB-Fed Board Conference *Domestic Prices in an Integrated World Economy*, Washington DC, 27–28 September 2007.

Morgan, K. (2004). 'The exaggerated death of geography: learning, proximity and territorial innovation systems', *Journal of Economic Geography*, 4, 3–21.

Musso A., L. Stracca, and D. van Dijk (2007). *Instability and Nonlinearity in the Euro Area Phillips Curve*, ECB working paper No. 811 (September).

OECD (2007). *Annual Employment Report*, Paris: OECD.

Olsen, K. (2006). *Productivity Impacts of Offshoring and Outsourcing: A Review*, OECD science, technology and industry working paper No. 2006(1).

Osbat, C., and M. Wagner (2008). 'Structural change and bilateral exchange rate pass-through for the euro area', paper presented at ECB workshop International Competitiveness: a European Perspective.

Ottaviano, G., D. Taglioni, and F. di Mauro (2007). *Deeper, Wider and More Competitive? Monetary Integration, Eastern Enlargement and Competitiveness in the European Union*, ECB working paper No. 847 (December).

Paloviita, M. (2008). *Estimating Open Economy Phillips Curves for the Euro Area with Directly Measured Expectations*, Bank of Finland Research discussion papers 16/2008.

Price, B., and B. Cournède (2007). 'Making the most of globalisation', *OECD Economic Outlook*, No. 81, Special Chapter (June).

Razin, A., and A. Binyamini (2007). *Flattening of the Short-run Trade-off Between Inflation and Domestic Activity: the Analytics of the Effects of Globalisation*, Kiel working paper No. 1363.

Rogoff, K. (2006). 'Impact of globalisation on monetary policy', in *The New Economic Geography: Effects and Policy Implications*, Federal Reserve Bank of Kansas City.

Rüffer, R., and L. Stracca (2006). *What is Global Excess Liquidity, and Does It Matter?*, ECB working paper No. 696 (November).

Rumler, F. (2007). 'Estimates of the open economy New Keynesian Phillips curve for euro area countries', *Open Econ Rev*, 18, 427–45.

Sbordone, A. (2008). *Globalization and Inflation Dynamics: The Impact of Increased Competition*, Federal Reserve Bank of New York staff report No. 324 (April).

Schumacher, D., J. Hatzius, and T. Yamakawa (2007). *Rising Income Inequality in the G3*, Goldman Sachs global economics paper No. 158 (July).

Taylor, J. (2000). 'Low inflation, pass-through, and the pricing power of firms', *European Economic Review*, 44, 1389–408.

White, W. (2008). *Globalisation and the Determinants of Domestic Inflation*, BIS working paper No. 250.

Wood, A. (1998). 'Globalisation and the rise in labour market inequalities', *The Economic Journal*, 108(450), 1463–82.

Woodford, M. (2007). 'Globalisation and Monetary Control', paper prepared for the NBER conference on the *International Dimensions of Monetary Policy*, 11–13 June 2007, Girona, Spain.

Wynne, M., and E. Kersting (2007). *Openness and Inflation*, Federal Reserve of Dallas staff paper No. 2 (April).

3   Trade and foreign direct investment in business services: a modelling approach

James R. Markusen

3.1   Introduction

Outsourcing and offshoring of services has attracted a lot of interest recently, perhaps in large part for the simple reason that it is a relatively new phenomenon.[1] But much of the interest is not just academic curiosity. Some concern is generated by the offshoring of white-collar services to relatively low-income countries such as India. It was one thing when low to moderately skilled manufacturing jobs were gradually lost to lower-income countries over the last two decades, but somehow the potential competition for and loss of white-collar jobs seems just as threatening.

There has been little new theory to guide us in understanding this expansion of trade and investment into new activities which were previously classified as non-traded. Possibly, no new theory is needed, and the new trade in services is just a particular case of our more general models. But at the very least, a more detailed development of this 'particular case' seems warranted given the empirical and policy attention it has received. The purpose of this paper is thus to inquire how theory might be adapted and developed to shed light on the new offshoring of white-collar services. Particular attention will be paid to small open high-skilled economies, and how they might be affected by increased trade in skilled services.

Defining services has always proved difficult and ambiguous, and I will instead simply indicate a range of activities that I have in mind. The policy debate in particular is not about things like transportation,

Prepared for the conference 'Globalization and the Macroeconomy', sponsored by the European Central Bank, 23–24 July 2007, Frankfurt.

[1] Terminology has not yet been standardised. 'Outsourcing' is unfortunately often used to refer both to moving an activity overseas (even to an owned subsidiary) and to moving an activity outside of the firm to a (local) independent contractor. I will use 'offshoring' to refer to moving an activity overseas and 'outsourcing' to refer to moving an activity outside the ownership boundaries of the firm. Moving an activity to a foreign subsidiary is thus offshoring but not outsourcing.

tourism or trade in capital. It is about business services provided to firms or in some cases directly to the purchasing firms' customers. These range from call centres and technical support, to business-process outsourcing (henceforth BPO), to software services such as programming to higher-end services including software design and medical services (e.g. reading and interpreting X-rays and MRI scans).

My starting point will be that increased trade in services is a result of changes in communications and information technology that allow for the geographic fragmentation of a formerly integrated multi-stage production process. These services have always been produced by firms, but they have traditionally been produced in-house or at least in-country (outsourced but not offshored). The ability to fragment production means that individual stages may be located in countries where cost and other conditions are most advantageous.

I think that there are really two separate questions here. The first is what sorts of activities can be offshored? This is not as easy as simply classifying them by skill intensity, for example. Evidence indicates that activity characteristics like codifiability, routinisation and the lack of need for face-to-face interaction are of great importance. This needs some thought and analysis. I have not seen any attempt to incorporate these features in a formal model, and it is important to do so to the extent that they are repeatedly emphasised in the international business literature.

The second question is what activities would a firm in a high-income country choose to offshore among those which are feasible to offshore? A trade economist's first reaction on this is to think about activities differing in factor intensities and locations differing in factor prices. Cost is minimised by locating activities where the factors they use intensively are cheap. A second reaction, derived from the theory of the multinational enterprise, is that activities (in the presence of scale economies) will be located where the market is large (Markusen, 1984, 2002).

These factors seem to work well for manufacturing, but they are somewhat less clear for white-collar services. In particular, we seem to have the problem that some skilled workers in information technology, for example, are cheap where they are scarce. Data and specific examples (e.g. Indian computer programmers) of this phenomenon are found in several of the articles in Brainard and Collins (2006). Second, the offshoring is often not to serve the local market, but to serve the firms back home.

I begin my analysis with a description of what I feel are the crucial empirical characteristics of the (newly traded) white-collar business services that need to be captured in theoretical models in Section 3.2.

Then I turn to the task of proposing such a model in Section 3.3. There I develop a two-country model (North and South) which tries to incorporate some of the features from the 'wish list' of Section 3.2. Two types of fragmentation, both initially infeasible, are considered. First, service production can be geographically fragmented from final goods production which uses the services as intermediates. Second, services themselves can be fragmented into an upstream headquarters activity and a downstream production activity.

The results I obtain are relatively optimistic for skilled-labour-abundant countries in an increasingly integrated world. At some basic level, increased ability to fragment production and trade services frees economies from constraints. Fragmentation allows firms in the high-skilled economy (henceforth North) crucial access to cheaper production of less-skilled phases of production, which increases the competitiveness of North's final goods producers, allowing an expansion that maintains or drives up demand for skilled labour. Second, I assume scale economies and firm-level product differentiation in services, and so access to foreign service providers for domestic final-goods producers and access to foreign producers by domestic service firms increases real productivity in North. The larger the range of services available, the higher the productivity of final goods producers or, alternatively, the lower the price index for a composite service input.

I believe that some progress is made with respect to tying together country characteristics, such as size and skilled-labour abundance, with technology characteristics such as factor intensities across activities, scale economies complementarities, trade costs and investment (or fragmentation) costs. Somewhat less progress is made on other issues, especially the notions of codifiability and routinisation, and thus on the problem of what activities it is feasible to offshore. I simply assume that service production requires an upstream, skilled-labour intensive activity that is the core of the firm. Then there is a routinised, downstream, less-skilled-labour-intensive activity that may (or may not) be geographically fragmented away from the headquarters. In a second theoretical section, I try to capture some of these ideas by introducing two classes of skilled workers: entrepreneurs or managers, and more routine skilled workers. The jobs of the latter are the downstream jobs that can be outsourced, and hence these are the workers who are vulnerable to offshoring. In some experiments, the wages of the entrepreneurs and the skilled workers change in opposite directions.

What general conclusions can be drawn as to the consequences of service offshoring for the future of a high-skilled economy? It seems possible that what will happen in services will resemble what has happened in manufacturing over the last two decades. In particular, it may be that middle-skilled activities, ones that can be codified and routinised, will tend to migrate to offshore locations like India. Higher-skilled activities and ones that require judgement, discretionary actions, and/or face-to-face interactions will likely stay and expand in the high-income countries. This suggests difficulties for middle-skilled white-collar workers, particularly those with specific skills in codifiable and routinised activities. This has some analogy to the loss of relatively routine production and assembly jobs over the last two decades in North America and Europe. Other policy implications of the theory are briefly discussed: within the context of the model, for example, foreign market access for the small-country's firms is crucial.

3.2   Adapting theory to the empirical characteristics of offshoring of white-collar services

There are a few things missing from most conventional trade models for our purposes. Most models used for theoretical, policy and empirical analysis tend to focus on a fixed number of tradable goods and services and border barriers that raise the cost of trade. Often missing in particular are: (1) the potential for trading new things, (2) the possibility of reversals in the direction of trade, (3) the modelling and importance of barriers to establishing foreign subsidiaries as opposed to simply border barriers to trade, (4) the possibility that factors of production can be cheap in countries where they are very scarce.

With respect to this last point, the simplest off-the-shelf two-good, two-factor Heckscher-Ohlin model is not going to offer insights as to why relatively skilled-labour-intensive services are being offshored to very skilled-labour-scarce countries. One of the most important tasks of theory, in my opinion, is to develop richer, but empirically plausible models as to why this phenomenon is taking place. Yet it is not necessarily the case that the factor-proportions approach to trade has to be abandoned, just that it must be enriched to include multiple goods and/or factors, scale economies, complementarities, or other factors to explain the skilled-wage/skill-abundance puzzle.

Reversal in the direction of trade is another phenomenon that traditional models are poorly equipped to handle. Trade in white-collar services is not new. The modern theory of the multinational has emphasised that parent companies are exporters of white-collar services, including management and engineering consulting, marketing, finance and so forth to their subsidiaries. One thing that is relatively new and which has generated much of the current interest is the reversal in the direction of trade that we are seeing. In some ways this is closely related to the previous point. Many traditional modelling frameworks, relying on marginal comparative-statics analysis, are ill equipped to tackle this type of problem (Markusen, 2002).

Here is a wish list of characteristics we might like to have in theoretical models of offshoring of white-collar services. Much of this is a revision and extension of a similar section in Markusen (2006), since the focus and objectives of the present chapter are quite similar to those of the 2005 Brookings Trade Forum:

(A) Expansion of trade at the extensive margin: new things are traded as a result of innovations in communications and technology or institutions (e.g. legal restrictions).

This poses a number of challenges to theory, especially since we are talking about non-marginal changes and discrete movements of something not previously traded to potentially lots of trade. Traditional comparative-statics analysis is of little use: it focuses on marginal changes in activities which are already in use in the benchmark.

(B) Vertical fragmentation of production: the new traded services tend to be intermediates, may be upstream, downstream or not part of a sequence.

Traded white-collar services often have a number of important characteristics that cannot be captured in the simplest off-the-shelf models which assume a set of final goods. One is that they may be firm-specific rather than bought and sold on arm's-length markets. Another is that they may form part of a particular production sequence, such as being a well-defined upstream (design) or downstream (after-sales service) component of overall production.

(C) Accommodation of location-specific and other complementarities.

There may be crucial complementarities among different elements of the production chain, such as between skilled labour and telecommunications equipment and infrastructure. In some cases, it may be the case that services must be produced in the same location as where they are used in downstream or upstream manufacturing activities. I am coining the term 'location-specific complementarities' to describe this. This doesn't mean that services, or at least the downstream end product, cannot be traded. But it does suggest that a national presence may be required: a firm has to open a local office or branch in a foreign country in order to service that country. These considerations may also imply another type of complementarity, that between liberalisation in services and increased trade in goods (Markusen, 1983).

(D) Firms or specifically owners of knowledge-based assets may off-shore skilled-labour-intensive activities that are complements to these assets.

A plausible worry is that skilled workers in the high-income countries are being hurt, while their companies are profiting from offshoring. This cannot be dismissed and requires investigation. To me, it calls for at least a three-factor model, or alternatively one in which firms possess specific factors or other assets which are complements to skilled labour. An example mentioned above is software engineers as complements to telecommunications equipment and network infrastructure, in which the third factor is physical capital. Or it could be that software engineers are complementary with managerial sophistication, organisation infrastructure and marketing channels. The complementary input is knowledge-based assets.

Without services trade you can train an engineer in India, but there is no demand for his or her skills: there is nothing useful to do. The necessary complementary physical or knowledge capital is missing. The implication is that, in the absence of offshoring, these skilled workers are cheap even though they are relatively scarce in comparison with the country with the complementary factors. Offshoring allowing trade in the third factor (or services of knowledge-based assets) causes that factor (or its services) to move to the skilled-labour-scarce country to combine with cheap skilled labour there. This set-up obviously has the elements of a story in which skilled labour is harmed in the high-income country, while owners of the complementary physical or knowledge-based assets benefit.

(E) Agglomeration of complementary intermediate services.

Related to but somewhat distinct from point (C) is the issue of whether or not the intermediate business services themselves are more productive when located near to each other, as opposed to just being located near the final user, which was the focus of (C). It might be beneficial for a user firm to be located near to both a firm specialising in networking hardware and one specialising in the networking software, but it might also be beneficial for the latter firms to be located near one another. This could be modelled using an input–output structure among the service firms, as in Venables (1996). This is somewhat beyond the scope of this paper, but it does raise some concerns for small economies. In particular, it raises the possibility of multiple equilibria and that whatever location gets a head start remains ahead. There is a potentially large market failure here that could call for strong government support for creating a local agglomeration (e.g. the business park concept).

(F) Barriers to trade and investment in services: very different to those for trade in goods.

For goods trade we typically think of transport costs and border barriers (chiefly tariffs and quotas) as the principal barriers to trade. However, this is generally not the case for trade and investment in services. Typically, the movement of professional persons for at least short periods of time is necessary for trade in services. More generally, a foreign commercial presence is required. Barriers to trade and investment in services are thus much more in the areas of (1) right of commercial presence, (2) national treatment of foreign firms, (3) immigration permission for foreign professionals, and (4) enforcement of contracts and protection of intellectual property. Second, many service industries face heavy regulation: banking, insurance, legal and accounting, and telecommunications. In some cases, these explicitly discriminate against foreign firms, but in other cases they are, however onerous, regulations that impinge equally on domestic and foreign firms. Thus in the policy arena, the issues for trade and investment in services are very different from those for trade in goods.

3.3   An analytical approach to services and service-trade liberalisation

The preceding section indicates the need for a modelling approach that is more sophisticated than many standard trade models and, in particular, an approach that allows for large discrete changes in the things that can be traded. In this section, I will specify a theoretical approach, which can be coded into a numerical simulation model, that attempts to capture many of the ideas outlined in the previous section.

Suppose we begin with a simple two-final-good, two-factor, two-country Heckscher-Ohlin model and then allow one good to geographically fragment into two separate production activities, one in each country. Further, one of those two activities, denoted services (S), may be allowed to geographically fragment into a more skilled-labour-intensive 'headquarters' activity and a less-skilled-labour-intensive 'office' activity.

If we assume free trade in goods, just considering free versus prohibitive fragmentation costs in services means that we do not need to specify which is the upstream and which is the downstream activity. For a much more comprehensive treatment of this case, see Markusen and Venables (2007). Here are the principal features of the model:

(1) Two factors of production: skilled (H) and unskilled (L) labour.
(2) Two final goods, three production activities:
    AG – unskilled-labour intensive agriculture
    MAN – skilled-labour intensive manufacturing, can fragment into
    VA – value added by skilled and unskilled labour
    SER – services.
(3) SER – can fragment into:
    HQ – headquarters, may serve several offices
    OF – office, produces the deliverable for the client
(4) Two competitive, constant returns economies:
    North – high-skilled abundant
    South – low-skilled abundant.
(5) There are three generic 'types' of services firms, each of which may be located in either country, hence there are six firm types in total:
    N – national firms, provide services to domestic manufacturers, may possibly be allowed to 'export' to other country
    M – multinational firms, have physical production presence in both countries, essentially a 'horizontal' multinational
    V – vertical firm, with headquarters in one country, a single office located in the other, may possibly be allowed to export back to the home country.
(6) There are 'trade costs' for M and V firms supplying services abroad (skilled workers have to fly abroad in one direction or the other).
(7) There are firm-level scale economies arising from jointness of knowledge-based assets: fixed costs for an M firm are less than double the fixed costs of N or V firms.
(8) Services are differentiated or 'specialised', each produced with-increasing returns to scale. A wider range of available services increases real productivity for final manufacturers, or lowers their price index for composite services.

To expand on the last point a bit, it is assumed that one unit each of two different services is more beneficial to firms than two units of only one of the services. Using two specialised lawyers for a day (e.g. one taxation and one contracts specialist) is better than having two days from a general-purpose lawyer that does both. But fixed costs limit the degree of special-isation and diversity than can exist in equilibrium for a small country, and thus access to the larger world market is always productive.

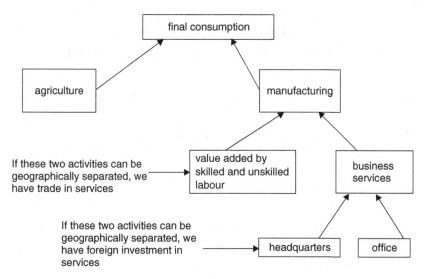

Figure 3.1 Structure of production

The model and the two types of fragmentation are illustrated in Figure 3.1. Consumption comes from the final goods, agriculture and manufacturing. Manufacturing is composed of 'value added' (direct contributions of skilled and unskilled labour) and services. It may be possible to do these in different locations, implying that trade in services is feasible. Services consist of a headquarters and an office. It may be possible to do these in different locations, implying that foreign investment in services is feasible.

We are interested in four equilibria, referred to as 'regimes'. Some regimes may not be technologically feasible or profitable, or they may not be allowed by regulation. The four are as follows:

> NN – No trade, no foreign investment (i.e. no M or V firms) allowed.
>
> TN – Trade in services (exports by N firms) allowed, no investment allowed.
>
> NI – No trade in services feasible or allowed, but investment feasible/allowed.
>
> TI – Trade and investment in services both allowed.

We can think of TN as allowing geographic fragmentation between services and manufacturing, but not allowing fragmentation within a service into headquarters and office. Under NI investment but not trade is feasible/allowed. Regime TI allows both to occur. TN permits what

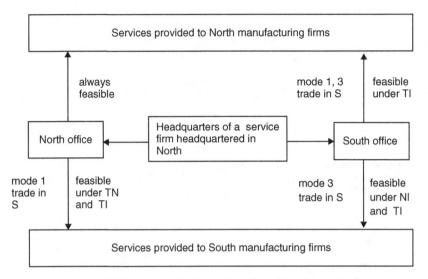

Figure 3.2 Types of trade in services for a North service firm

terminology refers to as Mode 1 trade in services: cross-border trade that does not involve an investment and involves minimal movement of persons. NI and TI permit what is called Mode 3, the establishment of a commercial presence (typically by a foreign direct investment) abroad. NI could occur, for example, if there are no government restrictions, but face-to-face contact is required so that investment via a foreign office is possible but exports of services are infeasible.

Figure 3.2 gives an example of the service provision by one firm, located in North. The top box is a manufacturing firm located in North and the bottom a manufacturing firm located in South. The domestic service firm has a headquarters in North (middle box of the diagram). It may have a domestic office in North which provides services to Northern firms (this is always allowed). That Northern office may provide services to Southern manufacturing firms, if trade in services (Mode 1) is allowed. The Northern firm may also establish a Southern office if investment in services is allowed (Mode 3). It can then provide services to local firms under regimes NI or TI. It can also provide exports services back to the Northern manufacturing firms under TI, but not under NI.

This completes the general description of the model. One crucial feature of the model is the choice of factor intensities for the different activities. I have experimented with this a lot, and there are some differences in results, of course. But many of the choices that seem 'reasonable' tend to yield similar results. In this paper, I will concentrate on a particular case which I find reasonable after reading a great deal of literature on offshoring of white-collar services, especially papers in the Brookings Trade Forum 2005 (Brainard and Collins, 2006). Here is my ranking of factor intensities (H/L intensity ratios), with the most skilled-labour intensive at the top, and the least-skilled-labour intensive at the bottom. Numbers are the values used in the numerical simulation model to follow, with the overall 'world' endowment normalised to 1.0

Fixed costs of service firm headquarters	4.4
Value added in manufacturing (direct use of H and L)	2.2
Overall manufacturing (value added plus intermediate services)	1.9
Overall service provision (headquarters plus office)	1.5
Service office (office)	1.1
World factor endowment ratio	1.0
Agriculture	0.5

My choice for a base case is that all activities in manufacturing and services are more skilled-labour intensive than the world endowment ratio at the calibration point (discussed below). Integrated or overall manufacturing is a bit more skilled-labour intensive than integrated services production. But the two components of services production lie at the extremes of the manufacturing-sector intensities. Headquarters is the most skilled-labour intensive and office activity is the least among the manufacturing-sector activities. This is equivalent to something like business-process outsourcing, one of the most common forms of offshored white-collar services. The high-end activity is quite sophisticated, whereas the downstream processing centres are only moderately skilled-labour intensive.

The second step is to calibrate a numerical model used to solve for these equilibria. I do this by assuming that the countries are identical, and that foreign production (type M and V firms) is not allowed, and that trade in services by N firms is prohibitively costly. This is then a benchmark equilibrium in which there is no geographic fragmentation of service production. Services are supplied solely to manufacturers in the same country. Units are chosen such that the number of national firms in each country is equal to one, and production of manufacturers and production of services in each country is equal to one. There is no trade in services allowed and, since the countries are identical, there is no trade in manufacturers either in this benchmark. Thus all trade quantities are zero in the calibrated equilibrium.

Table 3.1 *Country* i *small and skilled-labour abundant, simulation results under different service trade/investment restrictions (two-factor model)*

HS's H/L ratio = 2.78 HS's income share = 0.16	NN	TN	NI	TI
	level	level	level	level
National firms HS	1.00			
Horizontal firms HS			1.90	
Vertical firms HS				1.09
X production in HS	1.00	1.85	1.02	1.63
Final service production in HS	1.00		0.90	
Exports of X by HS	1.00	2.58	0.94	2.08
Exports of S from HS by HS firms				
Exports of S from HS by LS firms				
Imports of S from LS by LS firms		1.00		0.44
Imports of S from LS by HS firms				0.43
Skilled wage in HS	1.00	1.34	1.20	1.47
Unskilled wage in HS	1.00	0.96	0.97	0.84
Welfare in HS	1.00	1.14	1.08	1.13
Welfare in LS	1.00	1.03	1.01	1.03

There is quite a range of results for a model of this type, depending on differences in size and labour-force composition. Here, I will focus on results for the case in which one country is relatively small and quite skilled-labour abundant. This case gives a lot of regime switching and different results depending on the extent of its liberalisation and so it is instructive, if not general. Simulation results are reported in Tables 3.1 and 3.2. In the first of these, Table 3.1, North is skilled-labour abundant, having an endowment ratio H/L of 2.78, where the world as a whole has a ratio of one. North has a 0.16 share of total world income. The first block of rows gives the number of service firms active in equilibrium in North, the second block gives production quantities for manufacturing and services, the third block gives trade flows and the final block gives factor prices and welfare.

Before looking at the specific results, let me try to summarise the intuition. Despite the very different nature of the three liberalisation experiments skilled labour in North benefits significantly, unskilled labour has a smaller loss and aggregate welfare of North rises in all cases as does welfare in South.

(1) In TN where headquarters and office are bound together, liberalisation allows North to access the wide range of South services (by

Table 3.2 *Country i small and skilled-labour abundant, simulation results under different service trade/investment restrictions (three-factor model)*

HS's H/L ratio = 2.78 HS's income share = 0.16	NN	TN	NI	TI
	level	level	level	level
National firms HS	1.00	0.99		
Horizontal firms HS			0.75	
Vertical firms HS				1.04
X production in HS	1.00	1.16	1.05	1.65
Final service production in HS	1.00	0.86	0.95	
Exports of X by HS	1.00	1.18	1.00	2.09
Exports of S from HS by HS firms		1.00		
Exports of S from HS by LS firms				0.44
Imports of S from LS by LS firms		1.00		
Imports of S from LS by HS firms				0.44
Skilled wage in HS	1.00	1.18	1.04	1.45
Entre/management wage in HS	1.00	0.92	1.62	1.54
Unskilled wage in HS	1.00	1.08	1.04	0.86
Welfare in HS	1.00	1.10	1.08	1.13
Welfare in LS	1.00	1.03	1.01	1.03

imports). This leads to a substitution from services to manufacturing, the latter being more skilled-labour intensive overall than services, and so raises the return to skilled labour. Service production ceases in North in this particular example.

(2) In the NI scenario, horizontal multinational services firms replace the national firms. There is a large increase in the number of service firms headquartered in North, but a small fall in final (office) service production, and this again pulls up the wage of skilled labour in North.

(3) In the full TI liberalisation scenario, service production ceases in the North and much of this is offshored to the subsidiaries of the North firms. Final X production rises and this, combined with the large increase in headquarters, gives a big boost to the skilled wage in the North.

The first column of Table 3.1 computes a general equilibrium for regime NN with no trade or investment in services allowed. Quantities and prices are renormalised to one in the initial equilibrium. There are national firms in both countries; their numbers are similar (South not shown), reflecting the fact that North's small size is offset by its greater skilled-labour abundance. Manufacturing production and service production are also similar across the two countries (recall that these production quantities would all equal one when the countries are identical). Country North is a net exporter of manufacturing.

The intermediate liberalisation case TN, where trade but not investment in services is liberalised, is shown in the second column of Table 3.1. North becomes more specialised in manufacturing and stops producing services. Instead, North benefits from being able to import differentiated services from South, which increases productivity in final manufacturing production.

The substitution of manufacturing for final service production benefits skilled labour in North, which has a real income increase of 34 per cent. Unskilled labour loses 4 per cent, but North as a whole get an aggregate welfare gain of 14 per cent.

The third column of Table 3.1 gives the NI scenario in which it is not feasible to trade services (mode 1 not feasible or allowed), but foreign investment (mode 3) is feasible. This could be due, for example, to the need for face-to-face contact between the service firm and the manufacturing firm. Now there is a regime switch to horizontal firms in both countries, each having an office in both countries. The number of firms headquartered in North rises significantly relative to the base (NN) case: the small domestic market is no longer a constraint for North service firms. Production of both services and final manufacturers are not very different from the base case. Changes in factor prices and total welfare in North are somewhat similar to those in scenario NI, despite the very different patterns of production and trade in the two cases.

The right-hand column of Table 3.1 shows the full liberalisation scenario TI. Now the regime shifts to vertical service firms in North, with the latter dominating. North is once again more specialised in manufacturing production and stops producing services domestically.

North remains a net exporter of X and imports some services from South affiliates of North firms. This is the type of offshoring (but not outsourcing) often discussed in the business press: location of in-house service production in the foreign country used to serve the home market.

North is now the dominant location for the headquarters of service firms, though not production (office activities). This gives a further boost to manufacturing production and a big boost to the return to skilled labour. The latter now rises by 47 per cent over the benchmark NN equilibrium. Unskilled labour now has a bigger loss, and aggregate welfare gains for North are 13 per cent.

I believe that the results in Table 3.1 emphasise a couple of points. The first is being able to draw on foreign sources for intermediate inputs in a world of scale economies, product differentiation and complementarities. In the first transition, from NN to TN, North draws on foreign 'varieties', making it much more competitive in manufacturing production, which is itself very skilled-labour intensive by assumption. Both production and exports of manufacturing from North increase substantially. The ability to draw on the full range of foreign services lowers the aggregate price index for services in North and hence increases competitiveness in manufacturing.

Second, integration allows for foreign market access for domestic service firms, and allows them the advantage of specialising in the very skilled-labour-intensive headquarters activity only. In the TN case as just noted, there are a small number of service firms headquartered in North. But with full liberalisation (TI), almost all service firms are headquartered in North. Foreign market access for these firms, giving them the ability to actually produce in South where the demand for services is concentrated, makes a world of difference. Most of that foreign production of services by North type V and M firms goes to manufacturing production in country South with only a small proportion being exported back to North. The best jobs not only stay in North, they significantly increase in number, leading to a large increase in the real return to North skilled labour.

3.4   Fragmentation and specialisation in headquarter services

The model outlined above has a couple of limitations that are likely to be important in the context of service trade/investment liberalisation. One is that it is generally the case that, in equilibrium, a small, skilled-labour abundant country will have a lower wage for skilled labour than a large, skilled-labour scarce country. But part of the puzzle that is leading us to work on this trade is precisely that the latter countries seem to have much lower wages for workers with equivalent skills. There are many stories and indeed hard evidence that some computer-industry workers are paid much less in India than workers with equal skills in the USA or Europe. So why is skilled labour expensive where it is abundant? Of course, one simple answer is that they are not equally skilled, and US/European workers are either better or the firms they work for are better at extracting output.

The other empirical idea that has not been addressed here is the notion of some tasks being more tradable than others, especially those that are routine and codifiable. Workers may be equally skilled in the two activities, but those who work on routine tasks may be more vulnerable in the face of globalisation that the non-routine workers.

In this section, I present an extension to my basic model which tries to hit these two birds with one stone. I am going to assume that there are in fact two types of skilled workers. One type we continue to denote by H, and these will be routine workers who can work at a geographic distance from the firm's headquarters. The second type is denoted by E (as in entrepreneur), upper-level workers who are involved in tasks that are fundamental to the firm. Furthermore, we will assume that the E workers are 'upstream': they produce the firm-specific assets or alternatively they are used in the fixed costs of firm creation, the headquarters activity. H workers are 'downstream' in the office activity, involved in producing the firm's actual output like computer code, call centres, business processing and so forth. To keep things fairly simple, H workers are also used in manufacturing (or more correctly value added) and agriculture production. E workers are only used in service industry headquarters activities and are vital to supporting domestic service firms in equilibrium (for all types N, M and V). Horizontal-type M firms are assumed to need E workers from both countries, but mostly from the home country. For H workers in North working in a national firm, for example, their jobs can be 'offshored' by the E workers switching the firm to a M or V type, hiring foreign H workers to replace the domestic ones. Thus H workers are vulnerable to having their jobs offshored, but of course the domestic E workers must themselves compete against foreign firms.

Suppose that our small North is not only skilled-labour abundant, now referring to the total of H and E workers relative to unskilled workers, but also has a higher proportion of E workers in the total of H + E. The important thing to note in this context is that, when trade and especially foreign investment are not allowed, E and H workers are bound together in producing services: they are location-specific complements, meaning that they must not only be used together, but in the same location. Under our assumptions about factor endowments across the two countries, it is now the case that North will be better positioned for headquarters of type N services firms. However, service delivery is H-worker intensive, and the consequence of this is that country North will have higher wages for H workers than South. This is the result we need to capture the empirical fact that skilled workers (H type) are cheaper where they are more scarce, in South.

We can now do the same experiment we did in Table 3.1. The proportions of total skilled (E+H) to unskilled workers is the same in Table 3.2, but North has a higher E/H ratio than South. One difference now is that the number of North services firms will not be able to adjust much, since the E workers are only used in service headquarters production by assumption, and so they cannot be drawn in from other parts of the economy. But the increased demand for their services though exports or foreign investment in services is going to give a big boost to their wages. The North H workers, who must now compete with offshore H workers in South, may lose or may get a small boost through switching to the manufacturing sector.

The first column of Table 3.2 gives the NN regime. Even though North is small (16 per cent income share), its endowment makes it the centre for service firms. Final manufacturing production is similar in the two countries as is final service production (South not shown). Taken together, these results mean a smaller output per service firm in North, sacrificing some scale economies but allowing a greater degree of differentiation. North is the manufacturing exporter.

The introduction of trade but not investment in services in the second column of Table 3.2 does not actually change the types and numbers of active firms much. There is, however, some substitution in North toward manufacturing production and away from service production, with North exporting most of that increased service production. Recall that value added in manufacturing is more skilled-labour intensive than final service production. The consequence of these changes is that there is a redistribution within North away from E workers to H workers. The former lose 8 per cent while the latter gain 18 per cent.

The intuition behind this redistribution is probably that, in the absence of trade in services, the complementary bundling of H and E workers needed for service production and the complementary bundling of services and manufacturing value added supports higher wages for the E workers. When trade in services is permitted, the substitution of more manufacturing production for final service production lowers the aggregate demand for E workers at the old wage. But the H workers benefit from this change as their expertise is in more demand for service production. There is a welfare gain of 10 per cent for North.

In the second experiment (third column) of Table 3.2 (NI), we see a shift away from national firm production, with multinationals dominating in North. There is virtually no change in manufacturing and service production in North. E workers are big gainers in North as they provide services to both North and South offices of their firms. But the general efficiency gain also increases the wages of H workers in North and unskilled workers are small losers. The welfare gain of 8 per cent for North comes largely from the efficiency gains of having a larger variety of services to use in production.

The final experiment in Table 3.2 liberalises both service trade and investment (TI). As was the case in Table 3.1, we now have a mix of horizontal and vertical firms headquartered in North. There is now a shift toward manufacturing and away from final (office) service production relative to the base case. One again, there is a big gain for E workers yet H workers also gain a lot. The losers are again unskilled labour while the country as a whole gains a significant 13 per cent.

The results for the wages of H workers in North are interesting and contrast with those in the two-good model in Table 3.1. In allowing only trade in services, H workers now gain a lot less. This is essentially an efficiency gain that overwhelms a relative price change against H workers relative to E workers. When investment in services is not allowed, North suffers from a relatively inefficient service sector passed on in high costs to manufacturing producers because of the lack of service variety. Access to a broader range of services through investment (or to cheaper foreign services by not paying the trade cost) allows essentially an efficiency gain for the small country. This shows up in the increased final manufacturing production in Table 3.2 which is associated with an increased demand for skilled H workers. This tends to lift all real factor prices and now H workers are better off. The shift toward more X production, however, now reduces the wages of unskilled workers in North.

Again, I feel that the intuition for the results in Table 3.2 lie in the fact that, in the absence of trade or investment in services, North is handicapped in not having an efficient production sector for S due to its small size in Table 3.2 (i.e. lack of efficiency-increasing diversity), which is passed on in higher real costs (higher price index for services) to the manufacturing sector.

3.5   Summary and conclusions

This paper approaches the phenomenon of increased trade and foreign investment in white-collar services from the point of view of theory. The paper concerns how we think about these services and how we might model them.

After developing a list of characteristics that I think a reasonable theory might capture, I develop a two-country general-equilibrium model. This model has one final goods sector, manufacturing, that uses services as intermediates. Intermediates in turn have an upstream 'headquarters' activity and a downstream 'office' activity. The headquarters activity is assumed to be the most skilled-labour intensive, followed by value added in manufacturing production, followed by downstream service production, followed by agriculture (the other final goods sector).

In one experiment, manufacturing production is geographically bound together with service production, and headquarters and downstream production must similarly occur in the same location. Two types of fragmentation are possible. First, we allow services to be traded, used as input into manufacturing production in the other country. Second, we allow services themselves to geographically fragment into a headquarters and office location (termed investment in services). A numerical simulation approach compares the no-trade no-investment scenario (NN) to service trade but not investment feasible/permitted (TN), to trade infeasible but investment feasible (NI), and then to a full liberalisation scenario (TI) in which both trade and investment are permitted.

Liberalisation, or technical/institutional changes that allow trade and investment in services tend to benefit a relatively small, skilled-labour-abundant economy. There are several sources of these gains.

(1) Offshoring allows service firms to source from abroad the downstream part of service production that is costly at home. This improves their competitiveness in both markets.

(2) Access to foreign service providers through trade or investment increases the range of services available to domestic manufacturing producers, increasing their productivity or lowering the cost of the aggregate service intermediate.

(3) Access to foreign markets for the domestic services firms makes them more competitive, allowing them to spread their fixed costs over a larger output.

All three of these effects tend to favour skilled labour over unskilled labour. However, while the relative wage of skilled labour rises, the level of the real wage of unskilled labour may rise as well (not true for all scenarios), reflecting the fact that the real productivity gains from effects (2) and (3) above can lift all workers' real wages.

In a second experiment, I divide skilled labour into two types, entrepreneurs (E) or managers, and more general or routine skilled workers (H). I assume that E workers are only used in the upstream headquarters activity, whereas H workers are used in the downstream activity, in manufacturing and in agricultural production. Domestic service firms require local E workers, but the downstream tasks performed by the H workers can be done offshore by foreign H workers. Our small, skilled-labour-abundant North has a higher ratio of all skilled to unskilled workers than South and also a higher ratio of E workers to H workers.

For many variables, the results of this experiment are not that different from the experiment with only two types of labour. The big difference is with respect to factor rewards. Liberalisation now leads to an increase in the real price of E workers relative to H workers in the small economy when there is investment liberalisation. For some other levels of country size and endowment differences (not shown here), the real wages of H workers fall in North, as a result of their having to compete with offshore H workers.

This is exactly the scenario that some researchers and policy analysts have feared. The more routine skilled workers have their wages reduced at the expense of the top-level management and other workers. But when North is very small, there are some parameter values such that the efficiency gains dominate the relative wage changes, and all factors in the small, skilled-labour-abundant country can gain from liberalisation. But the E workers continue to gain much more.

I think that the intuition behind these results is that the lack of trade and investment in services 'bundles' E and H workers together in producing services and manufacturing: they are location-specific complements. The relative abundance of E workers in North pulls up the return to H workers. Fragmentation means that the E workers can seek out foreign H workers instead (offshore the H workers' jobs) and so the latter may (but not must) lose.

REFERENCES

Brainard, S. Lael, and Susan Collins (eds.) (2006). *Brookings Trade Forum 2005: Offshoring White-Collar Work*, Washington: The Brookings Institution.
Markusen, James R. (1983). 'Factor movements and commodity trade as complements', *Journal of International Economics*, 14, 341–56.
    (1984). 'Multinationals, multi-plant economies, and the gains from trade', *Journal of International Economics*, 16, 205–26.
    (2002). *Multinational Firms and the Theory of International Trade*, Cambridge: MIT Press.
    (2006). 'Modeling the offshoring of white-collar services: from comparative advantage to the new theories of trade and FDI', in Brainard and Collins (eds.), pp. 1–34.
Markusen, James R., and Anthony J. Venables (2007). 'Interacting factor endowments and trade costs: a multi-country, multi-good approach to trade theory', *Journal of International Economics*, 73, 333–54.
Venables, Anthony J. (1996). 'Equilibrium locations of vertically linked industries', *International Economic Review*, 37, 341–59.

4 Entry dynamics and the decline in exchange-rate pass-through

Christopher Gust, Sylvain Leduc and Robert J. Vigfusson

4.1 Introduction

It is well known that the degree of exchange-rate pass-through (pass-through herein) to import prices is low. The evidence surveyed in Goldberg and Knetter (1997) suggests that an average pass-through estimate for the 1980s would be roughly 50 per cent for the United States, implying that, following a 10 per cent depreciation of the dollar, a foreign exporter selling to the US market would raise its price in the United States by 5 per cent. Moreover, there is substantial evidence that the degree of pass-through to US import prices has declined considerably since the early 1990s, to a level of about 30 per cent.[1]

In Gust *et al.* (2010), we attempt to explain these findings by demonstrating that, in the presence of pricing complementarity, trade integration spurred by lower tariffs, transport costs and changes in relative productivities accounts for a significant portion of the decline in pass-through. In our framework, trade integration reduces pass-though because pricing complementarity induces an exporter to set a relatively high and variable mark-up when its costs are lower than its competitors and a low and unresponsive mark-up when its costs are relatively high. Pass-through thus declines solely because of mark-up adjustments along the intensive margin, as we abstracted from the entry and exit decisions of exporting firms.

In this paper, we instead examine how entry dynamics affect pass-through in the presence of declines in trade costs and changes in relative productivities across countries that help account for greater US openness. This is particularly important since the decline in pass-through has occurred at a time when the US economy has become increasingly

---

[1] Our empirical evidence is in line with the work of Olivei (2002) and Marazzi *et al.* (2005) for the United States. Ihrig *et al.* (2006) also document a fall in pass-through in other G7 economies, and Otani *et al.* (2003) find a decline in exchange-rate pass-through in Japan.

open with a greater concentration of foreign firms exporting to the United States.[2] Dornbusch (1987), for instance, shows that an increasing presence of foreign firms should reduce firms' pricing power in US markets, result in less variable mark-ups and therefore put upward pressure on pass-through to import prices.

Once we extend our previous analysis to incorporate such a mechanism, we find that the effect of entry on pass-through is quantitatively small and is more than offset by the adjustment of mark-ups that arise only along the intensive margin. However, even though entry has a relatively small impact on pass-through, it nevertheless plays an important role in accounting for the secular rise in imports relative to GDP. In particular, our model suggests that over three-quarters of the rise in the US import share since the early 1980s is due to trade in new goods. To have a more significant impact on pass-through, firms' entry in our framework would need to generate a much larger increase in the share of imports than is observed empirically. Thus, a key insight of this paper is that adjustment of mark-ups that occur along the intensive margin are quantitatively more important in accounting for secular changes in pass-through than adjustments that occur along the extensive margin.

The paper is organised as follows. The next section presents evidence on the decline in pass-through in the United States, while Section 4.3 describes the time-series properties of trade costs and documents changes in productivities in different regions of the world. The model is described in Section 4.4, and we relate our statistical measure of pass-through to the model in Section 4.5. Section 4.6 discusses the model's calibration and our results are presented in Section 4.7. The last section concludes.

4.2   US import prices and the real exchange rate

We first examine the statistical relationship between import prices and the exchange rate and document the increasing disconnect between these variables. Our analysis closely follows Gust *et al.* (2010), who provide a more detailed treatment of this relationship.

In our analysis, we focus on imports that are included in the end-use categories of automotive products, consumer goods and capital goods, excluding computers and semiconductors. We will refer to these categories as finished goods, which account for 45 per cent of the nominal value of total imports since 1987.

---

[2] See Kehoe and Ruhl (2002) and Hummels and Klenow (2005), among others, for the view that the extensive margin is an important characteristic of trade growth.

We concentrate on this more narrowly defined measure of import prices for two reasons. First, we exclude import prices of services, computers and semiconductors because of concerns about price measurement. Second, our preferred measure excludes import prices of foods, feeds, beverages and industrial supplies, because we view our model as less applicable to these categories. In particular, we model the determination of import prices as arising from the decisions of firms that are monopolistic competitors and have the ability to price discriminate across countries. In the context of our model, excluding these goods is sensible since for many of these goods the extent of monopolistic behaviour and price discrimination is limited.

We argue that the decline in pass-through can be understood using a real model and thus focus on real import prices and real exchange rates. Accordingly, we define the real price of imports as the ratio of the finished goods import price deflator to the US CPI (consumer price index) deflator. Henceforth we will refer to our relative price index of finished goods as the relative price of imports. For our measure of the real exchange rate we use the Federal Reserve's real effective exchange rate, which is constructed from data on nominal exchange rates and consumer price indices for thirty-nine countries.

We use the following statistic to summarise the relationship between these two series:

$$\beta_{p_m,q} = \frac{\mathrm{cov}(p_m,q)}{\sigma_q^2} = \mathrm{corr}(p_m,q)\frac{\sigma_{p_m}}{\sigma_q}, \tag{1}$$

where p_m denotes the relative price of imports and q denotes the real exchange rate. This statistic takes into account the correlation between the two series as well as their relative volatility and can be derived as the estimate from a univariate least squares regression of the real exchange rate on the relative import price. As shown in Table 4.1, our estimate of $\beta_{pm,q}$ has declined in the 1990s, reflecting both the decline in the relative volatility of import prices and the lower correlation between the two series. Further evidence of the increasing disconnect between these variables is shown in Figure 4.1 which plots estimates of $\beta_{pm,q}$ for the log-differenced data based on 10-year, rolling windows. (The line indicates the point estimate and the shaded region denotes the 95 per cent confidence region.) There is a gradual decline in $\beta_{pm,q}$ beginning in the mid 1980s.

Our summary statistic, $\beta_{pm,q}$, is closely related to estimates of pass-through in empirical studies. For instance, we get comparable estimates to Marazzi et al. (2005) regarding the change in the relationship

Table 4.1 *Volatility and correlation of relative import price and real exchange rate*[a]

Moment (differenced)	Full sample	1980:1–1989:4	1990:1–2004:4
a. $\beta_{pm,q}$ (a = b*c)	0.35	0.55	0.13
b. σ_{pm}/σ_q	0.47	0.60	0.25
c. $\text{corr}(q,p_m)$	0.75	0.92	0.51
Moment (HP-Filtered)			
a. $\beta_{pm,q}$ (a = b*c)	0.46	0.59	0.17
b. σ_{pm}/σ_q	0.54	0.61	0.29
c. $\text{corr}(q,p_m)$	0.85	0.95	0.60

[a] $\beta_{pm,q}$ denotes the regression coefficient from a univariate least squares regression of the real exchange rate on the relative import price. Differenced refers to data that has been log-differenced. HP-filtered series were computed by transforming the log of the variables (with $\lambda = 1600$).

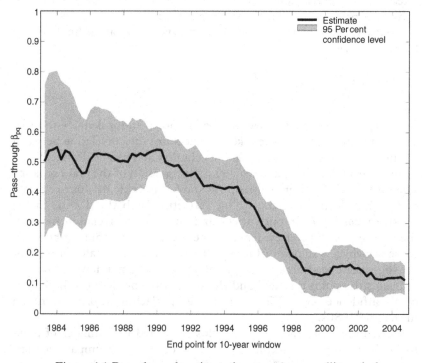

Figure 4.1 Pass-through estimated over a 10-year rolling window

between import prices and the exchange rate.[3] Overall, the evidence suggests that there has been an increasing disconnect between the price of imported finished goods and the exchange rate.[4]

4.3   Trade costs and productivity

In this section, we address the time-series evidence regarding whether tariffs and transport costs have fallen over time as well as discuss the behaviour for other forms of trade costs. We also examine the data on changes in the relative productivity of the United States vis-à-vis its trading partners.

Barriers to international trade take many forms, some less tangible than others. Typically, tariffs and transport costs come to mind as factors impeding the flow of goods across countries. However, international trade can also be hindered by the presence of legal and regulatory costs, distribution costs, and institutional and cultural barriers. Although tariffs and transport costs make up only a fraction of overall trade costs they remain an important factor underlying the movement towards greater trade integration. For instance, Baier and Bergstrand (2001) find that the decline in tariff rates and transport costs played an important role in post-World-War-II expansion in international trade for OECD countries.[5]

Data on tariffs and transport costs support the notion that trade costs have been falling over time. For the United States, detailed information on tariffs and transport costs are available from Feenstra (1996) and Feenstra et al. (2002) who have compiled product-level import data. Using this data, we compute tariffs and transport costs for finished-goods industries from 1980 to 2001. For each available industry, we measure trade costs as the sum of transport costs and tariffs and compute an industry-weighted average trade cost measure. (See the appendix of Gust et al. (2010) for the details of these calculations.)

---

[3] When estimating pass-through, Marazzi et al. (2005) control for movements in marginal costs using foreign CPIs and commodity prices. The results are also similar if different control variables are used. For instance, pass-through declines to the same extent when unit labour costs and domestic output are respectively used to control for changes in marginal costs and import demand, as in Campa and Goldberg (2004).

[4] This decline in pass-through is most evident for finished goods. The decline in pass-through for total imports is smaller and less precisely estimated.

[5] The fact that tariff and transport costs have been declining throughout the post-war period yields the implication in our model that, other things equal, exchange-rate pass-through to import prices should have declined throughout the post-war period. Unfortunately, our measure of import prices for finished goods industries does not extend back far enough to investigate this possibility.

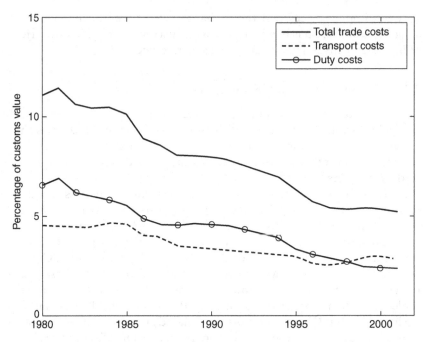

Figure 4.2 The decline in average transport costs and tariffs for US imported goods

Figure 4.2 reports that, over our sample period, the average trade cost across industries fell from 11.1 per cent of the custom value of the goods in 1980 to 5.2 per cent in 2001. The figure also decomposes our average trade cost measure into its tariffs and transport costs components. It shows that transport costs have declined somewhat since 1980 but that the fall in trade costs has been driven mostly by a reduction in tariffs.

Although tariffs and transport costs have the advantage of being relatively easier to quantify, it is more difficult to measure other forms of trade costs precisely since they are often not directly observable. As a result, researchers infer these costs by estimating gravity models of international trade. This literature finds mixed evidence regarding a possible decline in overall trade costs.[6] As a result, we take a conservative approach and focus only on the evidence regarding transport costs and tariffs.

---

[6] Using different data sets and methodologies, Rauch (1999), Coe et al. (2002) and Brun et al. (2005) find that trade costs have fallen continuously since the 1970s. On the other hand, Frankel (1997) and Berthelon and Freund (2004) find no evidence of a significant decline in trade costs.

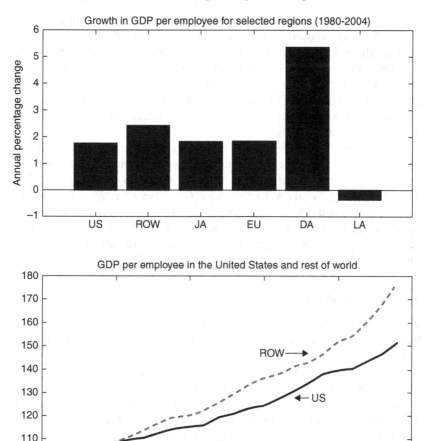

Figure 4.3 Growth in GDP per employee in the United States and the rest of the world

Since trade integration can also be triggered by improved product-ivity of exporting firms, we document changes in relative productivity across countries. The top panel of Figure 4.3 displays the annualised percentage change in GDP per employee for the United States (US), its foreign counterpart (ROW), and other regions around the world for the 1980–2003 period.[7] These indices are constructed using data on GDP per employee, and the ROW index is based on data for OECD and

---

[7] Although we would prefer a more disaggregated measure, we focus on productivity at the aggregate level due to data limitations for developing countries.

major developing countries. Growth in GDP per employee outside the United States outpaced US growth largely because of faster productivity growth in developing Asia (DA), which includes a number of rapidly developing countries such as China and South Korea. Productivity growth in Europe (EU) was roughly on a par with growth in the United States, while Japanese (JA) productivity growth was somewhat faster than in the United States, despite a marked deceleration in Japanese productivity in the 1990s.

With foreign labour productivity growth higher than US productivity growth over the last two decades, there has been considerable convergence of foreign productivity to the level of US productivity. The bottom panel of Figure 4.3 shows that GDP per employee outside the United States roughly doubled over the 1980–2003 period, while US GDP per employee rose about 40 per cent over this period. As a consequence, the level of foreign productivity has increased by 40 per cent relative to US productivity over the past twenty-five years.

4.4   The model

Our model is based on Gust *et al.* (2010) and consists of a home and a foreign economy. These two economies have isomorphic structures so in our exposition we focus on describing only the domestic economy. The domestic economy consists of two types of agents: households and firms. Households have utility that depends on the consumption of both domestically produced goods and imported goods. These goods are purchased from monopolistically competitive firms, who set prices flexibly each period. While the range of goods produced by these firms is exogenously given, the fraction of firms that export is determined endogenously. In particular, because a firm must pay both a fixed and variable cost to export its good, it may choose to sell its good only in the domestic economy. The key element we introduce into this environment is that a firm's demand curve has a non-constant elasticity so that exchange-rate pass-through to import prices may be incomplete.

4.4.1   Households

The utility function of the representative household in the home country is

$$E_t \sum_{j=0}^{\infty} \beta^j \left\{ \log\left(C_{t+j}\right) - \chi_0 \frac{L_{t+j}^{1+\chi}}{1+\chi} \right\}, \qquad (2)$$

where the discount factor β satisfies $0 < \beta < 1$ and E_t is the expectation operator conditional on information available at time t. The period utility function depends on consumption C_t and labour L_t. A household also purchases state-contingent assets b_{t+1} that are traded internationally so that asset markets are complete.

Households receive income from working and an aliquot share of profits of all the domestic firms, Ω_t. In choosing its contingency plans for C_t, L_t, b_{t+1}, a household takes into account its budget constraint at each date:

$$C_t + \int_s p_{bt,t+1} b_{t+1} - b_t = w_t L_t + \Omega_t. \tag{3}$$

In equation (3), $w_t = \dfrac{W_t}{P_t}$ is the household's real wage and $p_{bt,t+1}$ denotes the price of an asset that pays one unit of the domestic consumption good in a particular state of nature at date $t + 1$. (For convenience, we have suppressed that variables depend on the state of nature.)

4.4.2 Demand aggregator

There is a continuum of goods indexed by $i \in [0,1]$ in each economy. While a domestic household purchases all of the domestically produced goods, there are only $i \in [0, \omega_t^*]$ that are available for imports, where ω_t^* denotes the endogenously determined fraction of traded foreign goods. A household chooses domestically produced goods, $C_{dt}(i)$, and imported goods, $C_{mt}(i)$, to minimise their total expenditures:

$$\left[\int_0^1 P_{dt}(i) C_{dt}(i) di + \int_0^{\omega_t^*} P_{mt}(i) C_{mt}(i) di \right], \tag{4}$$

subject to $D\left(\dfrac{C_{dt}(i)}{C_t}, \dfrac{C_{mt}(i)}{C_t} \right) = 1$. In minimising its expenditures, a household takes the prices of the domestic, $P_{dt}(i)$, and imported goods, $P_{mt}(i)$, as given. (For convenience, we denote these prices in nominal terms, although prices are flexible in the model and we solve only for real variables.) In our model, there are no distribution services required to sell the imported goods to households. Accordingly, $P_{mt}(i)$ denotes both the retail import price for good i and price charged at the point of entry.

The function, $D\left(\dfrac{C_{dt}(i)}{C_t}, \dfrac{C_{mt}(i)}{C_t} \right)$, is a household's demand aggregator for producing a unit of C_t and is defined by:

$$\int_0^1 \int_0^{\omega_t^*} D\left(\frac{C_{dt}(i)}{C_t}, \frac{C_{mt}(j)}{C_t}\right) di \, dj = \left[\frac{1}{1+\omega_t^*} V_{dt}^{\frac{1}{\rho}} + \frac{\omega_t^*}{1+\omega_t^*} V_{mt}^{\frac{1}{\rho}}\right]^{\rho} - \frac{1}{(1+\eta)\gamma} + 1. \tag{5}$$

In this expression, V_{dt} is an aggregator for domestic goods given by:

$$V_{dt} = \int_0^1 \frac{1}{(1+\eta)\gamma}\left[(1+\omega_t^*)(1+\eta)\frac{C_{dt}(i)}{C_t} - \eta\right]^{\gamma} di, \tag{6}$$

and V_{mt} is an aggregator for imported goods given by:

$$V_{mt} = \frac{1}{\omega_t^*}\int_0^{\omega_t^*} \frac{1}{(1+\eta)\gamma}\left[(1+\omega_t^*)(1+\eta)\frac{C_{mt}(j)}{C_t} - \eta\right]^{\gamma} dj. \tag{7}$$

Our demand aggregator adapts the one discussed in Dotsey and King (2005) to an international environment and is discussed in more detail in Gust et al. (2006). It shares the central feature that the elasticity of demand is nonconstant (NCES) with $\eta \neq 0$, and the (absolute value of the) demand elasticity can be expressed as an increasing function of a firm's relative price when $\eta < 0$.

Expenditure minimisation by a domestic household implies that the demand curve for an imported good is given by:

$$\frac{C_{mt}(j)}{C_t} = \frac{1}{1+\omega_t^*}\left[\frac{1}{1+\eta}\left(\frac{P_{mt}(j)}{P_{mt}}\right)^{\frac{1}{\gamma-1}}\left(\frac{P_{mt}}{\Gamma_t}\right)^{\frac{\rho}{\gamma-\rho}} + \frac{\eta}{1+\eta}\right]. \tag{8}$$

In the above, Γ_t is a price index consisting of the prices of a firm's competitors defined as:

$$\Gamma_t = \left[\left(\frac{1}{1+\omega_t^*}\right)^{\frac{\gamma}{\gamma-\rho}} P_{dt}^{\gamma-\rho} + \left(\frac{\omega_t^*}{1+\omega_t^*}\right)^{\frac{\gamma}{\gamma-\rho}} P_{mt}^{\gamma-\rho}\right]^{\frac{\gamma-\rho}{\gamma}}, \tag{9}$$

and P_{dt} and P_{mt} are indices of domestic and import prices defined as:

$$P_{dt} = \left(\int_0^1 P_{dt}(i)^{\frac{\gamma}{\gamma-1}} di\right)^{\frac{\gamma-1}{\gamma}}, \tag{10}$$

$$P_{mt} = \left(\frac{1}{\omega_t^*}\int_0^{\omega_t^*} P_{mt}(j)^{\frac{\gamma}{\gamma-1}} dj\right)^{\frac{\gamma-1}{\gamma}}. \tag{11}$$

Expenditure minimisation also implies an analogous expression for the demand curve of domestic good i, which depends on prices, $P_{dt}(i)$, P_{dt} and Γ_t.

A property of our aggregator is that it nests an Armington aggregator so that the elasticity of substitution between a home and foreign good can differ from the demand elasticity for two home goods.[8] This separate elasticity for goods occurs when $\rho \neq 1$, which gives the model more flexibility to match estimates of the elasticity of substitution between home and foreign tradables as well as estimates of economy-wide mark-ups. More importantly, when $\eta \neq 0$, the demand curve has an additive linear term, which implies that the elasticity of demand depends on the price of good i relative to other prices. It is this feature that helps give rise to incomplete pass-through to import prices and implies that pass-through depends on the economy's structure including the underlying shocks.

The aggregate consumer price level is given by

$$P_t = \frac{1}{1+\eta}\Gamma_t + \frac{\eta}{1+\eta}\left[\frac{1}{1+\omega_t^*}\int_0^1 P_{dt}(i)di + \frac{1}{1+\omega_t^*}\int_0^{\omega_t^*} P_{mt}(j)dj\right]. \tag{12}$$

From this expression, it is clear that the consumer price level is equal to the competitive pricing bundle, Γ_t, when $\eta = 0$. In general, the consumer price level is the sum of Γ_t with a linear aggregator of prices for individual goods.[9]

4.4.3   Firms

The production function for firm i is linear in labour so that

$$Y_t(i) = Z_t L_t(i). \tag{13}$$

---

[8] More specifically, with $\eta = 0$, our demand aggregator can be thought of as the combination of a Dixit-Stiglitz and Armington aggregator. To see this, note that in this case we can rewrite our aggregator as:

$$C_t = (1 + \omega_t^*)\left[\frac{1}{1+\omega_t^*}C_{dt}^\rho + \frac{\omega_t^*}{1+\omega_t^*}C_{mt}^\rho\right]^{\frac{\gamma}{\rho}},$$

where $C_{dt} = \left(\int_0^1 C_{dt}(i)^\gamma di\right)^{\frac{1}{\gamma}}$ and $C_{mt} = \left(\frac{1}{\omega_t^*}\int_0^{\omega_t^*} C_{mt}(j)^\gamma dj\right)^{\frac{1}{\gamma}}$. As in Bergin and Glick (2005), our specification of the demand aggregator also rules out the 'love of variety' effect. However, a change in ω_t^* does increase the number of foreign varieties relative to home varieties in the consumption bundle, and thus 'home' bias in household preferences is endogenously determined in the model.

[9] The consumer price level can be derived from equating equation (4) to $P_t C_t$ and substituting in the relative demand curves. The price Γ_t can be derived from substituting the relative demand curves into equation (5).

In the above, Z_t is an aggregate, *iid* technology shock that affects the production function for all firms in the home country. A firm hires labour in a competitive market in which labour is completely mobile within a country but immobile across countries. Marginal cost is therefore the same for all firms in the home country so that real marginal cost of firm i is given by $\dfrac{w_t}{Z_t}$.

Firms in each country are monopolistically competitive and each firm sells its good to households located in its country. Profit maximisation implies that a firm chooses to set its price as a mark-up over marginal cost. As a result, the price of good i in the domestic market satisfies:

$$\frac{P_{dt}(i)}{P_t} = \mu_{dt}(i)\frac{w_t}{Z_t}, \quad i \in [0,1], \tag{14}$$

with $\mu_{dt}(i) \geq 1$. The mark-up $\mu_{dt}(i)$ can be expressed as:

$$\mu_{dt}(i) = \mu_{dt} = \left[1 - \frac{1}{|\varepsilon_{dt}|}\right]^{-1} = \left[\gamma + \eta(\gamma-1)\left(\frac{P_{dt}}{\Gamma_t}\right)^{\frac{\rho}{\rho-\gamma}}\right]^{-1}, \tag{15}$$

where $|\varepsilon_{dt}|$, is the absolute value of the elasticity of a domestic good given by:

$$\varepsilon_{dt} = \left[(\gamma-1)\left(1 + \eta\left(\frac{P_{dt}}{\Gamma_t}\right)^{\frac{\rho}{\rho-\gamma}}\right)\right]^{-1}. \tag{16}$$

In the above, we have dropped the index i, since we restrict our attention to a symmetric equilibrium in which all firms set the same price in the domestic market (i.e. $P_{dt}(i) = P_{dt}$, $\varepsilon_{dt}(i) = \varepsilon_{dt}$, and $\mu_{dt}(i)=\mu_{dt}$).

Equation (15) shows that a firm's mark-up depends on the price it sets relative to its competitors price Γ_t. When the (absolute value of the) demand elasticity is increasing in $\dfrac{P_{dt}}{\Gamma_t}$, the mark-up will be a decreasing function of this relative price. Consequently, a firm will respond to a fall in the price of its competitors by lowering its mark-up and price. A firm finds it desirable to do so, because otherwise it will experience a relatively large fall in its market share. An important exception to this pricing behaviour is the CES demand curve in which $\eta = 0$. In this case, a firm's mark-up does not depend on the relative price of its competitors.

Entry

Following Melitz (2003), Ghironi and Melitz (2004) and Bergin and Glick (2005), we allow for the endogenous entry and exit of firms into the export market. In particular, we assume that each period a firm faces a fixed and per-unit export cost and decides whether to export or not. Unlike these previous papers, which allow productivity to vary with a good's type, we assume that the fixed cost varies with the variety of the good.[10] In particular, we assume that the fixed cost is given by:

$$f_x(i) = f_x\left(\frac{1}{1-\alpha_x i} - 1\right), \quad \alpha_x \geq 0, \tag{17}$$

and is paid in units of labour. We view this fixed cost as reflecting the cost to a firm of making consumers aware of its product, setting up a distribution system and understanding the legal and regulatory environment of a foreign market. It seems reasonable to assume that these costs differ depending on the type of good.

Since an exporter must make its entry decision before the realisation of shocks in period t, a firm will choose to export if its expected profits from exporting exceed its fixed cost:

$$E_{t-1}\left[(\pi_{xt}(i) - f_x(i)w_t)\right] > 0, \tag{18}$$

where exporter i's per-unit profits in the foreign market are given by:

$$\pi_{xt}(i) = \left(q_t \frac{P_{mt}^*(i)}{P_t^*} - \frac{D_t w_t}{Z_t}\right) C_{mt}^*(i). \tag{19}$$

In the above, q_t is the real exchange rate expressed in units of the home consumption bundle per units of foreign consumption, $P_{mt}^*(i)$ is the nominal price of home good i denominated in foreign currency and $C_{mt}^*(i)$ is the demand for home good i by foreign households. (We use a star to denote foreign variables.) Also, D_t is an iceberg shipping cost which we assume to be a stochastic *iid* process.[11] Finally, our functional form for the fixed cost implies that only firms on the interval $i \in [0, \omega_t]$

---

[10] In our environment with variable mark-ups, heterogeneity in the technologies of firms would considerably complicate the analysis, since computing aggregate prices and quantities would involve accounting for a distribution of mark-ups. In contrast, because the fixed cost does not affect a firm's marginal pricing condition, we can still analyse a symmetric equilibrium in which all firms who decide to export choose the same price and mark-up.

[11] This assumption is not critical for our analysis. We assume that D_t is stochastic mainly to illustrate how pass-through differs depending on the type of shock.

will export their good where the marginal good ω_t satisfies equation (18) as an equality.

Similar to a firm's pricing decision in the domestic market, profit maximisation implies that a firm chooses its export price as a mark-up over marginal cost:

$$q_t \frac{P^*_{mt}(i)}{P^*_t} = \mu^*_{mt}(i) \frac{D_t w_t}{Z_t}, \quad i \in [0, \omega_t]. \tag{20}$$

In a symmetric equilibrium, all exporting firms will choose the same price and mark-up (i.e. $P^*_{mt}(i) = P^*_{mt}$ and $\mu^*_{mt}(i) = \mu^*_{mt}$). An exporter's mark-up is given by:

$$\mu^*_{mt}(i) = \mu^*_{mt} = \left[1 - \frac{1}{|\varepsilon^*_{mt}|} \right]^{-1} = \left[\gamma + \eta(\gamma-1)\left(\frac{P^*_{mt}}{\Gamma^*_t} \right)^{\frac{\rho}{\rho-\gamma}} \right]^{-1}, \tag{21}$$

where $|\varepsilon^*_{mt}|$ is the absolute value of the elasticity of a domestic good in the foreign market.

Comparing equations (14) and (20), we note that the law of one price (i.e. $\frac{P^*_{mt}(i)}{P^*_t} q_t = \frac{P_{dt}(i)}{P_t}$) will not hold when $D_t > 1$. In addition, because the demand elasticity can differ across markets (i.e. $\varepsilon_{dt} \neq \varepsilon^*_{mt}$), a firm will optimally choose to price discriminate. Price discrimination by firms is possible due to the presence of fixed and per-unit trade costs.

4.5   Defining pass-through

We consider two alternative definitions for import price pass-through. For the first, we define pass-through from the perspective of an individual exporter who views the exchange rate as exogenous. This definition considers how much an individual exporter changes his price in response to a 1 per cent change in the exchange rate, holding constant the other factors a firm takes as given: its marginal cost and the prices of other firms. Letting $p_{mt}(j) = \frac{P_{mt}(j)}{P_t}$ and $\xi_t = \frac{\Gamma_t}{P_t}$ denote the relative price of exporter i and the relative price of its competitors, respectively, a foreign exporter's pricing equation can be written as:

$$p_{mt}(j) = \mu_{mt}(j) D^*_t \frac{w^*_t}{Z^*_t} q_t, \tag{22}$$

where $\mu_{mt}(j)$ is given by an analagous expression to equation (21). The direct effect of an exchange-rate change on the price of foreign exporter i is given by $\kappa_{mt}(j) = \dfrac{\partial p_{mt}(j)}{\partial q_t} \dfrac{q_t}{p_{mt}(j)}$:

$$\kappa_{mt}(j) = \frac{1}{1 - \eta\mu_{mt}(i)\left(\dfrac{\rho(\gamma-1)}{\gamma-\rho}\right)\left(\dfrac{p_{mt}(j)}{\xi_t}\right)^{\frac{\rho}{\rho-\gamma}}} = \frac{1}{1 + (\mu_{mt}(j)-1)\dfrac{\partial\,|\varepsilon_{mt}(j)|}{\partial p_{mt}(j)}\dfrac{p_{mt}(j)}{|\varepsilon_{mt}(j)|}}. \qquad (23)$$

Because $\kappa_{mt}(j)$ measures only the direct effect of an exchange-rate change on an exporter's price, we refer to it as the direct pass-through measure.

From the expression directly after the equality, we can see that if $\eta < 0$ then direct pass-through will be incomplete.[12] In this case, a 1 per cent increase in q_t drives up a foreign exporter's cost when denominated in dollars; however, a firm does not raise its price a full 1 per cent because as the exporter's price rises relative to its competitors, it induces the exporter to accept a lower mark-up rather than give up market share.

Alternatively, the expression after the second equality in equation (23) indicates that direct pass-through depends on the level of the mark-up and the elasticity of the elasticity of demand, $\dfrac{\partial\,|\varepsilon_{mt}(j)|}{\partial p_{mt}(j)}\dfrac{p_{mt}(j)}{|\varepsilon_{mt}(j)|}$.

This expression is similar to the one derived by Eichenbaum and Fisher (2004) in a closed economy context. With $\eta < 0$, the elasticity of the elasticity of demand is positive and as a result $\kappa_{mt}(j) < 1$.

To facilitate comparisons of our model with the data, in addition to our direct pass-through measure, we also examine our model's implications for the second moment $\beta_{pm,q}$ previously defined (in log-differences) as:

$$\beta_{pm,q} = \frac{\text{cov}(\Delta p_{mt}, \Delta q_t)}{\text{var}(\Delta q_t)}. \qquad (24)$$

The relationship between $\beta_{pm,q}$ and $\kappa_{mt}(j)$ can be seen by log-linearising equation (22) around the non-stochastic steady state to write a foreign exporter's pricing decision as:

$$\hat{p}_{mt} = \kappa_m\left(\hat{D}_t^* + \hat{\psi}_t^* + \hat{q}_t\right) + (1 - \kappa_m)\hat{\xi}_t. \qquad (25)$$

---

[12] With $\eta < 0$, the demand curve is less convex than the CES case.

The symbol '$\hat{\xi}$' denotes the log-deviation of a variable from its steady state value and $\kappa_m = \kappa_m(i)$ evaluated at non-stochastic steady state. Using this equation, we can relate $\beta_{pm,q}$ and κ_m via:

$$\beta_{Pm,q} = \kappa_m + \kappa_m \left(\frac{\text{cov}(\Delta \psi_t^*, \Delta q_t)}{\text{var}(\Delta q_t)} + \frac{\text{cov}(\Delta D_t^*, \Delta q_t)}{\text{var}(\Delta q_t)} \right) + \left(1 - \kappa_m\right) \frac{\text{cov}(\Delta \xi_t, \Delta q_t)}{\text{var}(\Delta q_t)}. \quad (26)$$

According to equation (26), the univariate regression statistic, $\beta_{pm,q}$, is related to κ_m except that $\beta_{pm,q}$ takes into account any correlation of the real exchange rate with an exporter's costs and the pricing index of an exporter's competitors that occurs in general equilibrium. Thus, $\beta_{pm,q}$ takes into account both direct and indirect effects of an exchange rate change on an exporter's price.

In our analysis, we focus on comparing our model results to the data for $\beta_{pm,q}$ rather than κ_m. This reflects that $\beta_{pm,q}$ is a second moment that is easily measured in the data. In contrast, measuring κ_m is complicated by finding good measures of marginal costs and the prices of a firm's competitors as well as correctly specifying the equations for estimating κ_m and dealing with the endogeneity of the exchange rate and the prices of other firms.

4.6   Calibration

In order to investigate the role of trade costs and productivity differentials on pass-through, we log-linearise and solve the model around two different steady states. In the first, the home and foreign economies are identical, and both economies have relatively high trade costs. We call this our benchmark calibration. In the second, we lower trade costs as well as raise the level of foreign productivity, keeping the remaining parameters constant.[13] We call this the 2004 calibration.[14]

The value of η, which governs the curvature of the demand curve, is critical for our analysis. Faced with sparse independent evidence regarding this parameter, we calibrate it as a part of a simulated method of moments procedure. Specifically, we choose η along with

[13] While the level of foreign productivity is actually lower than US productivity, for simplicity we begin with a calibration in which the two economies are identical. This simplification seems reasonable, since our results for the decline in pass-through depend critically on the change in relative productivity in the two countries rather than their initial levels.

[14] In the initial steady state, each country's net foreign asset position is zero. Given this initial position, we then allow a country's net foreign asset position to respond endogenously in the second steady state to the deterministic change in trade costs and foreign productivity.

the standard deviations of the *iid* technology and trade cost shocks so that the model's implications for the volatility of output, the ratio of the volatility of relative import prices to the real exchange rate and the correlation between relative import prices and the real exchange rate match those observed in the 1980–1989 period. In doing so, we constrain the standard deviation of the technology shocks and trade costs shocks to be the same in both countries (i.e. $\sigma_z = \sigma_z^*$ and $\sigma_D = \sigma_D^*$). By construction, our model matches the observed value of $\beta_{pm,q}$ for the 1980s. With η pinned down based on the pre-1990s data, we then examine the fall in $\beta_{pm,q}$ arising from a fall in trade costs and a higher level of foreign productivity.

Table 4.2 shows our calibrated value of η as well as the calibrated values of other important parameters of the model. We choose γ to be consistent with an exporter's mark-up over marginal cost of around 20 per cent in the benchmark calibration. We set $\rho = 0.85$, which implies an aggregate trade-price elasticity for the benchmark calibration of 2.[15] The discount factor $\beta = 1.03^{-0.25}$, and the utility function parameter χ is set to 1.5, which implies a Frisch elasticity of labour supply of ⅔. We set χ_0 and χ_0^* to imply $L = L^* = 1$ in the benchmark calibration.

For the initial levels of technology, we choose $Z = Z^* = 1$. As shown in Figure 4.3, foreign productivity rose about 35 per cent relative to the level of US productivity from 1980 to 2000. Thus, we set $Z^* = 1.35$ in the 2004 calibration. Consistent with Table 4.2, we set $D = D^* = 1.1$ in the benchmark calibration and lowered $D = D^* = 1.05$ in the 2004 calibration.

For the fixed costs of trade we set $f_x = f_x^* = 0.46$ which implies that the import share in the home economy is about 10 per cent. Since we assume that trade is balanced in the initial steady state, the foreign economy has the same import share. We choose $\alpha_x = \alpha_x^* = 2.5$ so that after the fall in trade costs and increase in foreign productivity, the home country's import share rises about 4 percentage points (pp).

We also compare our benchmark calibration to one with CES preferences (i.e. $\eta = 0$). Table 4.2 reports the parameter values used for the

---

[15] We define the aggregate trade-price elasticity by differentiating aggregate import demand:

$$\omega_t^* C_{mt} = \frac{\omega_t^*}{1 + \omega_t^*} \left[\frac{1}{1 + \eta} \left(\frac{P_{mt}}{\Gamma_t} \right)^{\frac{\rho}{\gamma - \rho}} + \frac{\eta}{1 + \eta} \right] C_t,$$

with respect to $\dfrac{P_{mt}}{\Gamma_t}$ holding C_t and ω_t^* constant. With $\rho < 1$ in our benchmark calibration, this aggregate elasticity is lower than the elasticity of demand for individual good i, $|\varepsilon_{mt}(i)|$.

Table 4.2 *Parameter values and properties of calibrated models*

	NCES demand		CES calibration
	Benchmark calibration	2004 calibration	
ρ	0.85	0.85	1.7
η	-3.05	-3.05	0
γ	1.1	1.1	0.835
β	0.9926	0.9926	0.9926
χ	1.5	1.5	1.5
χ_0	0.79	0.79	0.83
$D=D^*$	1.1	1.05	1.1
Z	1	1	1
Z^*	1	1.35	1
f_x	0.46	0.46	0.37
α_x	2.5	2.5	2.5
$\sigma_Z = \sigma_Z^*$	0.0178	0.0178	0.0191
$\sigma_D = \sigma_D^*$	0.0094	0.0094	0.008
Home trade share	10.0%	14.0%	10.0%
Home firms' domestic mark-up (μ_d)	1.27	1.24	1.20
Foreign exporters' mark-up (μ_m)	1.20	1.38	1.20
Home trade-price elasticity	-2.0	-1.2	-2.0
Direct pass-through (κ_m)	0.48	0.36	1

CES calibration, which were selected in an analogous manner to our benchmark calibration. Table 4.3 shows that both the CES and benchmark calibration (by construction) match the observed volatility of output and correlation between import prices and the exchange rate in the 1980s. However, only the benchmark calibration with $\eta \neq 0$ has the flexibility to match the observed value of $\beta_{pm,q}$ in the 1980s. Although the benchmark calibration implies slightly more exchange rate volatility than the CES calibration, both versions of the model understate the amount of volatility relative to the data. Thus, while the NCES demand curves better account for the observed relationship between the relative import price and the real exchange rate, they do not by themselves explain other important aspects of the data emphasised in the international business cycle literature.[16]

---

[16] See Bergin and Feenstra (2001) for a discussion of how the interaction of NCES demand curves with sticky prices denominated in local currency can be helpful in accounting for exchange-rate dynamics.

Table 4.3 *Selected moments of data and calibrated models*[a]

	Data		Model		
Moment	1980– 1989	1990– 2004	Benchmark calibration	2004 calibration	CES calibration
a. $\beta_{pm,q} = \text{cov}(\Delta q, \Delta p_m)/\text{var}(\Delta q)$ (a = b*c)	0.55	0.13	0.55	0.40	1.08
b. $\sigma(\Delta p_m)/\sigma(\Delta q)$	0.60	0.25	0.60	0.43	1.17
c. $\text{corr}(\Delta q, \Delta p_m)$	0.92	0.51	0.92	0.92	0.92
$\sigma(y^{hp})$	1.74	0.98	1.74	1.71	1.74
$\sigma(q^{hp})$	4.98	2.70	1.91	1.96	1.74

[a] The superscript 'hp' denotes that a variable was transformed using the HP-filter (with $\lambda = 1600$).

4.7   Results

In this section, we first discuss the effects of falling trade costs and higher foreign productivity on pass-through.[17] We then present our main finding regarding how pass-through is influenced by firms' entry in the export market.

4.7.1   Trade integration and declining pass-through

Table 4.4 shows the effects of lowering per-unit trade costs and higher foreign productivity on pass-through and important steady-state prices and quantities. The table shows the value of the variables in steady state except for $\beta_{pm,q}$, which is obtained from log-linearising the model and computing the population moments of the model's variables given the shock processes. We start by looking at the effects of changing one variable at a time (columns 2, 3 and 5), before analysing their combined impacts (last column). As shown in the second column, a 5 pp fall in the trade costs of foreign exporters reduces the real marginal cost of exporting (denominated in terms of the home consumption bundle) by 3.5 per cent. Note that the fall in foreign exporters' real marginal cost, $qD^* \dfrac{w^*}{Z^*}$, is less than the decline in D^* as increased demand for the foreign good puts upward pressure on the real exchange rate, q,

---

[17] More details on the theoretical link between trade integration and pass-through can be found in Gust *et al.* (2006).

Table 4.4 *The effect of permanently lower trade costs and higher foreign productivity*[a,b]

	Lower D^*	Lower D	Lower D^*,D	Higher Z^*	Higher Z^*, Lower D^*,D
Foreign exporter trade cost (D^*)	-5	0	-5	0	-5
Home exporter trade cost (D)	0	-5	-5	0	-5
Foreign productivity (Z^*)	0	0	0	35	35
Home import share	0.7	0.2	0.9	3.3	4.0
Home firm mark-up at home (μ_d)	-0.3	-0.1	-0.3	-1.4	-1.7
a. Home import price (p_m)(a = b+c)	-1.6	-0.3	-1.9	-8.2	-9.9
b. Foreign exporter's mark-up (μ_m)	1.8	0.3	2.2	10.9	13.9
c. Foreign marginal cost ($qD^* \frac{w^*}{Z^*}$)	-3.5	-0.7	-4.1	-19.1	-23.8
Real exchange rate (q)	1.1	-1.1	0	-17.5	-17.7
Direct pass-through (κ_m)	-1.8	-0.4	-2.2	-9.5	-11.6
Pass-through ($\beta_{pm,q}$)	-2.3	-0.6	-2.9	-12.5	-14.7

[a] Entry refers to the log-difference for a variable from its value in the benchmark calibration. For the trade costs, home-trade share, κ_m, and $\beta_{pm,q}$, we report the percentage point difference. For Z^*, we report the arithmetic percentage change instead of the log-difference.
[b] Row a equals row b plus row c with any discrepancy due to rounding.

and on foreign wages. With lower costs, foreign exporters reduce their prices and the home country's import share rises 0.7 pp. Because foreign exporters' prices fall relative to their competitors (i.e. the domestic firms), they are able to increase their mark-ups and still gain market share. Conversely, the prices for domestic goods rise relative to their competitors, and domestic firms are forced to cut their mark-ups in reaction to stiffer competition from abroad.

With higher mark-ups on foreign goods, the strategic complementarity intensifies and foreign exporters become more willing to vary their mark-ups in response to cost shocks. Thus, the 5 pp decline in trade costs causes the direct pass-through measure κ_m to fall from 0.48 to 0.462, or 1.8 pp. This fall in κ_m also leads to a reduction in our statistical measure of pass-through, $\beta_{pm,q}$, of 2.3 pp. To understand the fall in

$\beta_{pm,q}$, recall that equation (26, reproduced below) implies that a fall in κ_m directly lowers $\beta_{pm,q}$:

$$\beta_{pm,q} = \kappa_m + \kappa_m \left[\frac{\mathrm{cov}(\Delta\psi_t^*, \Delta q_t)}{\mathrm{var}(\Delta q_t)} + \frac{\mathrm{cov}(\Delta D_t^*, \Delta q_t)}{\mathrm{var}(\Delta q_t)} \right] + (1 - \kappa_m) \left[\frac{\mathrm{cov}(\Delta\xi_t, \Delta q_t)}{\mathrm{var}(\Delta q_t)} \right].$$

Moreover, the decline in κ_m implies that there is less weight on the marginal cost term (the first term in square brackets) and more weight on the price competitiveness term (the second term in square brackets). The marginal cost term is larger than the price competitiveness term because ξ_t turns out to vary little. As a result, a fall in κ_m, by shifting a firm's emphasis in pricing away from cost considerations to considerations of price competitiveness, induces an even larger decline in $\beta_{pm,q}$.

A fall in D, the trade cost on domestic goods sold to the foreign economy, also lowers pass-through (third column of Table 4.4). In general equilibrium, increased foreign demand for home goods causes an appreciation of the home currency that reduces the cost of foreign exporters and leads to a fall in pass-through. The appreciation of the currency results in the real cost of foreign exporters (in home currency) falling by 0.7 per cent. This decline in costs triggers a fall in foreign exporters' prices relative to prices of domestic goods in the home market. As a result, exporters increase their mark-ups and prices of foreign goods decline only 0.3 per cent. At these higher mark-ups, κ_m declines 0.4 pp and $\beta_{pm,q}$ declines 0.6 pp.

The fourth column of Table 4.4 shows the combined effects of lowering trade costs in the home and foreign economies. In this case, foreign exporters' share of the domestic market expands by 0.9 pp and our statistical measure of pass-through declines about 3 pp.

The fifth column of Table 4.4 displays the effects of raising the level of foreign productivity by 35 per cent. Although there is a substantial increase in foreign real wages in response to the higher level of productivity, marginal costs in foreign currency fall. The foreign currency also depreciates; so, an exporter's marginal cost in home currency units falls almost 19 per cent. This large decline in foreign costs allows foreign exporters to both substantially reduce prices and expand their mark-ups at the expense of their domestic competitors. Consequently, the decline in $\beta_{pm,q}$ is a sizeable 12.5 pp.

The last column of Table 4.4 displays the decline in pass-through from the benchmark calibration to 2004 calibration in which the increase in foreign productivity is combined with the decline in D and D^*. Higher productivity and lower trade costs have a substantial impact on pass-through. Overall, $\beta_{pm,q}$ falls almost 15 pp, which accounts for about one-third of the observed decline. The fall in pass-through occurs even though the home market is simultaneously becoming more competitive: mark-ups on domestic goods fall 1.7 pp (see Table 4.2 for a more detailed comparison of the properties of the benchmark and 2004 calibrations). These results broadly capture the view that pass-through has fallen in the United States because of increased foreign competition, which in turn has reduced profit margins of domestic producers in the US market.[18]

4.7.2   The impact of entry on pass-through

We now assess the interaction of the intensive and extensive trade margins with the variable demand elasticity and their role in accounting for the decline in pass-through. To do this, we consider a version of our model that abstracts from entry altogether and then consider a version in which only foreign exporters make entry decisions. In each case, we consider a fall in domestic and foreign trade costs of 5 pp and an increase in foreign productivity of 35 per cent.

To better understand the relative importance of the intensive and extensive margins, Figure 4.4 plots a number of key variables as a function of the number of foreign exporters. We do so for three different cases: the benchmark calibration with relatively high trade costs and low foreign productivity (the dashed line), the 2004 calibration with low trade costs and high foreign productivity (the dotted line), and the 2004 calibration except only foreign exporters make entry decisions (the dashed-dotted line). The corresponding numerical results to Figure 4.4 are shown in Table 4.5.

Consider first the dashed lines in each panel. As the number of foreign exporters increases, per-unit profits of export good i decline due to lower demand for each individual good and a decline in an exporter's mark-up. This mark-up decline reflects that an increase in the number of foreign exporters drives up wages and production costs in the foreign economy, inducing a real home currency depreciation and a rise in the relative import price, p_m. Conversely, the mark-ups of domestic firms in the domestic market increase.

Both measures of pass-through increase as the number of foreign exporters rises. As discussed earlier, this increase reflects that a reduction in an exporter's mark-up is associated with an increase in direct

[18] In recent years, US producers have experienced increased profits. If we allowed US productivity to rise as in Figure 4.3 instead of fixing $Z = 1$ in both steady states, US profits would also rise despite a fall in domestic mark-ups of US producers.

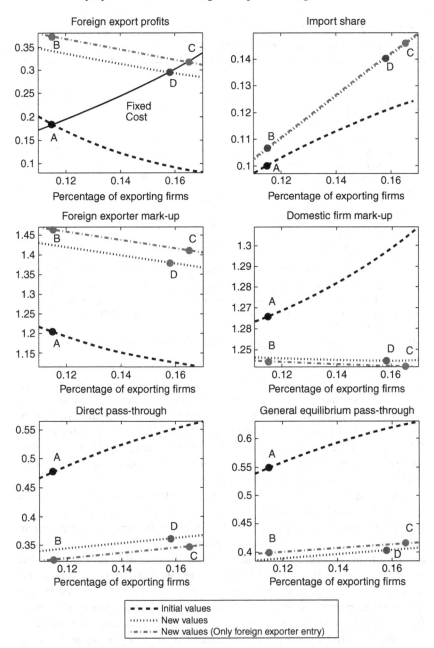

Figure 4.4 The effect of the intensive and extensive entry margins on pass-through

Table 4.5 *The effect of permanently lower trade costs and higher foreign productivity for alternative model versions*[a,b]

	Without entry	With only foreign exporter entry	With entry
Foreign exporter trade cost (D^*)	-5	-5	-5
Home exporter trade cost (D)	-5	-5	-5
Foreign productivity (Z^*)	35	35	35
Home import share	0.7	4.6	4.0
Home firm mark-up at home (μ_d)	-1.7	-1.9	-1.7
a. Home import price (p_m) (a = b+c)	-12.9	-11.0	-9.9
b. Foreign exporter's mark-up (μ_m)	19.8	16.1	13.9
c. Foreign marginal cost ($qD^* \dfrac{w^*}{Z^*}$)	-23.7	-19.2	-17.7
Real exchange rate (q)	-15.2	-13.0	-11.6
Direct pass-through (κ_m)	-15.2	-13.0	-11.6
Pass-through ($\beta_{pm,q}$)	-15.1	-13.4	-14.7

[a] Entry refers to the log-difference for a variable from its value in the benchmark calibration. For the trade costs, home trade share, κ_m, and $\beta_{pm,q}$, we report the percentage point difference. For Z^*, we report the arithmetic percentage change instead of the log-difference.

[b] Row a equals row b plus row c with any discrepancy due to rounding.

pass-through, κ_m. Also, an increase in the number of exporters in the domestic economy implies that there are more firms who change their prices in response to exchange-rate movements, which also increases pass-through in general equilibrium, $\beta_{pm,q}$. Thus, as in Dornbusch (1987), our model implies that, other things being equal, an increase in the number of foreign exporters leads to higher pass-through of exchange-rate changes to import prices.

Returning to the upper left panel, the equilibrium number of foreign exporters in the benchmark calibration is given by point A, where per-unit profits intersect with the fixed cost (the solid line). What happens when we lower trade costs and raise foreign productivity but completely abstract from the extensive trade margin? The equilibrium shifts from point A to point B, as the fall in export production costs raises the demand for an exporter's good as well as his profits. As shown in the upper right panel, the import share in the home economy also rises from about 10 per cent to 10.7 per cent. Lower production costs are also associated with an increase in the mark-ups of foreign exporters and, as shown in the second column of Table 4.5, a decline in pass-through of about 15.1 pp. Consequently, most of the decline in pass-through occurs along the intensive trade margin.

Now consider the case in which we allow for the entry of foreign exporters in response to the decline in the cost of exporting. In this case, the equilibrium shifts from point B to point C, as the increase in profits induces more exporters to pay their fixed entry cost. Accordingly, the import share now rises to about 14.6 per cent, so that the bulk of the increase in imports reflects new goods. There is some decline in the mark-ups of foreign exporters relative to point B. Although the two measures of pass-through rise from point C to point B, the effect is small relative to the decline in pass-through associated with the intensive margin.

When we further endogenise home exporters' entry decisions, the equilibrium moves from point C to point D, which corresponds to the last column in Table 4.5. Since foreign firms are 35 per cent more productive than in the initial equilibrium (point A), foreign demand for domestic goods falls and domestic exporters decide to exit the foreign market. Table 4.5 shows that this reduction in the number of domestic exporters implies a smaller appreciation of the domestic real exchange rate and as a result the profit and mark-up functions for a foreign exporter shifts down to the dotted line. At equilibrium point D, foreign exporters' mark-ups are smaller and, in turn, the direct measure of pass-through, κ_m, is higher than at point C. Despite this increase in κ_m, $\beta_{pm,q}$ falls, reflecting that there is less co-movement between the real exchange rate and foreign marginal cost (see equation (26)) with a decline in the number of domestic exporters in the foreign economy.

Overall, the entry of foreign exporters plays an important role in accounting for the large rise in the import share associated with a decline in trade costs and higher foreign productivity. An increase in the number of foreign exporters also has the *ceteris paribus* effect of raising pass-through. However, this effect is small relative to the decline in pass-through that results from mark-up adjustments that occur along the intensive margin in response to factors that increase trade integration.

4.8   Conclusion

We assessed the impact of firm entry on exchange-rate pass-through to import prices. This question is particularly important given the increased openness of the US economy and the considerable decline in the degree of pass-through to US import prices. Such a decline in pass-through implies that foreign exporters have become more willing to vary their mark-ups in order to keep their local prices competitive and maintain market share in the wake of large exchange-rate fluctuations.

One argument put forward by those more sceptical of the decline in pass-through is that the entry of foreign exporters associated with greater openness should reduce mark-ups, make them less variable and raise the degree of exchange-rate pass-through.

In our framework, we find that firm entry does indeed push up exchange-rate pass-through and is essential in accounting for the secular rise in the US import share. However, increased entry of foreign exporters has a relatively small impact on exchange-rate pass-through. The effects of higher foreign productivity and a reduction in trade costs on mark-up behaviour along the intensive margin are much more important quantitatively and appear to explain a considerable portion of the observed decline in pass-through to US import prices. Thus, it is not surprising that pass-through has declined as the US economy has become more open.

REFERENCES

Baier, S. L., and J. H. Bergstrand (2001). 'The growth of world trade: tariffs, transport costs, and income similarity', *Journal of International Economics*, 53, 1–27.

Bergin, P. R., and R. C. Feenstra (2001). 'Pricing-to-market, staggered contracts, and real exchange rate persistence', *Journal of International Economics*, 54, 333–59.

Bergin, P. R., and R. Glick (2005). *Tradability, Productivity, and Understanding International Economic Integration*, National Bureau of Economic Research working paper No. 11637.

Berthelon, M., and C. Freund (2004). *On the Conservation of Distance in International Trade*, World Bank policy research working paper No. 3293.

Brun, J.-F., C. Carrere, P. Guillaumont, and J. de Melo (2005). 'Has distance died? Evidence from a panel gravity model',*World Bank Economic Review*, 19, 99–120.

Campa, J. M., and L. S. Goldberg (2004). *Exchange Rate Pass-Through into Import Prices*, Centre for Economic Policy Research discussion papers No. 4391.

Coe, D. T., A. Subramanian, N. T. Tamirisa, and R. Bhavnani (2002). *The Missing Globalization Puzzle*, International Monetary Fund working paper No. 02/171.

Dornbusch, R. (1987). 'Exchange rates and prices', *American Economic Review*, 77, 93–106.

Dotsey, M., and R. G. King (2005). 'Implications of state-dependent pricing for dynamic macroeconomic models', *Journal of Monetary Economics*, 52, 213–42.

Eichenbaum, M., and D. M. Jonas (2007). 'Estimating the frequency of price reoptimization in Calvo-style models', *Journal of Monetary Economics*, Vol. 54(7), 2032–47.

Feenstra, R. C. (1996). *U.S. Imports 1972–1994: Data and Concordances*, National Bureau of Economic Research working paper No. 5515.

Feenstra, R. C., J. Romalis, and P. Schott (2002). *U.S. Imports, Exports and Tariff Data, 1989–2001*, National Bureau of Economic Research working paper No. 9387.

Frankel, J. A. (1997). *Regional Trading Blocs in the World Economic System*, Washington, DC: Institute for International Economics.

Ghironi, F., and M. J. Melitz (2005). 'International trade and macroeconomic dynamics with heterogeneous firms', *Quarterly Journal of Economics*, 120, 865–915.

Goldberg, P. K., and M. M. Knetter (1997). 'Goods prices and exchange rates: what have we learned?', *Journal of Economic Literature*, 35, 1243–72.

Gust, C., S. Leduc, and R. Vigfusson (2006). 'Trade integration, Competition, and the Decline in Exchange Rate Pass-through', *Journal of Monetary Economics*, Vol. 57(3), 309–24.

Hummels, D., and P. J. Klenow (2005). 'The variety and quality of a nation's trade', *American Economic Review*, 95(3), 704–23.

Ihrig, J. E., M. Marazzi, and A. D. Rothenberg (2006). *Exchange-Rate Pass-Through in the G-7 Countries*, Board of Governors of the Federal Reserve System international finance discussion papers No. 851.

Kehoe, T. J., and K. J. Ruhl (2002). *How Important is the New Goods Margin in International Trade?*, Federal Reserve Bank of Minneapolis staff report No. 324.

Marazzi, M., N. Sheets, and R. J. Vigfusson (2005). *Exchange Rate Pass-Through to U.S. Import Prices: Some New Evidence*, Board of Governors of the Federal Reserve System international finance discussion papers No. 833.

Melitz, M. J. (2003). 'The impact of trade on intra-industry reallocations and aggregate industry productivity', *Econometrica*, 71, 1695–725.

Olivei, G. P. (2002). 'Exchange rates and the prices of manufacturing products imported into the United States', *Federal Reserve Bank of Boston New England Economic Review*, 3–18.

Otani, A., S. Shiratsuka, and T. Shirota (2003). 'The decline in the exchange rate passthrough: evidence from Japanese import prices', *Monetary and Economic Studies*, 21, 53–81.

Rauch, J. E. (1999). 'Networks versus markets in international trade', *Journal of International Economics*, 48, 7–35.

5 Does the exchange rate belong in monetary policy rules? New answers from a DSGE model with endogenous tradability and trade frictions

Michael Kumhof, Douglas Laxton and Kanda Naknoi

5.1 Introduction

The benefits of exchange-rate flexibility lie in its ability to change the relative prices of goods in the presence of nominal rigidities. Friedman (1953) first argued that a flexible exchange-rate regime is desirable as a shock absorber, and this has been followed by a long subsequent literature. The implications for the conduct of domestic monetary policy have, however, been the subject of much debate. In the closed-economy literature, several important papers have found that welfare-optimising monetary policy results in a complete stabilisation of the domestic price level, with no trade-off between output gap stabilisation and domestic price stability.[1] Many key contributions to the recent open-economy literature have found conditions under which these results carry over to an open economy setting, meaning specifically that there is no need for monetary policy to explicitly consider the exchange rate.[2] However, these papers share a common set of assumptions that may be violated in practice. They include producer currency pricing, perfect exchange-rate pass-through and a lack of real rigidities in international trade. The literature has thus far concentrated on the pricing assumption, by replacing the producer currency pricing assumption with local currency pricing. It can then be shown that it becomes optimal to either have a completely fixed exchange rate, or at least to have a very significant role for the exchange rate in the monetary policy rule.[3]

---

[1] The key papers are King and Wolman (1996), Goodfriend and King (1997) and Rotemberg and Woodford (1997).

[2] See Obstfeld and Rogoff (2002), Benigno and Benigno (2003) and Gali and Monacelli (2005).

[3] See Smets and Wouters (2002), Devereux and Engel (2003) and Corsetti and Pesenti (2005).

The empirical evidence for the pricing assumption is a subject of much debate.[4]

In this study we argue that another and thus far overlooked set of factors may play a key role in determining whether the exchange rate should enter monetary policy rules. They concern the endogenous determination of the composition of trade, together with real rigidities in both exporting and importing. For real rigidities in importing we assume that there are costs, in terms of both cost and time, of initiating and reversing new import supplier relationships. For real rigidities in exporting, there is a cost to switching between purely domestic production on the one hand and production for both domestic and foreign markets on the other. We find that in a baseline model with producer currency pricing but without these features the optimised linear monetary policy rule has a zero weight on deviations of the real exchange rate from its long-run trend. When endogenous determination of the composition of trade is added together with export-switching costs, the exchange rate assumes an important role, with real appreciations requiring monetary easing. Adding real import rigidities significantly increases the optimal coefficient on the real exchange rate.

To derive these results we develop a two-country DSGE model that integrates the theory of comparative advantage of Dornbusch *et al.* (1977) into a monetary model with real rigidities and with sticky prices and wages. In this model the nominal exchange rate can play a much more fundamental role in facilitating or slowing down adjustments in the real economy. To illuminate the implications for monetary policy we subject the model to standard types of shocks. We then study macroeconomic performance using monetary policy interest rate rules that add a term for real exchange-rate deviations from trend to the conventional inflation and output gap terms.

The model builds on the monetary, stochastic general equilibrium model of comparative advantage of Naknoi (2008). Heterogeneity in productivity and proportional trade costs determine which goods are exported, imported or not traded in equilibrium. In this environment trade is significantly more responsive to shocks than in conventional

---

[4] Corsetti and Pesenti (2005) argue that an intermediate degree of pass-through may be most appropriate, with developing countries likely to be closer to a high pass-through than industrialised countries. Goldberg and Knetter (1997) and Campa and Goldberg (2005) find that in industrialised countries the degree of short-run pass-through to import prices is roughly 50 per cent, and close to 100 per cent in the long run. But for many developing countries the consensus is that pass-through to import prices is very much higher, for example Burstein *et al.* (2005).

models, which tend to under-predict the volatility of trade flows relative to GDP. In the short run, this endogeneity of the trade pattern amplifies the expenditure-switching effect of exchange rates, as firms transit into and out of exporting. At the same time, the transitions cause aggregate productivity to fluctuate, in the same manner as in the real models of Ghironi and Melitz (2005). These transitions generate additional output volatility that monetary policy must stabilise.

We also assume that it is costly to belong to the set of exporters. The cost is time-variant and generates smaller trade responses in the short run than in the long run. It is similar to the fixed cost of entering into exporting described in Ghironi and Melitz (2005). The assumption that exporters transit into and out of exporting in the short run is not far-fetched. Trade economists have identified year-to-year transitions into and out of exporting from micro data in the USA, Colombia and Mexico. For example, the duration of trade relationships of the USA with its trading partners at the product level is found to vary from three to five years.[5] These studies indicate that the exporting decision is not a long-run issue. It is better viewed as a medium-run phenomenon with some degree of persistence.

The model makes three departures from Naknoi (2008). First, we assume that importers take time and find it costly to build new relationships with foreign suppliers. This time to build markets assumption is similar to time to ship in Backus *et al.* (1994). It generates a low short-run elasticity of substitution between domestic goods and imported goods, despite a high long-run elasticity. Because this friction reduces the short-run real trade response, it has important implications for monetary policy.

Second, we introduce vertical integration, with endogenous tradability only observed at the level of intermediate goods.[6] This was introduced partly for realism, as it allows the model to generate observed trade to GDP ratios without postulating unrealistically high import shares in production and consumption. But in addition it doubles the effects of the time-to-build-markets assumption, which we make at both the intermediate and final goods levels.

Third, to obtain a fully specified business cycle model we introduce investment and capital accumulation. We assume time to build in investment subject to quadratic investment adjustment costs. Together with the assumption of habit persistence in consumption this implies

---

[5] See Aitken, Hanson and Harrison (1997), Roberts and Tybout (1997), Bernard and Jensen (2004), Besedes and Prusa (2006) and Das *et al.* (2007).

[6] Obstfeld and Rogoff (2000) argue that the expenditure-switching channel largely operates through relative prices in the intermediate goods sector.

that domestic demand responds sluggishly, thereby generating plausible responses to standard shocks.

To the best of our knowledge, our model is the first two-country monetary business cycle model that embeds endogenous tradability in a setting with significant nominal and real rigidities. Nominal rigidities in price and wage setting allow for a meaningful analysis of optimal monetary policy, which would not be possible in the flexible-price models of Bergin and Glick (2003) and Ghironi and Melitz (2005). We can therefore compare our results to those of the large literature on optimal monetary policy in open economies cited above.

We describe our model in the next section. Section 5.3 discusses calibration, Section 5.4 presents our results and Section 5.5 concludes.

5.2 The model

5.2.1 Outline

The model economy consists of two countries, referred to as Home and Foreign. The countries have identical preferences and identical final and intermediate goods technologies but different technologies in primary production. Countries differ in size, with the population of Home being α and that of Foreign $(1-\alpha)$.

Each economy consists of a representative household, a government and multiple layers of firms. Households consume, supply labour and accumulate capital. The most upstream level of firms is primary producers, who obtain capital and labour inputs from households, the latter subject to sticky nominal wages. Primary producers differ by their level of productivity relative to producers in the other country. They endogenously decide on three modes of activity, quitting production if they are not competitive with imports from abroad, producing only for the domestic market if they are competitive domestically but not abroad, and producing for both the domestic and the foreign market if their competitors abroad are not competitive. The next layer of production is intermediates firms, which combine domestic and foreign varieties and then sell them either domestically or abroad. The final layer is final goods producers, who combine domestic and foreign intermediates inputs with an exogenously non-tradable fixed input to produce final output for domestic consumers, investors and the government. We assume that international trade at each stage is subject to an iceberg-type trading cost τ, where a fraction $1-\tau$ of goods is lost in shipping. The government is Ricardian and decides on an interest-rate rule for monetary policy.

We include habit persistence in consumption and time-to-build capital lags in investment, which help produce the lagged and hump-shaped responses of real variables to real and monetary policy shocks found in macroeconomic data (see also Laxton and Pesenti, 2003). These are complemented by some theoretically less common real rigidities on the economy's supply side, including time-to-build-markets for imports and switching costs for exports.

5.2.2   Households

Households maximise lifetime utility, which has a constant relative risk aversion form with three arguments, consumption C (which exhibits habit persistence and is subject to preference shocks S_t^c), leisure $(\alpha - L)$ (where α is the time endowment) and real money balances m. Denoting the intertemporal elasticity of substitution by σ, we have

$$Max \quad E_0 \sum_{t=0}^{\infty} \beta^t \left\{ \frac{S_t^c \left(C_t - v C_{t-1}\right)^{1-\frac{1}{\sigma}} - 1}{1 - \frac{1}{\sigma}} + \psi \frac{\left(\alpha - L_t\right)^{1-\frac{1}{\sigma}}}{1 - \frac{1}{\sigma}} + \psi_m \frac{\left(m_t\right)^{1-\varepsilon}}{1-\varepsilon} \right\}.$$

Households' capital accumulation follows time-to-build technologies, with a six-period lag between the investment decision and the point at which the investment decision leads to an addition to the productive capital stock:

$$K_{t+1} = (1 - \Delta)K_t + I_{t-5}S_{t-5}^{inv},$$

where S_t^{inv} is an investment demand shock. Each investment decision represents a commitment to a spending plan over six periods, starting in the period of the decision and ending one period before capital becomes productive. Actual investment spending is therefore given by the share-weighted sum of investment decisions between periods t and $t-5$. Changes in investment starts are subject to an external adjustment cost that is quadratic in the rate of change of investment.

Households' income consists of real wages, real returns on capital, on fixed factors,[7] on risk-free international bonds that are subject to an endogenous risk premium term, and on risk-free domestic (and domestic currency denominated) bonds, in addition to lump-sum government redistributions and profit redistributions. Their expenditure consists of consumption spending and investment spending. Real and

---

[7] This is introduced to capture the role of exogenously non-traded goods in the economy, as the assumption that all goods are tradable under zero trading costs seems too extreme.

nominal rigidities are due to quadratic adjustment costs on investment, international bond holdings, and wage inflation.[8] These and all other adjustment costs are assumed to be redistributed back to households as lump-sum payments.

The optimality conditions for the household problem are a standard set of Euler equations for asset holdings and consumption, a complex set of intertemporal conditions for the optimal investment path, and a condition for optimal wage setting that penalises large jumps in the wage inflation rate.

5.2.3   Production

We describe the optimisation problem of each level of production, starting at the lowest level and building up to final consumption and investment goods. **Primary varieties (z) producers** have Cobb-Douglas production functions in labour and capital:

$$y_t(z) = a(z)x_t\lambda_t(z)^\gamma k_t(z)^{(1-\gamma)} = a(z)x_t v_t(z).$$

The first two elements of the production function are sector-specific productivity levels $a(z)$ and aggregate productivity levels x_t. The sector-specific productivity terms determine the pattern of comparative advantage between countries, a crucial ingredient in making tradedness of intermediate goods endogenous. For each variety z there is a continuum of producers who are perfectly competitive in their output and factor markets. Their price therefore satisfies the condition $p_t(z) = mc_t/x_t a(z)\chi_t$, where mc_t is the marginal factor cost (the cost of $v_t(z)$), determined from the appropriate cost-minimisation conditions, and χ_t is an export adjustment cost discussed below. When a good is produced in the Foreign country and shipped to the Home country or vice versa there are iceberg-type proportional trading costs τ_t that are identical across goods.[9] Therefore, in the absence of relative productivity differences, there would be no trade as each country would produce the entire range of consumption goods at home. But as soon as there are sufficiently strong comparative advantage patterns in productivity the effect of trading costs can be overcome, leading to trade. For a given pattern of comparative advantage, lower trading costs lead to more trade, or to a smaller range of non-traded goods, the latter being goods

---

[8] The latter follows Rotemberg (1982), as extended to costs of adjusting the rate of change of the wage by, among many others, Laxton and Pesenti (2003).
[9] Unlike adjustment costs, transport costs are not redistributed back to agents in a lump-sum fashion. They represent an actual loss in transit.

that are produced in both countries. We refer to the pattern of relative productivities along the spectrum of goods z as the comparative advantage schedule. Its shape is of crucial importance for our results. We normalise productivity in Foreign to one, $a^*(z) = 1\ \forall z$, and for Home we assume a productivity schedule that is exponentially declining in z according to $a(z) = Ne^{-nz}$.

The world trade pattern depends on the relative prices of Foreign and Home produced goods. A Home firm will produce a given variety only if its price does not exceed the price that an importer of the same variety is able to charge given his marginal cost and trading costs. Given the declining relative productivity pattern in Home there will therefore be a maximum level of z above which Home will rely entirely on imports instead of producing at home. We denote this time-varying level by z_t^h. Equally, there is a minimum z, denoted z_t^l, below which Foreign will rely on imports from Home. All goods varieties between z_t^l and z_t^h are non-traded, meaning they are produced in both countries.

We assume that entering the export trade involves additional costs such as extra marketing costs and costs of building a geographically larger distribution network. Conversely, exiting the export trade involves benefits that can be conceptualised as the scrap value of overseas sale operations as in the industrial organisation literature. The functional form of these costs and benefits is of the iceberg type, that is costs which melt a fraction of productivity $a(z)$ or $a^*(z)$ for new entrants, and which conversely add to the productivity iceberg for firms that exit. The dependence of such costs on entry and exit is captured by making them a function of the change in the range of varieties produced for exports between last period and this period. In particular, for Home exporters we have $\chi_t^l = 1 - \Phi^a(z_t^l - z_{t-1}^l)/z_{t-1}^l$, and for Foreign exporters we have $\chi_t^h = 1 - \Phi^a(z_{t-1}^h - z_t^h)/z_{t-1}^h$. The effect of these costs is to make exporters' relative productivity schedule steeper around the cut-off points z_{t-1}^l and z_{t-1}^h of the last period. In the case of a favourable domestic productivity shock, this means that some formerly non-traded varieties continue to be produced only for the domestic market even though before taking account of export adjustment costs the producer could now produce more cheaply than foreigners. But as soon as that non-traded goods producer decides to become an exporter he faces a lower level of productivity.

Intermediates producers use inputs of home export goods, non-traded goods and import goods. They are price-takers in both their input and output markets. They also face two real frictions, a quadratic cost of adjusting their inputs, and a time-to-build-markets constraint that these inputs can only be chosen k periods ahead. The solution to this problem features both a delayed and an inertial adjustment of input purchases to shocks, similar to investment under the time-to-build-capital assumption.

Final output producers are perfectly competitive price takers in their input markets and monopolistically competitive in their output market. They first combine domestic and foreign intermediates, subject to the same kind of time-to-build-markets technology as intermediates producers. They then combine the intermediates composite with the stock of the non-tradable fixed factor. Their price setting is subject to inflation adjustment costs, and their mark-ups follow a stochastic process. Their output is sold to consumers, investors and the government.

5.2.4   Government

Fiscal policy in both countries is monetary dominant in that fiscal lump-sum transfers are endogenous to the implications of monetary policy choices. Government spending is positive and constant. The benchmark monetary policy rule that we consider for the Home economy is an extended version of the Taylor (1993) rule that allows for interest-rate smoothing and adds an additional real-exchange-rate feedback term:

$$i_t = \left(i_{t-1}\right)^{\lambda_i} \left(\frac{\bar{\pi}}{\beta}\right)^{1-\lambda_i} \left(\frac{\pi_{4,\,t}}{\bar{\pi}}\right)^{\lambda_\pi} \left(\frac{gdp_t}{\overline{gdp}}\right)^{\lambda_y} \left(\frac{s_t}{\bar{s}}\right)^{\lambda_s}.$$

The inflation target is given by $\bar{\pi}$ so that $\bar{\pi}/\beta$ is the long-run nominal interest rate. The central bank is assumed to respond to deviations of the year-on-year inflation rate $\pi_{4,\,t} = \left(\pi_t \pi_{t-1} \pi_{t-2} \pi_{t-3}\right)^{\frac{1}{4}}$ from its target $\bar{\pi}$, and to the output gap and the real-exchange-rate gap. The output gap is defined as the deviation of GDP from a two-sided centred moving average of GDP with weights taken from the Hodrick-Prescott (HP) filter. While this measure of the output gap is imperfect, it helps to avoid some of the pitfalls with using alternative measures such as the flex-price output gap, or purely backward-looking measures that are based on one-sided versions of the HP filter that exclude the model's predicted levels of future GDP – see the appendix for more details about the HP filter and the weights that we use. In effect, because we are using the model's predictions to help measure the underlying trend level of output it will produce measures of the business cycle that can account partly for supply shocks that shift the level of potential output. The measures will also be much less erratic and jumpy than flex-price measures of the output gaps that are influenced by data measurement problems.[10] In addition, in empirical versions of these models that produce competitive forecasts, following this approach in real time will result in significantly smaller revisions in the measures of the business cycle than are obtained from one-sided applications of the Hodrick-Prescott filter, which ignore information from the model's forecast of future output – see Juillard *et al.* (2007). Finally, and critically for this paper, the last term of the Taylor Rule includes a measure of the real-exchange-rate gap measured in exactly the same way as we measure the output gap. Including the real-exchange-rate gap is not standard, but the purpose of this paper is of course to analyse whether this term should be included in a world with endogenous tradability and real trade frictions. The Foreign central bank is assumed to follow a similar interest-rate feedback rule, but without a real-exchange-rate feedback term.

5.3   Calibration

We calibrate the model with the euro area in mind, and therefore set the size of Home to be 25 per cent of the world economy. Unless otherwise mentioned, parameters are assumed to be the same across the two countries. Consumers discount the future at the rate of 1 per cent per quarter (4 per cent per year). The intertemporal elasticity of substitution and the degree of habit persistence are 0.5 and 0.85, respectively. These coefficients, together with adjustment costs on consumption and investment, generate the lagged and hump-shaped responses to interest hikes typically found in empirical models.[11] The elasticity of labour supply is set equal to 0.5, which is standard for the macroeconomic literature, but at the high end of microeconomic estimates.

Average mark-ups for both the euro area and the rest of the world are taken from Bayoumi *et al.* (2004). The steady-state labour market mark-up is set to 30 per cent in Home and 16 per cent in Foreign and in the goods markets it is set at 35 per cent in Home and 23 per cent in Foreign. Coefficients defining wage and price stickiness parameters

---

[10] Wage and price indices contain significant noise components that induce measurement errors into flex-price measures of the output gap, which is one reason why they have not had much impact in policy-making deliberations. Another reason is that they typically are constructed by assuming that all of the economy's state variables – such as the capital stock – have always been determined by a flex-price economy.

[11] Without the adjustment costs, higher parameter values may be needed. For example, Bayoumi *et al.* (2004) show that values as high as 0.2 and 0.97 are required for the intertemporal elasticity and habit persistence to generate the hump-shaped responses to interest-rate shocks that can be found in the ECB's Area-Wide Model (AWM) of the monetary transmission mechanism – see Fagan *et al.* (2001).

were chosen to produce plausible impulse responses to standard shocks. Elasticities of substitution between Home and Foreign traded goods were set equal to 1.5, as is standard in the macroeconomic literature. The elasticity of substitution between traded and exogenously non-traded goods is set to 0.8, following the evidence surveyed in Mendoza (2005).

Turning to time-to-build lags, following Murchison *et al.* (2004), we assume that it takes one quarter to plan an investment project and five quarters to complete it.[12] We assume that investment expenditure is spread equally over the six-period life of the investment project. In addition, we set the adjustment cost parameters that govern investment dynamics to be consistent with the hump-shaped pattern seen in response to interest-rate cuts that peak at around four to six quarters. The depreciation rate of private capital is 2.5 per cent per quarter.

To reflect the difficulties of building and maintaining international supplier relationships compared to domestic supplier relationships, we assume a time-to-build-markets lag of two quarters in both intermediate and final goods. We choose adjustment cost parameters to generate plausible dynamics of imports following shocks. Similarly, setting the export switching cost parameter to 0.2 generates plausible transitions between exporting and non-exporting firms following shocks. The model therefore generates small changes in trade volumes in response to temporary real-exchange-rate fluctuations, but large changes in response to permanent shocks, as has been observed in practice – see Erceg *et al.* (2003) and Laxton and Pesenti (2003). Finally, we set the parameters that determine the endogenous risk premium on bonds to ensure that changes in the risk premium are sufficient to prevent implausibly large current account deficits.

The model is calibrated so that standard components of GDP have sizes compatible with their average shares in GDP in the data. The only difficulty here is the share of exogenously non-traded goods in GDP, which we assume to be 25 per cent. Relative GDP in both countries

---

[12] Time-to-build dynamics are becoming an important feature of the new generation of macro models that are being designed inside central banks. For example, the work by Murchison *et al.* (2004) at the Bank of Canada builds on earlier work at the Fed by Edge (2000a, 2000b). For more information on the importance of time-to-build dynamics for the internal propagation mechanism of DSGE models, see Casares (2002), which provides a very useful study showing the effects on macroeconomic dynamics of adding time-to-build lags that range between one and eight quarters.

is fixed by adjusting the Home aggregate productivity parameter in accordance with relative GDP in the data. Government spending and private investment are each assumed to represent 18 per cent of steady-state GDP in each country. We fix the steady-state capital income share in GDP at 36 per cent in both Home and Foreign. Exports and imports are assumed to be balanced in steady state, with an overall 20 per cent exports and imports to GDP ratio in Home (and of course correspondingly smaller ratios in the larger Foreign), half of which is accounted for by intermediate goods and half by final goods. To calibrate trade in this way the parameters at our disposal are different from conventional models, at least at the level of intermediate goods. The parameter here is not an exogenous share parameter but the slope of the relative productivity schedule. We first choose trading costs to equal 15 per cent of the value of trade, and then obtain a slope coefficient of 0.4 as consistent with 20 per cent exports and imports to GDP ratios. This relatively flat slope reflects the fact that we assumed Home to represent a fairly large share of the world economy.

For monetary policy, we assume that the inflation targets in both Home and Foreign equal 2 per cent per annum. The coefficients of the monetary policy rule are of course the subject of our analysis.

We work with a fairly stylised representation of shock processes, which are assumed to be identical in both economies. Wage and price setting is subject to mark-up shocks whose magnitudes have been calibrated so that they determine most of the variation in the inflation process at the business cycle frequency. Following recent empirical work we assume that there is no serial correlation in these shocks – see Smets and Wouters (2003, 2007) and Juillard *et al.* (2007, 2008). In the same empirical work, demand shocks to consumption and investment have been found to be very significant for explaining variations in the real economy at business cycle frequency. Following Juillard *et al.* (2008) we assume that the consumption and investment shocks are positively correlated (0.50) and that there exists significant positive serial correlation in the consumption shocks. We also consider shocks to the uncovered interest parity equation, which have been found to be very important for explaining exchange-rate variability and for these shocks we assume that they are highly serially correlated (0.75). In the section on sensitivity analysis we consider different assumptions about the shock processes to examine how the results change under alternative assumptions. We do not consider other sources of shocks such as permanent productivity shocks or shocks that affect specialisation and openness, but leave the analysis of these additional shocks until the model has been fully estimated.

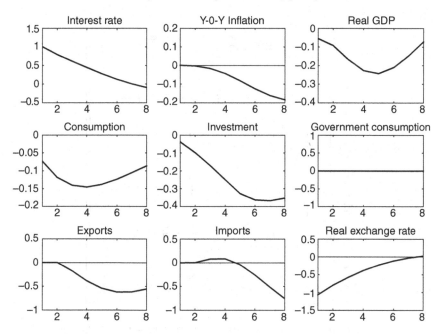

Figure 5.1 Home economy responses to a 100-basis-point interest-rate hike

Figure 5.1 reports the responses of the model to a persistent 100-basis-point hike in interest rates in the Home economy. The magnitude and hump-shaped response of GDP and consumption is similar to standard DSGE models such as the IMF's Global Economy Model (GEM) as well as reduced-form econometric models such as the ECB's Area-Wide Model (AWM) model – compare Figure 5.1 with Table 5.1. However, the model shows significantly smaller investment responses for temporary shocks. This mainly reflects the time-to-build capital assumption in the model, which tends to weaken the response of investment in response to temporary shocks. Conventional DSGE models such as GEM assume quadratic adjustment costs associated with changing the level of investment and abstract from time-to-build considerations – for a discussion of model properties with time-to-build dynamics see Murchison et al. (2004). Reduced-form models such as AWM are completely backward looking and so the responses to shocks should in principle represent an average response to temporary and permanent shocks. The model's responses to permanent shocks will typically be larger as it takes longer to increase the capital stock and firms have the incentive to incur the adjustment costs. Interestingly,

Table 5.1 *A comparison of the IMF's GEM monetary transmission mechanism with the ECB's AWM model*

| Variable | Model | Sum | Quarter | | | | | | | |
			1	2	3	4	5	6	7	8
Real GDP	GEM Home	-2.3	-0.2	-0.3	-0.3	-0.4	-0.4	-0.3	-0.3	-0.2
	AWM	-2.0	-0.1	-0.2	-0.2	-0.3	-0.3	-0.3	-0.3	-0.3
Consumption	GEM Home	-2.0	-0.1	-0.2	-0.3	-0.3	-0.3	-0.3	-0.2	-0.2
	AWM	-1.9	-0.0	-0.2	-0.2	-0.3	-0.4	-0.3	-0.3	-0.3
Investment	GEM Home	-7.5	-0.5	-0.9	-1.1	-1.2	-1.2	-1.0	-0.9	-0.7
	AWM	-7.8	-0.1	-0.5	-0.8	-1.2	-1.5	-1.4	-1.3	-1.2
Exports	GEM Home	-1.3	-0.1	-0.2	-0.2	-0.2	-0.2	-0.2	-0.1	-0.1
	AWM	-1.6	-0.1	-0.2	-0.3	-0.4	-0.3	-0.2	-0.2	-0.1
Imports	GEM Home	-3.3	-0.2	-0.4	-0.5	-0.6	-0.5	-0.4	-0.3	-0.3
	AWM	-4.9	-0.2	-0.5	-0.7	-0.9	-0.9	-0.7	-0.6	-0.6
Real exchange rate	GEM Home	3.5	1.2	1.0	0.7	0.4	0.2	0.0	-0.0	-0.0
	AWM	-1.0	0.5	0.3	0.0	-0.2	-0.5	-0.4	-0.4	-0.3
CPI	GEM Home	-0.5	-0.0	-0.0	-0.0	-0.1	-0.1	-0.1	-0.1	-0.1
	AWM	-0.4	-0.0	-0.0	-0.0	-0.0	-0.1	-0.1	-0.1	-0.1

the responses of imports and exports are significantly stronger in the model than in GEM and are more in line with the stronger responses of AWM.[13] Again, this reflects the key assumption in the model that the supply of exports is more responsive to relative prices as firms are allowed to choose to produce goods for either the export or domestic market.

5.4   Results

The main goal of this section is to assess under what conditions standard monetary policy reaction functions such as the Taylor Rule need to be modified to include information about the exchange rate. However, before proceeding to this analysis we first start by showing how the model is different from other standard DSGE models and why endogenous tradability matters.

5.4.1   How is the model different from other models?

Conventional monetary business cycle models cannot account for strong trends in trade volumes, nor can they explain how the monetary transmission mechanism changes over time as economies exploit greater specialisation. Our objective has been to develop a model that integrates trade theory into a monetary business cycle model. The basic assumption of the model is that trading costs restrict trade and result in lower levels of specialisation and productivity. Figure 5.2 reports results that show the long-run effects on welfare, trade, GDP, consumption, investment and labour effort of lower trading costs. In the base-case calibration a reduction in trading costs of 15 percentage points raises the export-to-GDP ratio by almost 42 percentage points. Since trading costs represent pure dead-weight losses, welfare improves significantly in both economies. In the Home economy GDP and investment rise by 9 per cent and 8.4 per cent, respectively. The increases in consumption economy are even larger (11.7 per cent) than the gains in GDP as the terms of trade improve in favour of the Home economy. The welfare improvement in the Foreign economy is significant, but much smaller than in the Home economy. This reflects the assumption that the Foreign economy is much larger than the Home economy (0.75 versus 0.25) so there are smaller potential gains from trade. In both economies higher welfare is a result of higher levels of productivity, which increase

---

[13] These responses are reported in Fagan *et al.* (2001) and Bayoumi *et al.* (2004).

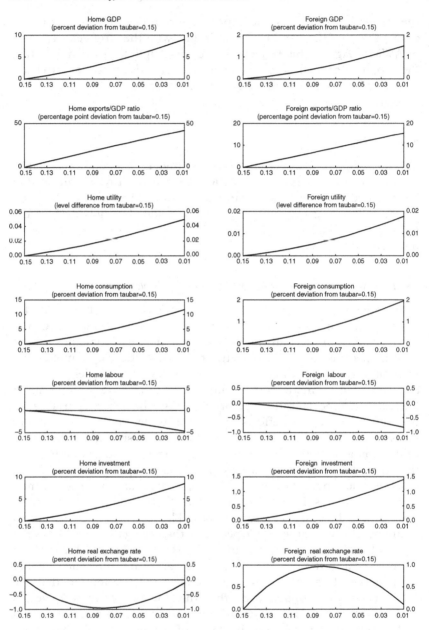

Figure 5.2 Long-run effects of reducing trading costs – base-case results

the sustainable level of real income. This results in an increase in the consumption of leisure – reduction in labour effort – that is one-half as large as the increase in consumption of goods and services.

Figures 5.3 to 5.6 provide some sensitivity analysis. The base-case calibration of the Home economy assumes that its relative size is 0.25. Figure 5.3 considers the case of a small open economy that only represents 1 per cent of the world's population. In this case the benefits of lower trading costs mainly accrue to the smaller economy and become larger. Indeed, in this case a 15 percentage point reduction in trading costs raises GDP by 14.8 per cent, about 5 percentage points more than in the base case when it represented 25 per cent of the world.

Figures 5.4 and 5.5 report results for cases where the elasticity of substitution between imported goods and domestically produced goods is 1.00 and 3.0, instead of the base-case assumption of 1.5. Higher trade elasticities strengthen the responsiveness of trade flows, but have very little additional effects. For example, in the base case a reduction in trading costs of 15 percentage points increases the export-to-GDP ratio by 41.9 percentage points and this effect declines to 41.3 percentage points when the elasticity of substitution is 1.0 and rises to 44.1 percentage points when it is 3.0. However, in these cases the effects on GDP and consumption are almost identical.

To isolate the different supply-side effects Figure 5.6 reports the results for a smaller labour supply elasticity (0.25 instead of the 0.50 that was used in the base case). This strengthens the effects on GDP (10.2 versus 9.0 per cent in the base case), consumption (13.2 versus 11.7 per cent) and investment (9.5 versus 8.4 per cent) as workers increase leisure relatively less in response to higher productivity. Welfare, however, improves by less than in the base case.

5.4.2   Optimal simple policy rules

We now optimise the feedback and smoothing coefficients in the Taylor monetary policy rule. To do so we consider a general loss function where policy makers are assumed to care about variability in inflation, output and exports:

$$L = L_1 \, \mathrm{var}(\pi 4) + L_2 \, \mathrm{var}(ygap) + L_3 \, \mathrm{var}(xgap).$$

The first two terms that place weights on inflation and output variability are standard. We argue there may be good reasons why policy makers might also care about variability in exports if there are significant frictions in shifting resources into the export sector. However, we do not make this element of the loss function critical for our results, rather

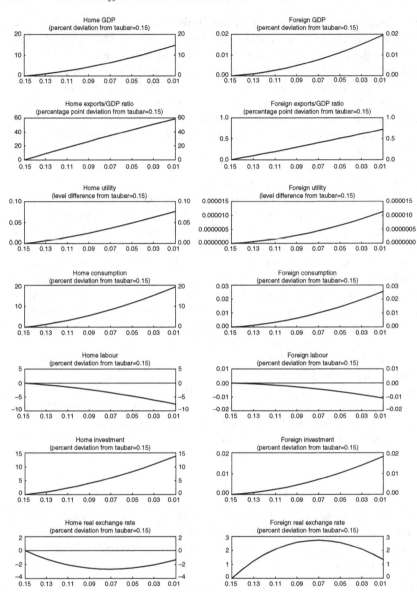

Figure 5.3 Long-run effects of reducing trading costs – smaller relative size of home economy

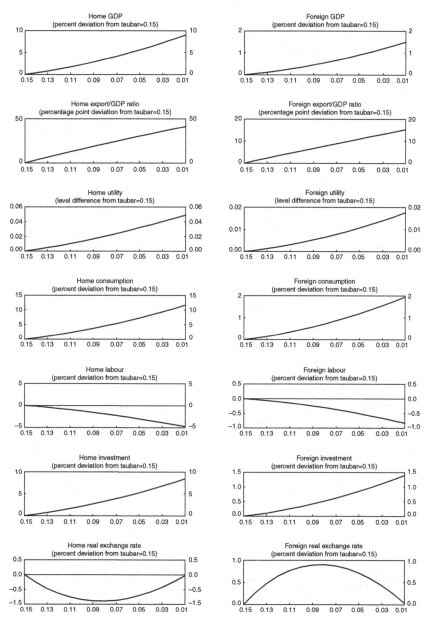

Figure 5.4 Long-run effects of reducing trading costs – lower elasticity of substitution between importables and domestically produced tradables

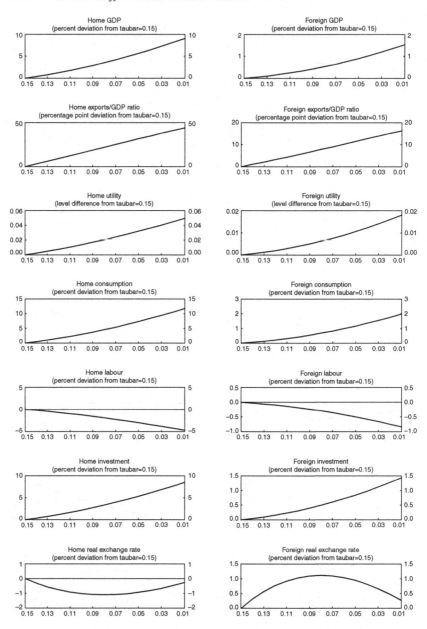

Figure 5.5 Long-run effects of reducing trading costs – higher elasticity of substitution between importables and domestically produced tradables

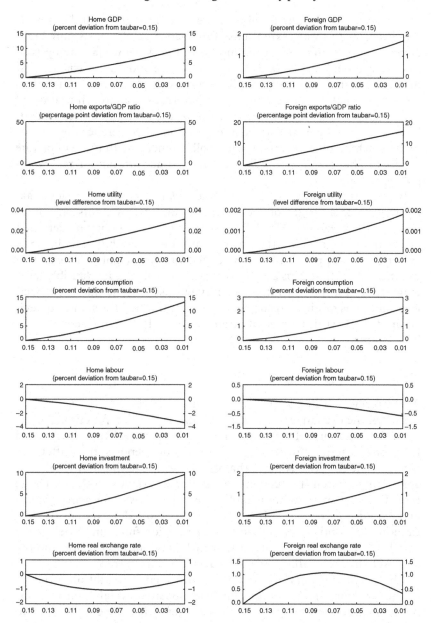

Figure 5.6 Long-run effects of reducing trading costs – less elastic labour supply

we simply report results for alternative sets of weights and discuss the implications. In future extensions of the paper we plan to explore higher-order approximations of the model and possibly welfare analysis so that we can analyse the level effects on welfare and other variables that may arise from excessive variability in exports. However, it should be recognised that loss functions are a more flexible approach that is not dependent on the specific form chosen for the utility function. In addition, it allows for a simple characterisation of preferences for policy makers, whose objectives may not wholly coincide with those of private agents, a phenomenon that is important in accounting for real-world policy making.

For expositional purposes we define *inflation nutters* as policy makers that place a weight of 1 on inflation and zero weights on output and export variability. We define *output gappers* as policy makers that place equal weights on inflation and output gap variability; and *output-export gappers* as policy makers that place equal weights on variability in inflation, output gaps and export gaps. To rule out implausibly large magnitudes for interest-rate variability we also assume that the objective function is minimised subject to a constraint that the standard deviation of the first difference of interest rates is less than or equal to 50 basis points.[14]

5.4.3   Base-case results

The top row of Table 5.2 reports the base-case results for *inflation nutters* when the exchange rate is included in the reaction function and the second row reports the results for *inflation nutters* when it is excluded from the reaction function. The third row reports the difference between the first two rows so that it is easier to see the additional variability imposed on the economy by ignoring variation in the exchange rate. The next six rows in the table repeat the analysis for *output gappers* and *output-export gappers*. In each line we report the value of the loss function, the optimal parameters in the reaction function as well as the standard deviations for year-on-year inflation, output, exports and the real exchange rate, all measured as deviations from trend.

The results for *inflation nutters* produce a large weight on inflation in the reaction function and significant positive weights on the output gap and the exchange rate. This suggests that the output gap and exchange-rate gaps have significant information content that is useful

---

[14] This is only slightly higher than the standard deviation of the first difference of short-term interest rates in the euro area.

Table 5.2 *Optimal simple rules under different loss functions: baseline*

	Loss	λ_i	λ_π	λ_{ygap}	λ_{sgap}	$\sigma\pi$	σ_{ygap}	σ_{xgap}	λ_{sgap}
Inflation nutter	0.44	0.92	1.09	0.14	0.06	0.67	0.81	2.61	1.91
	0.48	0.88	0.68	0.13		0.69	0.87	2.81	2.47
Difference	0.03	-0.04	-0.41	-0.01		0.02	0.06	0.20	0.56
Output gapper	0.89	0.94	0.49	0.24	0.06	0.71	0.62	2.48	1.69
	1.03	0.92	0.29	0.18		0.73	0.70	2.70	2.23
Difference	0.14	-0.02	-0.20	-0.06		0.02	0.08	0.22	0.54
Output-export gapper	6.25	1.18	0.38	0.15	0.14	0.91	0.67	2.23	1.05
	8.25	0.95	0.20	0.18		0.77	0.68	2.68	2.22
Difference	1.99	-0.22	-0.18	0.04		-0.14	0.01	0.45	1.17

for helping to reduce variability in inflation. However, when we focus on the role of the latter by comparing the differences between the first two rows we can see that excluding the exchange rate results in a very small increase in the inflation variability of two basis points. Note, however, that there are significant increases in the variability of output and especially exports by ignoring exchange-rate developments, so that while the losses of *inflation nutters* are little affected by ignoring output and exchange-rate gaps, *inflation nutters* would impose significant losses on *output gappers* and *output-export gappers*. Indeed, the parameter estimates on inflation are much larger than is typically observed in reaction functions, suggesting that policy makers are not *inflation nutters*, but instead place significant weight on real variables when they deliberate about interest-rate decisions. Indeed, when we move to the cases of *output gappers* and *output-export gappers* we observe a significant decline in the weight on the inflation term and an increase in the weight on the output gap in the case of *output gappers* and an increase in the weight on the real-exchange-rate gap for the case of *output-export gappers*. For the case of the *output-export gappers* there is a significant reduction in variability in both output and exports at the cost of higher variability in inflation, while for the *output gappers* excluding the exchange rate increases variability in both output and inflation. At this point the obvious question to ask is how these results are different from conventional monetary business cycle models that abstract from endogenous tradability. The next subsection answers that question.

Table 5.3 *Optimal simple rules under different loss functions: exogenous tradability*

	Loss	λ_i	$\lambda\pi$	λ_{ygap}	λ_{sgap}	$\sigma\pi$	σ_{ygap}	σ_{xgap}	σ_{sgap}
Inflation nutter	0.30	0.87	1.06	0.06	0.01	0.55	0.63	1.08	2.68
	0.31	0.86	0.99	0.06		0.55	0.63	1.08	2.77
Difference	0.00	-0.00	-0.07	-0.00		0.00	0.00	-0.00	0.09
Output gapper	0.57	0.87	0.81	0.28	0.01	0.60	0.46	0.98	2.42
	0.58	0.86	0.70	0.25		0.60	0.46	0.98	2.58
Difference	0.00	-0.01	-0.10	-0.03		0.00	0.00	0.00	0.16
Output-export gapper	1.51	0.85	0.60	0.32	0.02	0.64	0.43	0.96	2.36
	1.51	0.85	0.54	0.28		0.64	0.43	0.96	2.53
Difference	0.01	-0.01	-0.06	-0.04		-0.00	0.01	0.00	0.17

5.4.4   *The role of endogenous tradability*

It is straightforward to exclude endogenous tradability from the model by simply deleting the equations that determine the evolution of z_t^l and z_t^h, and then exogenising these variables. This and eliminating trade frictions turns the model into the standard open-economy model that has been used extensively in the literature. Table 5.3 repeats the analysis above when we exclude endogenous tradability. Strikingly, the parameters on the exchange-rate gap decline to practically zero and there is very little difference in all cases between the loss functions where the exchange-rate gap enters the reaction function and those cases where it does not. This confirms earlier results obtained from other DSGE models that assume producer currency pricing, where the exchange rate has not been found to play a significant contribution in conventional monetary reaction functions. A comparison of Tables 5.2 and 5.3 shows that shutting down this mechanism results in significantly less variability in inflation, output and exports.

To illustrate the differences in the two models we report the impulse response functions (IRFs) for an expansionary consumption shock in the Home economy. Figure 5.7 reports the results for the *output-export gapper* under the assumption of exogenous tradability and Figure 5.8 reports the results under endogenous tradability. In both cases we compare the IRFs with and without the exchange-rate gap in the reaction function. With exogenous tradability the IRFs are virtually identical

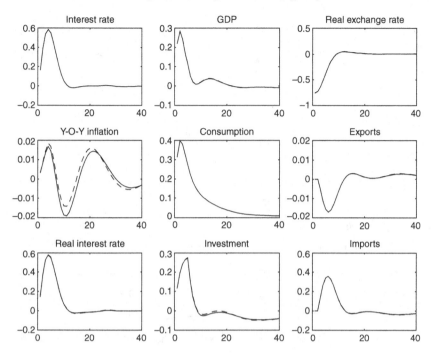

Figure 5.7 Impulse response functions without endogenous tradability (dashed line is without exchange rate in reaction function)

for interest rates, GDP, the real exchange rate, consumption, investment and trade volumes and, in fact, the only discernible difference is in the plot for year-on-year inflation. However, with endogenous tradability there are significant differences in the IRFs. The results without the exchange-rate gap produce a much stronger tightening in real monetary conditions (higher interest rates and a more appreciated real exchange rate) which works to constrain the expansionary effects on GDP, consumption and investment. Note, however, that it also results in a larger contractionary effect on exports and produces a significant undershoot of inflation from the target.

5.4.5   Implications of lower trading costs

Table 5.4 reports the results when trading costs are reduced from 0.15 in the base case to 0.10. As shown in Figure 5.2, this raises the steady-state exports to GDP ratio by about 15 percentage points. A comparison

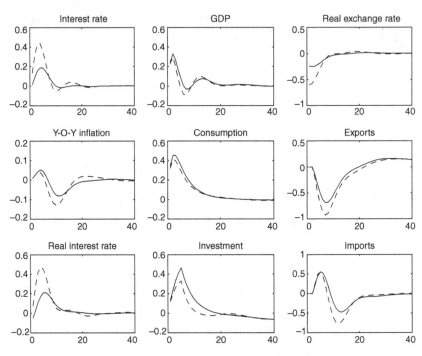

Figure 5.8 Impulse response functions with endogenous tradability
(dashed line is without exchange rate in reaction function)

Table 5.4 *Optimal simple rules under different loss functions: tau = 0.10*

	Loss	λ_i	λ_π	λ_{ygap}	λ_{sgap}	σ_π	σ_{ygap}	σ_{xgap}	λ_{sgap}
Inflation nutter	0.42	0.91	1.19	0.10	0.06	0.65	1.00	1.94	1.99
	0.44	0.88	0.75	0.11		0.66	1.07	2.08	2.46
Difference	0.22	-0.03	-0.44	0.01		0.02	0.07	0.14	0.47
Output gapper	0.99	0.95	0.45	0.21	0.06	0.71	0.70	1.66	1.57
	1.16	0.93	0.23	0.16		0.72	0.80	1.84	2.10
Difference	0.18	-0.01	-0.22	-0.06		0.01	0.11	0.18	0.53
Output-export gapper	3.53	1.05	0.32	0.21	0.10	0.82	0.67	1.55	1.28
	4.45	0.97	0.15	0.16		0.79	0.77	1.80	2.07
Difference	0.93	-0.09	-0.18	-0.05		0.03	0.10	0.25	0.79

of these results with the base-case results reveals interesting differences. Export variability declines because as economies become more open they require smaller adjustments in exports and imports in percentage terms to accommodate domestic demand shocks. It is important to emphasise that this prediction is based on comparing the dynamics around two steady states and it may be difficult to distinguish this effect in real data from other effects when economies are in the process of moving from one steady state to another, either because of changes in openness or long-run shifts in their net foreign asset positions. Not only is welfare permanently higher as a result of lower trading costs, but there are significantly smaller losses for policy makers that are *output-export gappers*.

5.4.6   Decomposition of base-case results for individual types of shocks

The advantage of simple monetary policy rules as guidelines for monetary policy is that they depend on a short list of variables. As such they are easier to understand and communicate than fully optimal rules, which will depend on the full list of model shocks that is being considered. The optimised weights in simple monetary policy rules will represent *average* responses to shocks that will generally not be optimal for supply and demand shocks. To better understand the base-case results reported in Table 5.2 we re-compute the optimal parameters in the simple policy rule under different assumptions about the shocks, focusing on different types of shocks. Indeed, for this purpose we separate the shocks used in the base case into three types of shock. The first type are demand shocks, which result in a positive short-run covariance between output and inflation. The second type of shocks are wage and price mark-ups, which result in a negative short-run covariance between output and inflation. Lastly, to understand the role of uncovered interest parity (UIP) shocks we consider these shocks separately.

Demand shocks only

Table 5.5 reports the results when we exclude all shocks except the two demand shocks in each region. For the case of *inflation nutters* and *output gappers* we observe very large parameters on both inflation and the output gap. And in both cases such policy rules are capable of reducing inflation variability to very low levels (below 0.2). These results should not be surprising given that monetary policy is best equipped to deal with such shocks as there is very little conflict between stabilising inflation and stabilising output. However, the fact that we do

Table 5.5 *Optimal simple rules under different loss functions: demand shocks only*

	Loss	λ_i	$\lambda\pi$	λ_{ygap}	λ_{sgap}	$\sigma\pi$	σ_{ygap}	σ_{xgap}	λ_{sgap}
Inflation nutter	0.03	1.13	29.27	1.24	3.19	0.18	0.52	1.55	0.46
	0.04	0.73	2.29	0.17		0.20	0.53	1.82	1.08
Difference	0.01	-0.40	-26.98	-1.07		0.03	0.01	0.27	0.62
Output gapper	0.26	2.00	28.23	4.62	8.20	0.18	0.48	1.50	0.34
	0.28	0.74	1.10	0.25		0.22	0.48	1.77	0.93
Difference	0.01	-1.26	-27.13	-4.37		0.04	-0.00	0.28	0.59
Output-export gapper	2.11	2.00	0.66	-0.18	0.25	0.53	0.55	1.23	0.41
	3.29	-0.00	3.57	0.36		0.27	0.48	1.73	0.78
Difference	1.18	-2.00	2.91	0.54		-0.26	-0.07	0.50	0.37

not observe such enormous feedback responses in the real world might indicate that it is not straightforward for policy makers to identify pure demand shocks. Interestingly, in both these cases the real exchange rate still plays a significant role in reducing inflation variability, except for *output-export gappers*, where the primary effect is in reducing export variability.

Supply shocks only
Table 5.6 reports the results for the cases where we eliminate all the shocks expcet the wage and price mark-up shocks. As supply shocks are the dominant source of shocks for explaining variability in inflation it should not be surprising that inflation variability is much higher than was the case for demand shocks. Here we observe a much less significant role for the exchange rate than for demand shocks.

UIP shocks only
Table 5.7 completes the analysis and reports the results for the cases where we eliminate all shocks expcet UIP shocks. In this case we should again expect to see a large role for the exchange rate, which is confirmed by larger coefficients on the exchange-rate gap in the rule.

5.4.7   What about a forward-looking Taylor Rule?

In constructing internal forecasts several central banks rely upon forward-looking Taylor Rules, which include a one-year-ahead forecast

Table 5.6 *Optimal simple rules under different loss functions: mark-up shocks only*

	Loss	λ_i	λ_π	λ_{ygap}	λ_{sgap}	σ_π	σ_{ygap}	σ_{xgap}	σ_{sgap}
Inflation nutter	0.37	0.79	1.72	0.17	0.07	0.61	0.61	1.34	1.33
	0.38	0.76	1.16	0.12		0.61	0.65	1.38	1.51
Difference	0.00	-0.03	-0.56	-0.06		0.00	0.04	0.04	0.17
Output gapper	0.50	0.94	1.29	0.94	0.11	0.66	0.26	1.02	0.93
	0.51	0.88	0.74	0.58		0.67	0.27	1.00	1.07
Difference	0.01	-0.06	-0.55	-0.35		0.01	0.00	-0.02	0.14
Output-export gapper	1.29	1.14	0.08	0.49	-0.00	0.78	0.17	0.80	0.98
	1.29	1.15	0.08	0.49		0.78	0.17	0.80	0.97
Difference	0.00	0.01	-0.00	0.00		-0.00	0.00	0.00	-0.01

Table 5.7 *Optimal simple rules under different loss functions: UIP shocks only*

	Loss	λ_i	λ_π	λ_{ygap}	λ_{sgap}	σ_π	σ_{ygap}	σ_{xgap}	σ_{sgap}
Inflation nutter	0.02	0.95	1.16	0.00	0.11	0.15	0.24	1.39	1.08
	0.03	0.97	0.97	0.41		0.16	0.28	1.65	1.83
Difference	0.01	0.01	-0.19	0.41		0.02	0.04	0.25	0.75
Output gapper	0.06	0.94	1.11	0.64	0.12	0.18	0.16	1.38	1.16
	0.07	0.91	0.69	0.75		0.19	1.19	1.59	1.73
Difference	0.01	-0.03	-0.42	0.11		0.01	0.03	0.21	0.56
Output-export gapper	1.44	1.97	2.30	0.93	0.26	0.48	0.22	1.08	0.62
	2.19	1.06	0.00	0.45		0.49	0.16	1.39	1.55
Difference	0.75	-0.91	-2.30	-0.48		0.01	-0.06	0.31	0.93

of inflation rather than a contemporaneous measure of inflation. One potential interpretation of the earlier results is that the output gap and exchange-rate gap include significant information content for helping to forecast future inflation developments and that this is the main explanation for why these variables have been found to be useful in minimising the objective function. To address this issue we repeat the analysis above, but replace the inflation term in the reaction function

Table 5.8 *Optimal simple rules under different loss functions: four-quarter-ahead inflation in the rule*

	Loss	λ_i	$\lambda\pi$	λ_{ygap}	λ_{sgap}	$\sigma\pi$	σ_{ygap}	σ_{xgap}	λ_{sgap}
Inflation nutter	0.44	1.07	1.48	-0.00	0.02	0.66	0.81	2.61	2.10
	0.45	1.02	1.12	0.02		0.67	0.83	2.69	2.30
Difference	0.01	-0.05	-0.36	0.02		0.01	0.02	0.08	0.20
Output gapper	0.88	0.97	0.74	0.17	0.04	0.71	0.61	2.45	1.73
	0.94	0.94	0.51	0.14		0.71	0.66	2.59	2.10
Difference	0.06	-0.03	-0.23	-0.03		-0.00	0.05	0.14	-0.36
Output-export gapper	6.16	1.30	0.76	0.08	0.17	0.88	0.68	2.22	1.04
	7.64	0.93	0.45	0.15		0.72	0.65	2.59	2.08
Difference	1.49	-0.38	-0.31	0.06		-0.16	-0.02	0.37	1.04

with the model's one-year-ahead forecast of inflation. The results are reported in Table 5.8. In most cases the value of the loss function is smaller, and for the cases of *inflation nutters* and *output gappers* there is a smaller weight on the exchange-rate gap. Also, relative to the base case, the loss function for the reaction functions that include and exclude the exchange-rate-gap term diminishes, suggesting that the exchange rate has information that helps to project future movements in inflation that is useful for helping to minimise the loss function. However, for the case of the *output-export gappers* excluding information about the exchange rate still has significant deleterious effects on the value of the loss function as it can result in excessive variability in exports.

5.4.8   *Sensitivity analysis*

Tables 5.9 and 5.10 explore the sensitivity of our results to changes in the baseline calibration that change the steady-state size of exports. Table 5.9 raises the steady-state exports-to-GDP ratio in the final goods sector from 10 per cent to 50 per cent by changing the corresponding production function share parameter. This implies that any shock can be accommodated with a smaller relative change in exports, therefore the volatility of exports falls relative to the baseline. But because exports are more volatile than other components of GDP, the overall volatility of output increases. We find that this change in specification reduces the optimal coefficient on the real-exchange-rate gap, especially for the *output-export gapper*. The reason is that export volatility accounts for a

Table 5.9 *Optimal simple rules under different loss functions: final goods exports equal 50%*

	Loss	λ_i	λ_π	λ_{ygap}	λ_{sgap}	$\sigma\pi$	σ_{ygap}	σ_{xgap}	λ_{sgap}
Inflation nutter	0.36	0.92	1.30	0.06	0.04	0.60	1.09	1.05	2.46
	0.37	0.89	0.94	0.07		0.61	1.16	1.10	2.86
Difference	0.01	-0.03	-0.36	0.01		0.01	0.07	0.06	0.40
Output gapper	0.94	0.96	0.52	0.21	0.06	0.68	0.69	0.84	1.63
	1.09	0.94	0.25	0.16		0.69	0.79	0.92	2.19
Difference	0.15	-0.02	-0.27	-0.05		0.01	0.09	0.07	0.56
Output-export gapper	1.63	1.00	0.45	0.21	0.07	0.71	0.67	0.82	1.51
	1.92	0.96	0.20	0.17		0.72	0.77	0.90	2.17
Difference	0.28	-0.04	-0.25	-0.05		0.00	0.10	0.08	0.66

Table 5.10 *Optimal simple rules under different loss functions: intermediate goods export share equal 30% and steeper comparative advantage schedule*

	Loss	λ_i	λ_π	λ_{ygap}	λ_{sgap}	$\sigma\pi$	σ_{ygap}	σ_{xgap}	λ_{sgap}
Inflation nutter	0.35	0.89	1.20	0.07	0.03	0.59	1.01	1.67	2.34
	0.36	0.87	0.95	0.07		0.60	1.05	1.74	2.63
Difference	0.01	-0.02	-0.25	0.00		0.01	0.05	0.07	0.29
Output gapper	0.85	0.93	0.54	0.24	0.05	0.67	0.63	1.33	1.67
	0.95	0.92	0.33	0.18		0.67	0.70	1.44	2.13
Difference	0.10	-0.02	-0.22	-0.06		0.00	0.07	0.11	0.47
Output-export gapper	2.52	1.00	0.37	0.24	0.08	0.74	0.60	1.27	1.42
	2.99	0.94	0.22	0.19		0.71	0.68	1.42	2.11
Difference	0.47	-0.06	-0.15	-0.06		-0.03	0.08	0.15	0.69

smaller share of losses, therefore stabilising exports by responding to the real exchange rate becomes less important. But of course this needs to be heavily qualified, in that the loss function weight on export volatility would presumably change as exports become a more important sector of the economy.

Table 5.10 is more interesting. Here we raise the steady-state exports-to-GDP ratio in the intermediate goods sector from 10 per cent to

30 per cent, but this is not accomplished through changing a share parameter. Instead, for a given trading cost, c, we need to change the pattern of comparative advantage. To allow more goods to be traded, this pattern needs to be more pronounced, in other words the comparative advantage schedule has to become steeper. Specifically, in our calibration we go from $n = 0.4$ to $n = 0.8$. Relative to the change in the exports-to-GDP ratio, which is only half that of the previous example, we observe much larger reductions in export volatility and in the optimal coefficient on the real exchange rate, and not only for the *output-export gapper*. In fact, in the limit, this type of change would lead to exogenous tradability, as with a near vertical comparative advantage schedule the range of traded goods would no longer be sensitive to shocks and to the real exchange rate. We have also examined the sensitivity of our results to removing different combinations of endogenous tradability, export adjustment costs and import adjustment costs. The picture that emerges is that these effects are cumulative, in that the more of them that are combined, the larger is the optimal monetary response to the real-exchange-rate gap.

5.5   Conclusions

This paper develops a DSGE model that integrates the theory of comparative advantage or endogenous tradability into a monetary model with nominal and real rigidities. We find that without endogenous tradability there is no role for the exchange rate in optimised monetary policy rules. But with endogenous tradability the exchange rate can play a much more fundamental role in facilitating or slowing down adjustments in the real economy, and it enters the optimised policy rule. The role of the real exchange rate in the policy rule is even more significant when trade is subject to export and import frictions.

We performed sensitivity analysis to see what are the key assumptions that give the exchange rate an important role in the monetary policy rule. Looking forward, we plan to extend this analysis by taking higher-order approximations of the model so that we can study the level effects on welfare and economic activity that may be associated with excessive variability in trade flows.

Appendix: HP Filter Weights

The Hodrick-Prescott (HP) filter has been used extensively to obtain measures of output gaps in spite of the problems associated with using such a procedure in real time when the filter at the end of the sample becomes a one-sided backward-looking filter – see Laxton and Tetlow (1992). In an empirically estimated DSGE model of the US economy Juillard *et al.* (2007) show that the severity of this end-of-sample problem can be mitigated significantly by using the model's multi-period forecasts of GDP. In their paper this is implemented by writing down the Kalman-filter representation of the HP filter, but an equivalent procedure can be obtained by simply constructing the two-sided weights and then coding this equation directly.

The HP filter estimates obtained from series y_i of length T are obtained by minimising the following function, where λ represents a parameter that penalises changes in the second difference of the computed trend series τ_i:

$$Z = \sum_{i=1}^{T}(y_i - \tau_i)^2 + \lambda\sum_{i=1}^{T-2}[(\tau_{i+2}-\tau_{i+1}) - (\tau_{i+1}-\tau_i)]^2.$$

Choosing τ_i to minimise Z requires $\partial Z/\partial \tau_i = 0$ for all i from 1 to T and then stacking the equations. Let τ and y represent vectors of length T, and let A represent a matrix with elements that are only a function of the HP curvature restriction λ:

$A\tau = y.$

Once the A matrix has been obtained the estimates of the trend series can be computed by simply finding the inverse of A. The elements of this matrix will also simply be a function of the curvature restriction λ:

$\tau = A^{-1}y.$

We will refer to A^{-1} as the weighting matrix. Assuming that $T = 49$ observations and $\lambda = 1600$, the dotted line in Figure 5.9 plots the first row of the weighting matrix that would determine the value of τ_i in the first period. Obviously, the estimates in this period can only depend on the current and future values of the series y, since by assumption it represents the first observation. The HP filter treats the end of the sample in a similar way except in this case the weighting scheme only depends on current and past values of the series – see the dashed line in Figure 5.9. Note that in this case the weight is quite high on the current and recent observations, which is why end-of-samples estimates from the HP filter tend to get pulled around a lot by movements in the actual series. The solid line in Figure 5.9 represents the weights in the middle of the sample ($i = 25$), in which case the weights are a symmetric function of past and future values of the series. The differences in weights

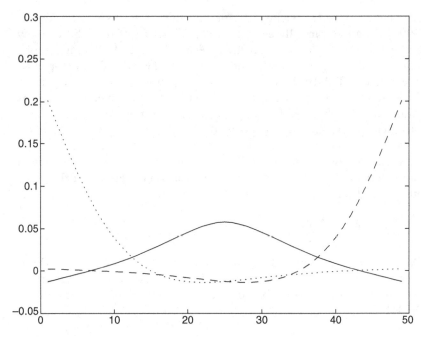

Figure 5.9 Hodrick-Prescott filter weights

between the in-sample estimates and end-of-sample estimates are enormous, explaining why HP output gaps can be revised substantially as new data are released and the sample is updated. Juillard *et al.* (2007) show that some of these problems with the HP filter can be overcome by using the weights from the middle of the sample and the model's forecasts for the series.

REFERENCES

Aitken, B., G. Hanson, and A. Harrison (1997). 'Spillovers, foreign investment and export behavior', *Journal of International Economics*, **43**(1–2), 103–32.

Backus, D., P. Kehoe, and F. Kydland (1994). 'Dynamics of the trade balance and the terms of trade: the J-curve?', *American Economic Review*, **84**(1), 84–103.

Bayoumi, T., D. Laxton, and P. Pesenti (2004). *Benefits and Spillovers of Greater Competition in Europe: A Macroeconomic Assessment*, ECB working papers No. 341.

Benigno, G., and P. Benigno (2003). 'Price stability in open economies', *Review of Economic Studies*, **70**, 743–64.

Bergin, P., and R. Glick (2003). *Endogenous Nontradability and Macroeconomic Implications*, NBER working papers No. 9739.

Bernard, A., and J. Jensen (2004). 'Why some firms export', *Review of Economics and Statistics*, **86**(2), 561–9.

Besedes, T., and T. Prusa (2006). 'Ins, outs and the duration of trade', *Canadian Journal of Economics*, **39**(1), 266–95.

Burstein, A., M. Eichenbaum, and S. Rebelo (2005). 'Large devaluations and the real exchange rate', *Journal of Political Economy*, **113**(4), 742–84.

Campa, M., and L. Goldberg (2005). 'Exchange rate pass-through into imports prices', *Review of Economics and Statistics*, **87**(4), 679–90.

Casares, M. (2002). *Time-To-Build Approach in A Sticky Price, Sticky Wage Optimizing Monetary Model*, ECB working paper series No. 147.

Corsetti, G., and P. Pesenti (2005). 'International dimensions of optimal monetary policy', *Journal of Monetary Economics*, **52**(2), 281–305.

Das, S., M. Roberts, and J. Tybout (2007). 'Market entry costs, producer heterogeneity and export dynamics', *Econometrica*, **75**(3), 837–73.

Devereux, M., and C. Engel (2003). 'Monetary policy in the open economy revisited: price setting and exchange-rate flexibility', *Review of Economic Studies*, **70**(4), 765–83.

Dornbusch, R., S. Fischer, and P. Samuelson (1977). 'Comparative advantage, trade, and payments in a Ricardian model with a continuum of goods', *American Economic Review*, **67**(5), 823–39.

Edge, R. (2000a). *The Effect of Monetary Policy on Residential and Structures Investment Under Differential Project Planning and Completion Times*, Board of Governors of the Federal Reserve System international finance discussion papers No. 671.

(2000b). *Time-to-Build, Time-to-Plan, Habit-Persistence, and the Liquidity Effect*, Board of Governors of the Federal Reserve System international finance discussion papers No. 673.

Erceg, C., L. Guerrieri, and C. Gust (2003). *SIGMA: A New Open Economy Model for Policy Analysis*, draft paper prepared for the Annual Central Bank Modelers' Workshop, Amsterdam.

Fagan, G., J. Henry, and R. Mestre (2001). *An Area-Wide Model (AWM) for the Euro Area*, ECB working papers No. 42.

Friedman, M. (1953). 'The case for flexible exchange rates', in *Essays in Positive Economics*, Chicago University Press, pp. 157–203.

Gali, J., and T. Monacelli (2005). 'Monetary policy and exchange rate volatility in a small open economy', *Review of Economic Studies*, **72**, 707–34.

Ghironi, F., and M. Melitz (2005). 'International trade and macroeconomic dynamics with heterogeneous firms', *Quarterly Journal of Economics*, **120**(3), 865–915.

Goldberg, P., and M. Knetter (1997). 'Goods prices and exchange rates: what have we learned?', *American Economic Review*, **35**(3), 1243–72.

Goodfriend, M., and R. King (1997). 'The new neoclassical synthesis and the role of monetary policy', *NBER Macroeconomics Annual*, **12**, 231–83.

Juillard, M., O. Kamenik, M. Kumhof, and D. Laxton (2007). 'Measures of potential output from an estimated DSGE model of the United States', paper presented at a workshop on *Issues in Measuring Potential Output*, Ankara Turkey, 16 January 2007.

(2008). 'Optimal price setting and inflation inertia in a rational expectations model', *Journal of Economic Dynamics and Control*, **32**(8), 2584–621.

King, R., and A. Wolman (1996). 'Inflation targeting in a St. Louis model of the 21st century', *Federal Reserve Bank of St. Louis Review*, **78**(3), 83–107.

Laxton, D., and P. Pesenti (2003). 'Monetary policy rules for small, open, emerging economies', *Journal of Monetary Economics*, **50**, 1109–46.

Laxton, D., and R. Tetlow (1992). *A Simple Multivariate Filter for the Measurement of Potential Output*, Technical Report No. 59 (Ottawa: Bank of Canada), June.

Mendoza, E. (2005). *Real Exchange Rate Volatility and the Price of Nontradables in Sudden-Stop-Prone Economies*, NBER working papers No. 11691.

Murchinson, S., A. Rennison, and Z. Zhu (2004). *A Structural Small Open-Economy Model for Canada*, working paper, Bank of Canada.

Naknoi, K. (2008). 'Real exchange rate fluctuations, endogenous tradability and exchange rate regimes', *Journal of Monetary Economics*, **55**(3), 645–63.

Obstfeld, M., and K. Rogoff (2000). 'New directions for stochastic open economy models', *Journal of International Economics*, **50**(1), 117–53.

(2002). 'Global implications of self-oriented national monetary rules', *Quarterly Journal of Economics*, **117**(2), 503–35.

Roberts, M., and J. Tybout (1997). 'The decision to export in Colombia: an empirical model of entry with sunk costs', *American Economic Review*, **87**(4), 545–64.

Rotemberg, J. (1982). 'Sticky prices in the United States', *Journal of Political Economy*, **90**, 1187–211.

Rotemberg, J., and M. Woodford (1997). 'An optimization-based econometric framework for the evaluation of monetary policy', *NBER Macroeconomics Annual*, **12**, 297–316.

Smets, F., and R. Wouters (2002). 'Openness, imperfect exchange rate pass-through and monetary policy', *Journal of Monetary Economics*, **49**, 947–81.

(2003). 'An estimated stochastic dynamic general equilibrium model of the euro area', *Journal of the European Economic Association*, **1**(5), 1123–75.

(2007). 'Shocks and frictions in U.S. business cycles: a Bayesian DSGE approach', *American Economic Review*, **97**(3), 586–606.

Taylor, J. (1993). 'Discretion versus policy rules in practice', *Carnegie-Rochester Conference Series on Public Policy*, **39**, pp. 195–214.

6　Globalisation and inflation in the OECD economies

Isabell Koske, Nigel Pain and Marte Sollie

6.1　Introduction

Over the past twenty-five years consumer price inflation has moderated considerably in all OECD economies, and also worldwide. The decline in OECD inflation from above 10 per cent in the early 1980s to around 2 per cent over the decade from 1995–2005 has been accompanied by a reduction in the variability of inflation and cross-country dispersion. These developments have coincided with a marked increase in the extent of globalisation, with the production of many goods and services becoming increasingly internationalised and the level of trade in goods and services between the OECD and non-OECD economies rising as a share of OECD GDP.

Ultimately, inflation should be determined by monetary policy. But many other factors can influence inflation, and in the short to medium term it can be difficult to assess whether any observed moderation in inflation results from monetary policy, structural factors such as globalisation or just good fortune. Globalisation itself, as reflected in trade and FDI, potentially affects inflation through a variety of channels (IMF, 2006a; Kohn, 2006). Enhanced trade integration with lower-cost economies may help to hold down domestic inflation by depressing trade prices and increasing the share of imports in domestic demand. Related to this, enhanced product market competition may have reduced the mark-ups of domestic producers. These forces and the internationalisation of production may also have helped to raise

Isabell Koske is a member of the Structural Surveillance Division and Nigel Pain a member of the Macroeconomic Policy Division of the OECD Economics Department. Marte Sollie was a secondment to the OECD Economics Department at the time of writing. The authors are grateful to Pete Richardson, Mike Feiner, Jørgen Elmeskov and other colleagues in the OECD Economics Department as well as participants of the ECB July 2007 Conference on 'Globalisation and the Macroeconomy' for helpful comments and suggestions. The paper has also been published in OECD Economic Studies, Vol. 2008, pp. 117–48. Errors are the responsibilities of the authors alone. The views expressed in this paper are those of the authors and do not necessarily reflect those of the OECD or its member countries.

the cyclical influence of global capacity utilisation on domestic price inflation (Borio and Filardo, 2007). Against this must be set the extent to which the strong globalisation-related growth in many non-OECD economies, and especially China, is putting upward pressure on the prices of many commodities.

This paper explores some of these issues in order to quantify the contribution of particular aspects of globalisation to the decline in OECD inflation. In doing so, the study extends the recent literature on this topic in several respects. In particular, wider allowance is made for possible price-level effects from globalisation, a larger number of countries are included in the sample and the separate impacts of commodity and non-commodity import prices are considered.

The analysis suggests that the inflation process in OECD countries did indeed change in the mid 1990s, around the time at which the extent of globalisation began to rise markedly. Accounting for this structural change leads to several important findings. Of these, the most notable is that the impact of import prices on consumer prices is higher after the break in all countries. In addition, the short- to medium-term response of inflation to domestic cyclical output variations is found to have declined over the past decade, implying an increase in the sacrifice ratio. By contrast, inflation has become more sensitive to foreign economic conditions, working through import prices.

A simulation exercise reveals that globalisation has, on balance, contributed to lower inflation in most OECD economies. Although strong GDP growth in the non-OECD economies has pushed up real oil and metals prices in OECD economies, this has been more than offset by the disinflationary impact of declining import prices of goods and services. Nonetheless, the net effect is small, with globalisation having been associated with a decline in the rate of consumer price inflation of between 0 to one quarter of a percentage point per annum since 2000.

The paper is organised as follows. First, it provides a short overview of inflation-related developments and some key indicators of the world economy that are drawn on in the analytical work. Next, it presents the findings of recent studies on the impact of non-OECD economies on consumer and import price inflation in OECD economies. The paper then continues by discussing the key findings from new estimates of the influence of non-OECD economies on selected commodity prices. The wider importance of globalisation and international trade for consumer price inflation is addressed in the subsequent section, which first reviews the range of evidence based on existing studies and then provides new estimates based on an econometric analysis of the factors determining consumer price inflation in the OECD economies. This is

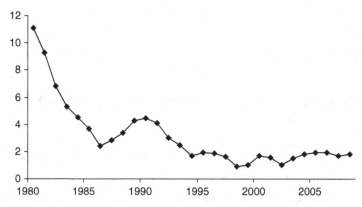

Figure 6.1 Consumer price inflation in the G7 economies
(percentages)
Source: OECD Economic Outlook database.

followed by an evaluation of the overall impact of commodity and non-commodity prices on consumer prices, using these new estimates in a scenario analysis. The final section summarises the key findings and concludes with a number of policy implications.

6.2   Recent trends in inflation and global economic conditions

Over the past twenty-five years inflation has fallen considerably across OECD countries. In 1980 the annual inflation rate was over 10 per cent in many OECD countries, compared with an average annual rate of 2 to 3 per cent since the second half of the 1990s (see Figure 6.1). Much of this decline occurred during the first half of the 1980s when average inflation fell by more than 1 pp per annum. Inflation rates continued to decline in subsequent years, though much more slowly. This fall in average inflation rates has been accompanied by a decline in inflation variability and also in inflation expectations. On average across OECD countries, the standard deviation of annual consumer price inflation has declined from above 3 per cent in the early 1980s to around 0.5 per cent in recent years.

A number of different factors have contributed to the fall in both average inflation and inflation variability; the focus here is on the role of external factors. Figure 6.2 compares the evolution of the aggregate price deflator for imported goods and services with domestic producer prices in manufacturing over the period 1980 to 2005. On average,

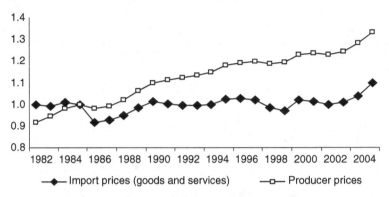

Figure 6.2 Import prices and producer prices in G7 economies
(1985 = 1)
Note: The producer price index covers all manufacturing goods.
Sources: OECD Economic Outlook database, OECD Main Economic
Indicators database.

import prices declined relative to producer prices during this period.[1]
Non-commodity import prices have risen at a very moderate rate
since the early 1990s and in some countries have even declined. More
recently, the modest rate of non-commodity import price inflation has
been partly offset by rising prices for commodity imports.

Low import price inflation in OECD countries can in part be attributed to the rising trade integration of low-cost countries from Asia and
Latin America. Since the beginning of the 1990s the share of non-
OECD countries in total world trade has increased markedly: from
about a quarter of total world trade in 1990 to about a third in 2005.
The rise in the trade share of non-OECD countries reflects the increasing openness of these countries as well as higher GDP growth rates
compared with OECD countries. Between 1980 and 2005 the GDP of
non-OECD countries grew by 5 per cent per annum on average, compared with growth of 3 per cent per annum in the OECD countries.

The integration of non-OECD countries into international trade and
production networks has also progressed since the mid 1990s, albeit
from a low level. One indicator of this is the global stock of FDI relative to global GDP, which increased throughout the 1990s (see Molnar
et al., 2008, Figure 1). Although this increase was mainly due to higher

[1] Using disaggregated EU import price data (classified at the 8-digit level) Kaplinsky
(2005) demonstrates that the proportion of sectors in which import prices fell between
1988 and 2001 is higher the lower the per-capita income of the country of origin.

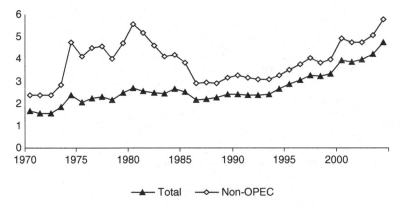

Figure 6.3 OECD imports from non-OECD countries – per cent of GDP, current prices
Source: OECD International Trade Statistics database and Economic Outlook database.

intra-OECD flows, inward FDI to non-OECD countries also picked up, particularly in the mid 1990s. Coinciding with the rise in international FDI flows, imports of OECD countries from non-OECD countries also rose markedly from the mid 1990s onwards (see Figure 6.3). In part, this trend reflects the recent strengthening of oil and other commodity prices. But it mainly reflects the increasing extent of international sourcing of finished and intermediate goods and services from the non-oil-producing countries in the non-OECD.

During 2002 to 2005 the prices of several commodities moved towards or past historical peaks in real terms, when expressed relative to weighted world export prices in US dollars (Figure 6.4).[2] These increases have been especially marked for real oil and metals prices. Between the fourth quarter of 2003 and the fourth quarter of 2005, oil prices rose by 74 per cent in real terms, with metals prices increasing by 47 per cent in real terms.[3] Additional increases occurred in 2006. The size and persistence of recent increases is unusual but, as can be seen from Figure 6.4, not outside all historical experience.

In contrast to oil and metals prices, the real prices of agricultural raw materials, foods and tropical beverages did not increase significantly

[2] The rise relative to domestic output or consumer prices is less marked, with trade prices having declined in real terms (Pain *et al.*, 2005).
[3] The price series for metals and agricultural commodities are composite indicators produced by the Hamburg Institute for World Economics (HWWA). The oil price series is the price of Brent crude.

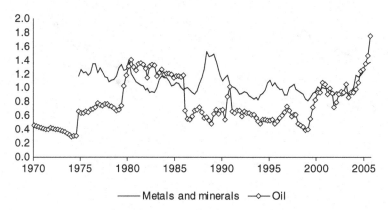

Figure 6.4 Real oil and metals prices – deflated by world export prices in US dollar terms (2000 = 1)
Source: OECD Economic Outlook database.

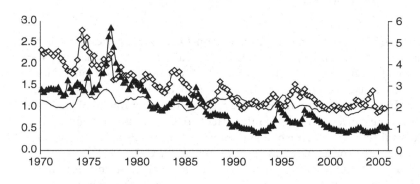

Figure 6.5 Real agricultural prices – deflated by world export prices in US dollar terms (2000 = 1)
Source: OECD Economic Outlook database.

over 2002–2005 and remained well below historical peaks at the end of 2005 (Figure 6.5). The broad agricultural commodity groups also comprise bio fuels, so that changes in oil prices may be propagated to other commodity prices (IMF, 2006b). Up to the end of 2005, however, any such spillovers appear to have been limited.

6.3   Imports from emerging markets and inflation

The increasing importance of China and other lower-cost producers in global production networks is likely to have placed downward pressure on the global prices of many goods and services, and hence import prices in OECD countries, through several different channels. This section discusses the findings from a number of studies that have sought to estimate the initial impact of imports from lower-cost producers on either domestic inflation or on the growth rate of import prices.

6.3.1   Estimates of the direct impact of imports from non-OECD Asia on OECD consumer price inflation

Using a simple accounting framework, a recent study by the OECD shows that over the past decade imports from China and, to a lesser extent, other dynamic Asian economies, have placed downward pressure on the rate of consumer price inflation in the United States and the euro area (OECD, 2006). In the reported calculations this arises from two sources: an increase in import penetration by lower-price Asian producers, and the differences between the rate of growth of their export prices and producer prices in the importing economies. Overall, the combined impact effect of imports from China and other dynamic Asian economies is estimated to have reduced domestic inflation in the United States by 0.1 pp per annum on average from 1996 to 2005. In the euro area, it is estimated to have reduced domestic inflation by 0.3 pp per annum between 2000 and 2005. Prior to that point, the effect was negligible.

Although this would appear to suggest that trade with lower-cost producers is placing downward pressure on domestic prices in OECD economies, the eventual effect on inflation is less clear as the calculations show only *ex ante* effects. The extent to which they eventually lead to lower consumer price inflation will depend on the effect they have on the behaviour of other competitors and domestically generated inflation.[4] The latter will depend on whether the initial impacts are accommodated by the stance of monetary policy in the importing economy. Deflationary pressures on the general price level can, at least in principle, be offset eventually by monetary policy relaxation, although this does depend on the extent to which they are recognised, estimated accurately and acted upon promptly.[5]

Such estimates provide only a partial view of the effects on OECD economies of increased trade with lower-cost producers in Asia and elsewhere. In particular, there is no allowance for any offsetting effects

---

[4] Kamin *et al.* (2006) find little evidence that the rising share of Chinese goods in the United States has had a marked impact on producer price inflation.

[5] To this extent, domestically generated inflation may end up being higher than otherwise. In this sense, the impact of higher trade with low-cost producers is inflationary (Rogoff, 2006).

of higher world commodity prices that may result from strong growth in comparatively commodity-intensive economies such as China.

6.3.2   Estimates of the direct impact of imports from the non-OECD on OECD import price inflation

The results of OECD (2006) are broadly comparable with those reported in other recent studies of the impact of the switch of sourcing to low-cost countries, although most of these other studies consider the impact on trade prices in the importing country rather than on consumer prices. For the United Kingdom, estimates suggest that the move to low-cost producers during the period 2000–2004 reduced the rate of world export price inflation to the United Kingdom[6] by 0.55 pp per annum on average (Nickell, 2005).[7] For the United States, Kamin *et al.* (2006) estimate that the growing share of imports from China lowered import price inflation by around 0.8 pp per annum on average between 1993 and 2002, all else being equal. The direct impact of this on consumer price inflation during this period would have been small, at around 0.1 pp or less, similar to the estimates in OECD (2006).[8]

Over the decade 1993–2002, only Japan and Korea are estimated to have experienced a reduction in import prices as a result of trade with China similar to that in the United States (Kamin *et al.*, 2006). For the median OECD economy, import price inflation is estimated to have declined by only 0.13 pp per year on average. Many of these economies, especially those in Europe, have a smaller share of their trade with Asian economies than the United States and Japan do. On the other hand, these economies are likely to have received additional benefits from low-cost imports from other economies, especially those in Central and Eastern Europe, and the size of any effect is likely to have become larger in more recent years due to the further rapid increase in import penetration by lower-cost producers.

The *ex ante* effects of low-cost production on trade prices are likely to be concentrated in particular sectors of the economy. Using data for the euro area from 1995 to 2005, estimates produced by the European Central Bank indicate that the combined impact of the rising import

---

[6] World export prices are a weighted average of the export prices of those countries that export to the United Kingdom in US dollars.

[7] Related findings for Norway, Sweden and New Zealand are reported by Melick and Galati (2006) and Hodgetts (2006).

[8] Thus implicitly, the findings in OECD (2006) can be regarded as consistent with a view that trade with China and the other dynamic Asian economies will have lowered import price inflation in the United States and the euro zone by at least 1 per cent per annum.

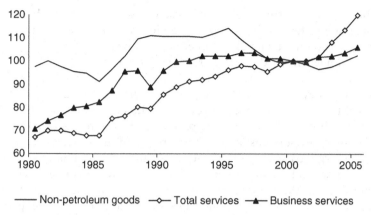

Figure 6.6 Goods and services import prices in the USA – US Import prices (2000 = 100)
Source: Bureau of Economic Analysis, United States.

penetration of low-cost producers in the manufacturing sector, and the differentials in inflation between them and other producers, has dampened euro area manufacturing import price growth by approximately 2 pp per annum (ECB, 2006). In contrast to the studies discussed above, these calculations also include an allowance for the impact of production in regions other than Asia.[9] Feyzioğlu and Willard (2006) find that the impact of trade with China on inflation in the United States and Japan is relatively strong on particular items such as household furnishings and food, rather than on the general consumer price level.

Overall, it appears reasonable to conclude that rising levels of imports from all lower-cost producers will have acted directly to reduce non-commodity import price inflation by up to 1 to 2 per cent per annum in most OECD economies over the past decade, with globalisation-related effects in goods prices also being reflected in some services prices as well. To date, there have been no studies of the impact of service sector offshoring on the prices of imported services in the OECD economies. Some possible evidence on this is provided in Figure 6.6, which shows import price deflators from the United States national accounts. Up until the early 1990s the price of imported business services, a category which will include imported services that were moved offshore from the United States, rose faster than the prices of other service imports.

[9] The group of 'low-cost' producers considered in ECB (2006) includes the new member states and candidate countries of the EU, the CIS, Latin America, Africa and all Asian countries other than Japan.

But since that time, prices of business service imports have broadly stagnated whereas those of other service imports have continued to rise, suggesting that a globalisation effect may be present.[10]

Changes in the domestic price level that stem from developments in only a few sectors of the economy may be less likely to generate a monetary policy response than equivalent changes in the domestic price level that are widespread throughout the economy (Rogoff, 2006). If so, the initial impact of an appreciation in the terms of trade (due to declining import costs) may be to push inflation below the medium-term target trajectory of the monetary authorities. The extent to which it does so, and the time over which this is allowed to persist, will depend not only on the behaviour of import prices but also on whether there are adverse effects on policy credibility and inflation expectations (Bean, 2006).

6.4   The impact of non-OECD output growth on commodity prices

Strong growth in China and other emerging markets in recent years has coincided with a sizable increase in global commodity prices. This section discusses the extent to which these developments are related, focusing in particular on the linkages between macroeconomic conditions, including the relatively higher rate of growth in non-OECD economies, and oil and non-oil commodity prices. Using the 'reduced form' equations for a selection of commodities reported by Pain *et al.* (2006), calculations are reported of what might have happened to commodity prices over the past five years if the non-OECD economies had not grown faster than the OECD economies. Such calculations, although only illustrative, help to evaluate the impact of growth in emerging markets on commodity prices and may thereby also help to indicate whether prices will continue to rise beyond the current high price levels or whether these are only temporary.

6.4.1   *Demand growth in the non-OECD countries*

Earlier periods of rapid growth in real oil prices in the mid and late 1970s were characterised by marked constraints on oil production, notably by producers in OPEC. In contrast, the present upturn in oil prices

---

[10] Business services prices are measured using the deflator for imports of 'other private services' in the United States national accounts.

has occurred at a time when the growth rates of both oil consumption and oil production have accelerated (IEA, 2006, Table 1). Over the decade to 2001 global oil demand rose by 1.4 per cent per annum on average. In the subsequent four years demand growth accelerated to an average rate of 2 per cent per annum.

The acceleration in global demand is more than accounted for by developments in non-OECD economies, where demand growth accelerated to just under 4 per cent per annum on average from 2001 to 2005, after averaging 1.5 per cent per annum in the previous decade. In China, average annual demand growth rose from just under 6.5 per cent to just below 9 per cent per annum. By 2005 the non-OECD economies accounted for 40 per cent of total global oil consumption, with one-fifth of this being due to China.[11]

The acceleration in oil demand in the non-OECD economies in recent years reflects in part strong output growth, especially in industrial sectors, a higher level of energy consumption per unit of output than the average OECD economy (OECD, 2005; Markandya et al., 2006) and rising private usage of motor vehicles. Strong world trade growth may also have contributed because of the associated growth in demand for aviation and shipping transportation.

Although the growth in final demand for oil would appear to have been the primary factor behind the recent rise in oil prices, this need not mean that other factors have been absent. Almost certainly there has been increasing precautionary demand as well, with concerns about possible supply disruptions in the Middle East and the possibility of short- to medium-term supply shortages because of low rates of past investment and natural disasters all acting to raise risk premiums. Speculation may also have played a role (IMF, 2006b).

The non-oil commodity group contains a wide range of different commodities, with few common elements in their prices. Metals and, to a lesser extent, agricultural raw materials are the most likely to be affected by a rise in the level of activity in commodity-intensive economies, as well as by the business cycle. China has also been a significant influence behind the strong global growth in demand for many metals over the past few years. During the period 2002–2005, the growth in demand from China accounted for almost all of the increase in global demand for nickel and tin, and over half of the increase in demand for

---

[11] Insofar as certain commodity-intensive activities have moved from other countries (including OECD countries) to China, the growth of Chinese demand for commodities may give an exaggerated impression of the net impact on demand for commodities of the emergence of China. For this reason, total non-OECD output measures are used in the empirical work, rather than just measures for China.

aluminium, copper and steel, reflected in marked increases in the share of China in total global consumption.[12]

6.4.2   *Estimates of the impact of output growth on commodity prices*

To obtain a more precise estimate of the impact of the recent rapid output growth in the non-OECD countries on commodity prices, reduced-form price equations were estimated by Pain *et al.* (2006) for five main commodity groups – oil, metals and minerals, agricultural raw materials, food and tropical beverages. The oil price measure used was the price of Brent crude, while for the remaining commodity groupings the price variables considered are the aggregate price indices compiled by the Hamburg Institute of World Economics (HWWA).[13] The equations relate real prices to measures of the level and growth of global activity, as well as measures of the share of world trade and world GDP accounted for by non-OECD economies.[14] Measures of the global output gap, and output gaps in the OECD and the non-OECD economies were also included in the analysis.[15] It is well established that the global output gap is an important factor behind the cyclical behaviour of commodity prices, especially when output growth is above potential (Adams and Ichino, 1995; Rae and Turner, 2001).[16]

The econometric estimates in Pain *et al.* (2006, Appendix 2) provide significant empirical evidence that the present upturn in real oil and metals prices has been amplified by the rapid output growth in emerging markets. For oil, two statistically similar specifications were obtained. In the first, the effects of strong growth in the non-OECD

---

[12] Although China and other emerging markets also make a significant contribution to global demand for other agricultural commodities (IMF, 2006b), the speed of response in supply can act to offset the impact of demand pressures on prices. Observed prices may also rise rapidly for reasons unconnected to demand pressures, such as weather-related supply fluctuations.

[13] The weightings on individual commodities within these broad price indices will reflect global demand, rather than country-specific factors. In some cases important commodities for particular countries may not be included in the aggregate price measures at all.

[14] A broader set of control variables were also considered initially for other possible macroeconomic influences, such as the US effective exchange rate and real short-term interest rate (Adams and Ichino, 1995; Hua, 1998).

[15] The output gap is measured as the ratio of actual GDP to potential GDP.

[16] The global output gap used in estimation is a GDP-weighted average of separately estimated output gaps for the OECD and the non-OECD economies. The OECD output gap is calculated using a production function approach to assess potential output. The non-OECD output gap was derived using a measure of potential output derived from a Hodrick-Prescott filter.

economies are reflected in a long-run levels term in the volume of world GDP and in a dynamic term in the share of the non-OECD economies in the level of world trade. A limitation of this equation, estimated over a sample from the mid 1980s to 2005, is that the long-run income elasticity is very high, at 1.7 per cent, almost certainly reflecting the strong growth in oil demand and real oil prices over the estimation sample.

The second specification sought to test directly for the possible recent impact of strong growth in the non-OECD economies by including a variable for the differential between the rates of GDP growth in the non-OECD and the OECD starting in 2001. The coefficient on this term is both positive and statistically significant. Incorporating the additional measure also causes the long-run income elasticity to halve, although it remains significantly different from zero (at the 10 per cent level).[17]

For metals prices in real terms, recent demand-related pressures were also found to be best reflected by the differential between the rates of GDP growth in the non-OECD and the OECD. In effect, this corresponds to the rate of change of the non-OECD share of world GDP. The level of world GDP and the non-OECD trade share measure were not found to be significant determinants of metals prices. No significant effects from any of these variables were found for the three agricultural commodity prices either. The differences between these findings and those for oil prices are likely to stem from supply being more elastic for non-oil commodities, with any initial increase in demand more rapidly offset by an expansion in supply.

An implication of these results is that a period in which growth in the non-OECD economies is faster than that in the OECD economies will ultimately have only a temporary positive impact on the level of real metals prices. In contrast, the impact on real oil prices will be permanent because the higher level of global GDP that results is implicitly taken to imply a permanent increase in the level of oil demand with supply being less than fully elastic. In practice it seems unlikely that the longer-term difference in the impact on metals and oil prices would be as pronounced as this, even if such a feature is present in the comparatively short sample used for estimation.

Fluctuations in output gaps are also found to have a significant short- to medium-term influence on each of the commodity prices by Pain

---

[17] Significant econometric results for oil prices could be obtained only when using a sample beginning in the mid 1980s. The findings were inconclusive when the estimation period was lengthened by including the acceleration in oil prices in the 1970s. One possible explanation for this is that supply-side factors were the dominant influence on prices in these earlier periods.

et al. (2006), although there are marked differences in the size and direction of the effect on individual commodities. An increase in global output relative to trend is found to raise initially the real price of each commodity group. This change quickly fades for the prices of food and tropical beverages, but is found to persist for several years for oil prices and, to a lesser extent, metals and agricultural raw materials prices. For oil prices, the impact of an increase in the global output gap is found to be larger if it coincides with an increase in the non-OECD output gap, consistent with what might be expected given the different industrial structures in the OECD and the non-OECD.

6.4.3   *Estimates of the impact of non-OECD growth on commodity prices*

In order to quantify the impact of the strong growth in the non-OECD economies on commodity prices in recent years the econometric equations were simulated under two assumptions. Firstly, that the share of the non-OECD in world trade remained unchanged from the average level in the year 2000, and secondly that GDP in the non-OECD economies grew only at the rate of OECD GDP from 2000. The resulting calculations of the change in prices are only suggestive, but serve to illustrate the possible orders of magnitude involved. As the non-OECD share of world trade and GDP rose throughout the period from 2001–2005, the alternative path implies an increasingly large divergence from the actual outturn.[18] As a result, the impact on real prices of the change also increases in size over time.

For oil prices, the impact of holding the non-OECD trade share fixed at its level in 2000, and letting non-OECD GDP grow in line with OECD GDP, is to bring about a decline relative to baseline of just over 40 per cent in the level of the real oil price by the end of 2005 (Figure 6.7a) when using the second oil price equation. In nominal terms this is equivalent to a decline to just under $35 per barrel in the price of oil in the fourth quarter of 2005. Although this represents a sizable difference from the actual outturn, it does not entirely remove the strong growth in oil prices after 2002, as can be seen from Figure 6.7b. In the alternative oil price specification without the extra variable for the growth differential from 2001, the real oil price was lowered by some 20 per cent by the end of 2005 from its baseline level.

---

[18] By the fourth quarter of 2005, world GDP in constant prices is around 10 per cent below its actual value as a result of allowing non-OECD GDP to grow at the rate of OECD GDP from 2000 onwards.

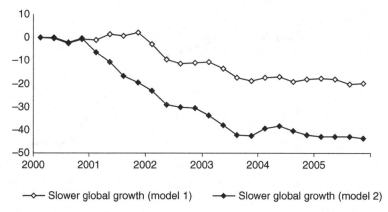

Figure 6.7a Removing the impact of non-OECD growth on real oil prices – percentage deviations from baseline

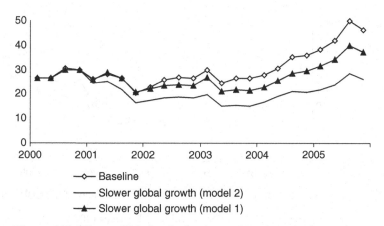

Figure 6.7b The profile of real oil prices – $ per barrel, 2000 prices

For metals prices, corresponding estimates are also based on the assumption that GDP in the non-OECD economies grew at the rate of OECD GDP from 2000. The resulting changes in the profile of metals prices are smaller than for oil prices, with the real metals price being about 10 per cent lower by the fourth quarter of 2005 than would otherwise have been the case. This accounts for only a small fraction of the actual growth in metals prices after 2002 (Figures 6.8a and 6.8b).

The alternative profile of oil prices also has a small impact on the prices of agricultural raw materials, reducing these prices by between 1

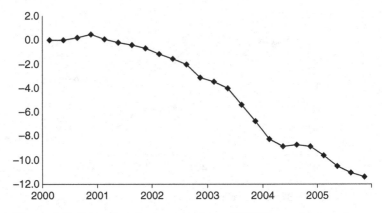

Figure 6.8a Removing the impact of non-OECD growth on real metal prices – percentage deviations from baseline

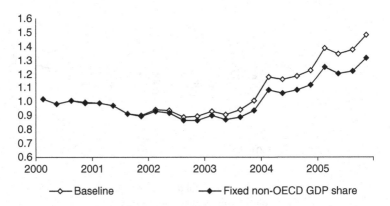

Figure 6.8b The profile of real metals prices (2000 = 1)

and 1.5 per cent over the course of 2003–2005 in the scenario in which oil prices declined by just over 40 per cent by the end of 2005. The prices of food and tropical beverages remain unchanged.

Other analytical studies have also suggested that strong output growth could have a sizable effect on commodity prices. A related scenario for future oil demand in China is considered in CBO (2006), with oil demand in China from 2006 to 2010 rising by 7.5 per cent per annum, similar to the rate seen from 2000 to 2005. This is estimated to be associated with an increase of $14 per barrel in real oil prices, which would be equivalent to an increase of almost 25 per cent on the average price of a barrel of Brent crude oil in 2005. Adams and Ichino (1995) estimate that a sustained rise of 0.5 pp in the annual rate of growth of world GDP is associated with increases of almost 12 and 10 per cent in real oil and metals prices respectively, after six years.

The scenario analysis of the impact of reduced levels of activity in the non-OECD economies does not consider short-term cyclical influences on prices, with world and non-OECD output gaps being left unchanged. However, if slower growth originated at least in part from the demand side, it could be argued that they should also weaken.[19] In order to evaluate the sensitivity of commodity prices to cyclical changes in output gaps, a second set of scenarios were constructed in which the output gap was changed for a short period of time. Two alternative paths were considered, a 2 percentage-point reduction in output lasting for one year and a 1 percentage-point reduction in demand relative to potential lasting for two years. Both changes would imply relatively large movements in the world output gap compared with those seen over the estimation period.

The results of this exercise, again holding world export prices and all other factors constant, also illustrate the different sensitivities of each real commodity price to cyclical influences (Figure 6.9). The largest and most persistent effect is on real oil prices, with prices reduced by up to 20–25 per cent in the two scenarios, and returning back to their baseline levels only after five years. The real prices of agricultural raw materials and metals initially fall by up to 8 and 10 per cent, respectively, before rising and returning above the baseline level after two years, which is consistent with what might be expected in these markets as supply responds to the initial demand-driven reduction in prices. The real prices of food and tropical beverages initially decline by between 5 and 10 per cent in the first year in which the output gaps are reduced, before rising above previous levels in the second year.

Overall, it is clear that the recent period of strong output and trade growth in the non-OECD economies and, by extension, the increasing internationalisation of production and offshoring from the OECD to the non-OECD economies, has placed significant upward pressure on the prices of many commodities. This is especially so for oil. The impact varies across commodities and has also built up over time. However, it is equally clear that growth in the non-OECD is not the only factor behind the recent acceleration in commodity prices after 2002.

---

[19] To this extent, the results reported above may suggest a slight underestimation of the effects on real commodity prices.

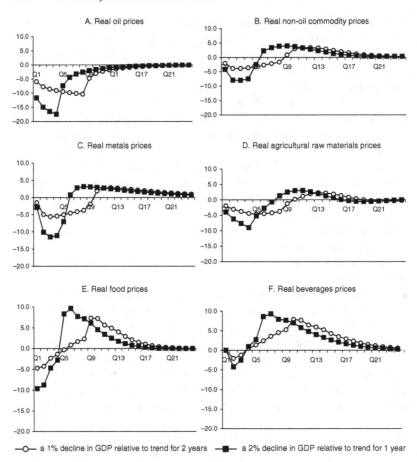

— ○ — a 1% decline in GDP relative to trend for 2 years   — ■ — a 2% decline in GDP relative to trend for 1 year

Figure 6.9 Real commodity prices – per cent effect of a temporary increase in output gaps

6.5   The impact of globalisation on consumer price inflation

This section provides an overview of the main findings from existing studies and then presents new empirical estimates of the wider impact of globalisation on consumer price inflation in OECD economies. The new evidence includes tests of whether inflation dynamics changed in the mid 1990s when the extent of globalisation began to increase. Given that the determinants of domestic inflation processes are found to have changed around that time, the following section then explores the size of the impact of globalisation by conducting a scenario analysis, which explicitly distinguishes between the impact via non-commodity and commodity import prices.

6.5.1   Existing studies of globalisation and inflation

Although there is a sizeable literature on the determinants of inflation in OECD countries (Melick and Galati, 2006), only a few papers assess the impact of globalisation on inflation directly. Other studies find evidence of structural changes in the inflation process that may possibly be related to aspects of globalisation, but this is not tested explicitly.

Several general conclusions emerge from this literature. First, imports from low-cost countries contribute to lower domestic inflation via both a direct accounting effect and also an indirect effect, whereby lower-cost imports put pressure on domestic producers in import-competing industries to lower their prices. The size of this indirect effect appears to be positively related to the intensity of foreign competition. Second, increased trade integration appears to have changed the intensity of the response of inflation to cyclical output fluctuations in OECD economies. With the prices of many domestic goods being determined increasingly by global demand and supply conditions, domestic inflation has become less sensitive to measures of domestic economic slack and more sensitive to measures of foreign economic slack. Third, global competition is generally found to have reduced the extent to which exporting firms are passing through exchange-rate changes into domestic currency prices. Finally, inflation persistence seems to have declined in many countries over the past decades, helped by greater central bank credibility. A more detailed overview of several recent studies is given below.

The existing literature also suggests that the results of these studies vary across countries and are sensitive to the sample period that is used. The general conclusions drawn in the previous paragraph do not necessarily apply to all OECD countries. In particular, the evidence of changes in inflation persistence and the relative influence of domestic and foreign economic conditions on inflation is sensitive to the countries included in the estimation sample.[20] For these reasons, the empirical work below allows for the possibility of different coefficients across countries, rather than simply imposing common coefficients on all.

[20] See, for instance, the different findings for each of six OECD economies in Debelle and Wilkinson (2002).

Trade openness and inflation

Several studies have examined the relationship between trade openness and the level of inflation, both for the economy as a whole and for particular manufacturing industries. One approach has been to directly estimate the 'mechanical' impact of imported goods from lower-cost economies on inflation in the importing economies (Kamin *et al.*, 2006; OECD, 2006). They typically find that lower-cost imports place a modest, *ex ante* downward impact on consumer price inflation, with a more marked impact on import price inflation. These effects are found to vary over time and across countries. More generally, the impact of enhanced trade openness on consumer price inflation has also been found to be sensitive to the countries included in the estimation sample. Typically, smaller estimates are found for developed economies than for developing ones (Temple, 2002; Wu and Lin, 2006).

The impact of globalisation on inflation is explored in IMF (2006a), using a Phillips-curve framework in which current inflation is related to lagged inflation, import price inflation, the change in the oil price and the output gap. To account for the impact of globalisation, interaction terms are introduced, with past inflation being interacted with a measure of monetary credibility, import price inflation being interacted with import penetration, and the output gap being interacted with openness, monetary credibility, average inflation and a wage bargaining index. The model is estimated for a panel of eight countries (the G7 countries and Australia) over the period 1960 to 2004. The sensitivity of inflation to the domestic output gap is found to have fallen over the sample period.[21] The key factor behind this decline is found to be trade openness. In general, import prices are found to have only a small influence on domestic inflation. Although a fall in import prices drives down consumer price inflation initially, the effect vanishes after about two years.

A number of studies have shown that industry-level price inflation is significantly related to measures of import competition (Gamber and Hung, 2001; Chen *et al.*, 2004; IMF, 2006a). Gamber and Hung (2001) relate price inflation in forty-four industries in the United States to import price inflation and an interaction term between import price inflation and industry-level import penetration, which is a measure of the intensity of foreign competition. Both terms are found to have statistically significant coefficients, suggesting that the impact of import prices on domestic prices is positively related to the intensity of foreign competition. In a related study, using data for a sample of manufacturing

---

[21] For 2004, the estimation results imply an inflation-output elasticity of 0.2 compared with a value of 0.3 for 1960 and 1983.

industries in seven European Union member states, Chen *et al.* (2004) estimate that the observed increase in openness over the sample period reduced industry mark-ups by 1.6 pp on average.[22] Although the impact of the mark-up and productivity effects at the sectoral level is marked, reducing inflation by 0.3 pp per annum on average in the industries concerned, the impact is minimal at the economy-wide level.

The determinants of changes in producer prices for sixteen manufacturing industries in eleven OECD countries are also explored in IMF (2006a). It is found that changes in relative producer prices in a certain sector (measured by the deviation of producer prices in that sector from average producer prices across all sectors) are negatively related to changes in that sector's exposure to globalisation as measured by its import-to-production ratio. On average, a 1 percentage-point increase in the import-to-production ratio is estimated to reduce relative producer prices by 0.1 per cent.[23] The contribution of increased openness to lower inflation appears to be twice as strong in low-tech sectors as in high-tech sectors. Moreover, the impact has increased over time; about 40 per cent of the decline in relative prices of the manufacturing sector since 1995 is explained by openness, compared with only 25 per cent during the 1980s and early 1990s.

The influence of foreign capacity on domestic inflation

A number of studies have sought to test directly whether measures of foreign output gaps or capacity utilisation have a direct impact on domestic inflation. The findings from such studies have been mixed. For the United States, some have found little evidence that foreign capacity utilisation has a significant impact on domestic inflation (Corrado and Mattey, 1997; Tootell, 1998), but others have come to the opposite conclusion (Gamber and Hung, 2001). More recent multi-country studies also yielded mixed results. For example, while the studies by Borio and Filardo (2006) and Vega and Winkelried (2004) suggest that measures of foreign economic slack play an important role in explaining inflation dynamics in OECD countries, Ihrig *et al.* (2007) find insignificant or incorrectly signed coefficients on foreign output gaps in Phillips-curve equations for a set of eleven industrial countries.

Borio and Filardo (2007) test whether the gap between headline and core inflation is related to measures of the global output gap. Using a

---

[22] Openness is also found to be associated with an increase in productivity of 11 per cent, consistent with the hypothesis that the least productive domestic firms are forced to exit from the market as a result of additional import competition.

[23] In addition to this direct effect, the study detects a small indirect effect of globalisation on producer prices that works through increased productivity growth.

sample of sixteen OECD economies it is found that the global output gap is significant, with its inclusion reducing the significance of the domestic output gap.[24] Moreover, a rolling regression exercise suggests that the importance of global measures of economic slack has risen over time.[25] To some extent these findings are not surprising. The gap between headline and underlying inflation includes energy and food prices, where global conditions on commodity prices have an important influence on domestic pricing. As discussed above, estimates of the global output gap have a significant positive relationship with commodity price inflation.

A related approach to the possible link between global economic conditions and national inflation rates is pursued by Ciccarelli and Mojon (2005). This study uses a dynamic factor approach to obtain a measure of global inflation from the national inflation rates of twenty-two economies. This measure is then found to be an attractor of national inflation rates, suggesting that national inflation rates are indeed sensitive to economic conditions in other countries. This leaves open the issue of what is driving global inflation.[26]

A possible corollary to the finding that inflation has become more sensitive to global conditions over time is that it may have become less sensitive to domestic conditions. The latter appears to be a common finding from many empirical studies for individual OECD economies (Melick and Galati, 2006), although it is not a universal one. For the United States, Dexter *et al.* (2005) demonstrate that the breakdown in the relationship between domestic capacity utilisation and domestic inflation found in other empirical studies disappears once controls are included for the effects of international trade. Ihrig *et al.* (2007) find evidence of a decline in the sensitivity of inflation to movements in the domestic output gap, but do not find significant evidence that this is due to globalisation.

Changes in exchange-rate pass-through to domestic prices
A number of recent studies have sought to test the proposition by Taylor (2000) that global competition should reduce the extent to

---

[24] This result is robust to the inclusion of three control variables (import prices, oil prices and domestic unit labour costs).
[25] The rolling regression results use pooled estimates across countries. As noted by Borio and Filardo (2006), the pre-conditions for obtaining unbiased parameters are not fulfilled in the data set used and these results should therefore be interpreted with care.
[26] There are some preliminary results in the paper which suggest that the constructed measure of global inflation is significantly correlated with measures of global real and monetary conditions.

which exporting firms are able to pass through exchange-rate movements into the domestic currency prices charged to importers. This
has been found to have considerable empirical support (see, for
example, Olivei, 2002, Gagnon and Ihrig, 2004 and Marazzi *et al.*,
2005). The third study estimates that exchange-rate pass-through to
United States import prices has declined from above one-half during
the 1980s to around one-fifth during the last decade. This decline
is found to be due to both a shift of imports away from commodities to manufacturing goods which tend to have lower pass-through
rates (Campa and Goldberg, 2003; Pain *et al.*, 2005) and to a general
decline in the exchange-rate pass-through across all product categories (Olivei, 2002). Gust *et al.* (2006) demonstrate in a dynamic general equilibrium model that this observed decline in the exchange-rate
pass-through stems mainly from the increasing trade integration of
the United States. For Japan, a decline in exchange-rate pass-through
is found to be spread across products, rather than being due to a shift
in the composition of imports (Otani *et al.*, 2003). For the euro area,
Campa *et al.* (2005) find that a structural break in the exchange-rate
pass-through into import prices is evident only in a small number of
manufacturing industries. Overall, these results provide indirect evidence that the competitive impact of enhanced openness may matter
and that it might vary across economies.

Changes in inflation persistence
An important issue for monetary policy is whether past inflation has
a significant role in determining present inflation (i.e. whether inflation is persistent) or whether expectations of future inflation are more
important.[27] A higher degree of inflation persistence implies that stabilising inflation following economic 'shocks' may require higher temporary costs to output. This has led to a series of studies testing whether
the persistence of domestic inflation has changed over time. Again, the
findings differ by country, by period considered and by the estimation
technique used (Melick and Galati, 2006).[28]

---

[27] It is possible that future expectations are based, at least in part, on past inflation.
[28] For example, Rudd and Whelan (2005) and O'Reilly and Whelan (2005) find little evidence that inflation persistence in the United States and in the euro area has
changed over time, whereas Cogley and Sargent (2001), Clark (2003), Levin and
Piger (2004) and Altissimo *et al.* (2006) all suggest that inflation persistence is markedly lower in recent years. Debelle and Wilkinson (2002) find that inflation persistence has declined in Australia and New Zealand, but has risen in the United Kingdom
and the United States. Cecchetti and Debelle (2006) report only weak evidence of a
decline in inflation persistence in recent years, even after allowing for a break in the
mean of inflation.

Altissimo *et al.* (2006) find that inflation persistence in the euro area has declined substantially since the 1970s once changes in the mean of inflation are allowed for and that the breaks in the mean coincide with shifts in the monetary policy regime. The link between changes in inflation persistence and changes in monetary credibility is confirmed by IMF (2006a) for a set of eight OECD countries. According to these estimates, strengthened monetary credibility reduced inflation persistence (as measured by the coefficient on lagged inflation) from 0.7 in the early 1980 to 0.6 in 2004.

6.5.2   *Testing for the impact of globalisation*

The empirical analysis in the present study differs from the above studies in several respects. First, the above studies examine the relationship between globalisation and inflation within an extended Phillips-curve framework. Such a framework does not allow for a potential effect of measures of globalisation on price levels. The present study attempts to overcome this by estimating an error-correction model for consumer prices, relating prices to import prices, unit labour costs and the domestic output gap.[29] It thus accounts explicitly for a possible price-level effect from globalisation, as reflected in the level of import prices. Second, the present study takes a broader view than many others by examining a range of possible effects from globalisation for a large set of OECD countries. Finally, the econometric analysis is complemented by a scenario analysis which quantifies some of the possible impacts of globalisation on domestic inflation, with import price inflation split into commodity and non-commodity components. This provides a richer analysis of underlying inflation dynamics than previous studies.

The empirical work examines the impact of globalisation as reflected in the price of imported goods and services. This is done using an error-correction model for the private consumption deflator in twenty-one OECD economies over the period 1980–2005,[30] with consumer prices

---

[29] In this respect, the present study is very similar to that of Ihrig and Marquez (2004), who use an error-correction model to examine the contribution of productivity advancements and labour market slack to low inflation in OECD countries. However, in contrast to the present study, Ihrig and Marquez (2004) look entirely on domestic factors as drivers of the decline in inflation and do not address the extent to which globalisation lies behind the decline.

[30] The countries included in the analysis are: Australia, Austria, Belgium, Canada, Denmark, Finland, France, Germany, Greece, Ireland, Italy, Japan, Korea, the Netherlands, Norway, Portugal, Spain, Sweden, Switzerland, the United Kingdom and the United States. All data are taken from the OECD Economic Outlook database if not otherwise specified.

being related to import prices, unit labour costs and the domestic output gap:

$$\Delta lnP_{i,t} = (\alpha_{0i} + \varphi_{0i}D) + (\alpha_{1i} + \varphi_{1i}D)(lnP_{i,t-1} - (\alpha_{2i} + \varphi_{2i}D)M_{i,t-1}^{SH} lnP_{i,t-1}^{M}$$

$$- (1 - (\alpha_{2t} + \varphi_{2i}D)M_{i,t-1}^{SH})lnC_{i,t-1}) + \sum_{j=1}^{4}(\beta_{ji} + \phi_{ji}D)\Delta lnP_{i,t-1}$$

$$+ \sum_{j=0}^{4}(\gamma_{ji} + \lambda_{ji}D)\Delta lnP_{i,t-j}^{M} + \sum_{j=0}^{4}(\delta_{ji} + \kappa_{ji}D)\Delta lnC_{i,t-j}$$

$$+ (\alpha_{3i} + \varphi_{3i}D)GAP_{i,t-1} + \varepsilon_{it}$$

The subscript i denotes the country and the subscript t the time period. The variables are defined as follows: P represents domestic prices measured by the private consumption expenditure deflator,[31] P^M represents import prices measured by the deflator of imports of goods and services, C represents domestic costs, proxied by unit labour costs of the total economy, GAP is the domestic output gap, and ε is an error term. The equations also include seasonal dummies as well as time dummies to account for changes in indirect taxes and similar events. Static homogeneity is imposed on all equations so that the mark-up of prices over costs is independent of the price level. Dynamic homogeneity is not directly imposed on the system. A test of this restriction is carried out after estimating the system and found to be strongly rejected by the data.

Initial parameter stability tests revealed evidence of a significant structural break in the parameters in the consumer price equations in the mid 1990s. To overcome this, two modifications were found to be necessary. The first was to interact the long-run import price coefficient with the share of imports in domestic demand, denoted M^{SH} in [1].[32] This implies that the long-run coefficient on import prices rises over time in most countries in the sample, in line with increases in import penetration, with an equivalent decline in the long-run coefficient on domestic unit labour costs. But even with this modification, there continued to be evidence of parameter instability in the mid 1990s. The

---

[31] The private consumption deflator provides a broader measure of inflation than many national consumer or retail price series, and is in principle more directly comparable across countries because it comes from the system of national accounts.

[32] A similar approach has been adopted in a number of related studies (see, for instance, Gamber and Hung, 2001 and IMF, 2006a). The import content of consumption is calculated as $M_{i,t}^{SH} = (M_{i,t} - \eta_i X_{i,t})/(M_{i,t} + Y_{i,t} - X_{i,t})$, where M denotes total imports, X denotes total exports, Y denotes domestic output and η is the share of imports used in the production of export goods. Estimates of η_i are taken from Pain et al. (2005, Table 7).

second modification was thus to allow for separate parameter estimates before and after 1995 by introducing a dummy variable D that is equal to unity from 1995 onwards. This overcomes the parameter instability when there is only a single set of parameters for the whole estimation period.[33]

The set of equations is estimated jointly using the seemingly unrelated regression procedure (SUR), first proposed by Zellner (1962). Cross-country restrictions are imposed as the data permit.[34] In the empirical model the long-run coefficient on the import price term will reflect not only the direct weight of imports in private consumption, but also the wider influence of import competition on the prices set by actual and potential competitors.[35] The unit labour costs term will reflect indirect effects from globalisation via wages and productivity.[36]

6.5.3   Summary of empirical results

The empirical analysis highlights a number of important ways in which the behaviour of consumer prices appears to have changed over the past decade. Of these, the most notable is the extent to which import prices have become a more important determinant of consumer prices over time in all OECD countries, implying that foreign economic conditions have become a more important influence on domestic inflation. At the same time, domestic inflation is found to have become less sensitive to temporary changes in the domestic output gap. Other notable changes include evidence that inflation persistence has declined in most OECD countries and that the speed of adjustment towards the 'desired' price level has slowed over the past decade.

During the first part of the sample period, from 1980 to 1994, the data support the formation of two country groups for the interaction

---

[33] For simplicity, only the results of the final specification are summarised in the main part of the paper.

[34] Imposing a single set of parameters common to all countries, as in other studies (IMF 2006a Borio and Filardo, 2007), was strongly rejected by the data.

[35] For further analysis of the wider impacts of low-cost countries on euro area inflation see Chapter 7.

[36] Specification [1] has two important implications for the behaviour of the mark-up over marginal costs. First, the mark-up behaves pro-cyclically, increasing during an economic upturn and falling during an economic downturn. This proposition is in line with the empirical evidence provided by Haskel et al. (1995) and Ghosal (2000). Second, the reaction of the mark-up to changes in the import content of consumption depends on the ratio between import prices and unit labour costs: $\partial ln(P_i/C_i)/\partial M_i^{SH} = \alpha_{2i} ln (P_{i,t}^M/C_{i,t})$. If import prices are initially higher (lower) than unit labour costs, the mark-up increases (decreases) with a rise in the import content of consumption.

term between import prices and import penetration. The long-run coefficients on the two interaction terms are very different, having values of 2.1 and 0.4 respectively (Table 6.1).[37] In the second part of the sample period, from 1995–2005, the long-run coefficient on the interaction term is found to rise to a common value of 2.6 for both groups of countries (Table 6.2).[38] This suggests that during the more recent period domestic producers have increasingly taken greater account of foreign competitors when setting their prices, so that import prices have a larger influence on domestic prices than their share in domestic demand would suggest.[39] The results also imply that the sensitivity of consumer prices to import prices will differ considerably across countries, reflecting differences in import penetration.[40]

The domestic output gap is found to have a significant impact on consumer price inflation in all of the countries in the sample, with the size of the initial impact being smaller in the more recent period. On average across countries, a rise in the domestic output gap by 2 pp for four consecutive quarters raises inflation in the following two years by 0.1 pp per annum less in the second part of the sample (1995–2005) than in the first part (1980–1994). This is similar to, but slightly smaller than, the finding reported in IMF (2006a).

The model employed in the analysis automatically incorporates an indirect effect from foreign economic conditions, as mediated through

---

[37] A coefficient of unity would indicate that the weight on import prices was exactly as might be expected given the share of imports in domestic demand.

[38] For the G7 economies, the size of the coefficient on the interaction term implies that domestic costs have a bigger influence on domestic consumer prices than do import prices. Not surprisingly, for most of the smaller economies in the sample domestic costs have a smaller weight than import prices, implying that domestic prices in these countries are to a large extent driven by world market prices in the long run. The size of the coefficient also implies that the direct (long-run) impact of a change in world oil prices is very similar to the present shares of energy in total private consumption expenditure in OECD economies.

[39] This interpretation rests on the assumption that import prices are weakly exogenous to the system. Testing for weak exogeneity of import prices is not feasible in the current setting as it would require including a full set of import price equations in the system being estimated. If import prices were not exogenous, the rise in the coefficient could also reflect an increase in pricing to market by importers. However, it is possible to establish that the current change term in import prices is exogenous to the system, as shown by a Wu-Hausman test (the respective p-value is 0.11). The test entails regressing the current change in import prices on a set of explanatory variables that are clearly exogenous to the system and then testing whether the residuals from this regression have any explanatory power in addition to the variables already included in the system.

[40] Earlier attempts at imposing a common long-run coefficient on import prices in each country were rejected by the data, confirming that there are significant differences across countries in the influence of import prices.

Table 6.1 *Regression results 1980–1994*

	α_0	α_1	α_2	β_1	β_2	β_3	β_4	γ_0
AUS	-0.031 [0.216]	-0.047 [0.000]	2.07 [0.000]		0.084 [0.000]	0.263 [0.000]		0.061 [0.000]
AUT	0.016 [0.657]	-0.022 [0.000]	0.378 [0.007]	0.118 [0.000]	0.269 [0.000]	0.263 [0.000]		0.020 [0.000]
BEL	0.091 [0.000]	-0.022 [0.000]	2.074 [0.000]	0.858 [0.000]	-0.426 [0.000]	0.099 [0.000]		0.182 [0.000]
CAN	0.039 [0.017]	-0.059 [0.000]	2.074 [0.000]	0.118 [0.000]				0.020 [0.000]
DNK	0.029 [0.172]	-0.059 [0.000]	0.378 [0.007]	0.118 [0.000]	0.084 [0.000]		0.303 [0.000]	0.182 [0.000]
FIN	0.039 [0.176]	-0.047 [0.000]	2.074 [0.000]	-0.172 [0.000]	0.084 [0.000]	0.099 [0.000]		0.020 [0.000]
FRA	0.025 [0.02]	-0.059 [0.000]	0.378 [0.000]	0.480 [0.000]		0.099 [0.000]		0.084 [0.000]
DEU	0.079 [0.052]	-0.022 [0.000]	0.378 [0.007]	0.118 [0.000]	0.269 [0.000]			0.104 [0.000]
GRC	0.552 [0.000]	-0.047 [0.000]	0.378 [0.007]		0.084 [0.000]		0.408 [0.000]	0.020 [0.000]
IRL	-0.008 [0.871]	-0.022 [0.000]	2.074 [0.000]	0.118 [0.000]	0.084 [0.000]		0.212 [0.000]	0.084 [0.000]
ITA	0.047 [0.014]	-0.059 [0.000]	2.074 [0.000]	0.232 [0.000]		0.099 [0.000]		0.061 [0.000]
JPN	0.049 [0.159]	-0.022 [0.000]	0.378 [0.007]		0.084 [0.000]	0.099 [0.000]	0.212 [0.000]	0.020 [0.000]
KOR	0.038 [0.402]	-0.047 [0.000]	0.378 [0.007]	-0.172 [0.000]		0.099 [0.000]	0.303 [0.000]	0.061 [0.000]
NLD	0.057 [0.362]	-0.022 [0.000]	0.378 [0.007]	-0.213 [0.000]	0.084 [0.000]		0.212 [0.000]	0.084 [0.000]
NOR	0.037 [0.356]	-0.059 [0.000]	2.074 [0.000]		-0.426 [0.000]	0.099 [0.000]		0.020 [0.000]
PRT	0.081 [0.000]	-0.047 [0.000]	2.074 [0.000]	0.480 [0.000]	0.084 [0.000]			0.104 [0.000]
ESP	0.103 [0.013]	-0.047 [0.000]	2.074 [0.000]	-0.172 [0.000]	0.269 [0.000]	0.099 [0.000]		
SWE	0.074 [0.331]	-0.022 [0.000]	2.074 [0.000]	0.118 [0.000]		0.099 [0.000]	0.212 [0.000]	0.104 [0.000]
CHE	0.033 [0.315]	-0.022 [0.000]	2.074 [0.000]	0.480 [0.000]	0.084 [0.000]			0.061 [0.000]
GBR	0.013 [0.795]	-0.022 [0.000]	2.074 [0.000]			0.099 [0.000]	0.303 [0.000]	0.020 [0.000]
USA	0.095 [0.001]	-0.022 [0.000]	2.074 [0.000]	0.118 [0.000]		0.099 [0.000]	0.212 [0.000]	0.104 [0.000]

Note: The numbers in parenthesis are the *p*-values of exclusion restrictions on the coefficients.

γ_1	γ_2	γ_3	γ_4	δ_0	δ_1	δ_2	δ_3	δ_4	α_3
0.012	-0.022			0.059		0.033			0.00068
[0.011]	[0.009]			[0.000]		[0.000]			[0.000]
0.116		0.060	-0.105	0.016	0.027		0.020		0.00031
[0.000]		[0.000]	[0.000]	[0.103]	[0.019]		[0.043]		[0.001]
-0.141	0.060	-0.046	0.022	0.193	-0.130		0.020		0.00012
[0.000]	[0.023]	[0.012]	[0.000]	[0.000]	[0.000]		[0.043]		[0.000]
0.039				0.193		0.077	0.020	0.032	0.00025
[0.000]				[0.000]		[0.000]	[0.043]	[0.025]	[0.000]
				0.016	0.072				0.00025
				[0.103]	[0.000]				[0.000]
0.039		0.021	0.022	0.016	0.027	0.077		0.032	0.00026
[0.000]		[0.016]	[0.000]	[0.103]	[0.019]	[0.000]		[0.025]	[0.000]
-0.033	0.028			0.016	0.072				0.00025
[0.000]	[0.000]			[0.103]	[0.000]				[0.000]
-0.033		0.060		0.104		0.033	0.020		0.00012
[0.000]		[0.000]		[0.000]		[0.000]	[0.043]		[0.000]
	0.028		0.022			0.033	0.020	0.032	0.00068
	[0.000]		[0.000]			[0.000]	[0.043]	[0.025]	[0.000]
	0.060	-0.046	0.111	0.059		0.033			0.00051
	[0.023]	[0.012]	[0.000]	[0.000]		[0.000]			[0.000]
0.012				0.016	0.027	0.033			0.00033
[0.011]				[0.103]	[0.019]	[0.000]			[0.001]
0.012				0.104	0.027				0.00012
[0.011]				[0.000]	[0.019]				[0.001]
0.039						0.033		0.032	0.00026
[0.000]						[0.000]		[0.025]	[0.000]
0.037	0.028	0.021	0.022	0.193	0.072	0.077	0.020		0.00031
[0.001]	[0.000]	[0.016]	[0.000]	[0.000]	[0.000]	[0.000]	[0.043]		[0.000]
0.037				0.016		0.077		0.235	0.00025
[0.001]				[0.103]		[0.000]		[0.000]	[0.000]
-0.033			0.022	0.104	-0.130		0.020	0.032	0.00020
[0.000]			[0.000]	[0.000]	[0.000]		[0.043]	[0.025]	[0.000]
0.037	0.028	0.021		0.016	0.180	0.033	0.020	0.032	0.00020
[0.001]	[0.000]	[0.016]		[0.103]	[0.001]	[0.000]	[0.043]	[0.025]	[0.000]
			0.022	0.059	0.072	0.033	0.020		0.00009
			[0.000]	[0.000]	[0.000]	[0.000]	[0.043]		[0.000]
				0.059	0.027	0.033			0.00012
				[0.000]	[0.019]	[0.000]			[0.001]
0.039	0.028		0.022	0.193	0.072	0.077	-0.145	0.032	0.00009
[0.000]	[0.000]		[0.000]	[0.000]	[0.000]	[0.000]	[0.000]	[0.025]	[0.000]
				0.016			0.020		0.00012
				[0.103]			[0.043]		[0.001]

Table 6.2 *Regression results 1995–2005*

	α_0	α_1	α_2	β_1	β_2	β_3	β_4	γ_0	γ_1
AUS	0.047	-0.020	2.608		0.084	0.263		0.061	0.012
	[0.000]	[0.000]	[0.000]		[0.000]	[0.000]		[0.000]	[0.011]
AUT	0.096	-0.020	2.608	0.118		0.263		0.020	0.116
	[0.012]	[0.000]	[0.000]	[0.000]		[0.000]		[0.000]	[0.000]
BEL	0.029	-0.020	2.608	0.363	-0.257	0.099		0.182	-0.141
	[0.465]	[0.000]	[0.000]	[0.000]	[0.000]	[0.000]		[0.000]	[0.000]
CAN	0.094	-0.020	2.608	0.118				0.020	
	[0.060]	[0.000]	[0.000]	[0.000]				[0.000]	
DNK	0.224	-0.020	2.608	0.118	0.084			0.182	
	[0.002]	[0.000]	[0.000]	[0.000]	[0.000]			[0.000]	
FIN	0.069	-0.020	2.608		0.084	0.099		0.020	
	[0.291]	[0.000]	[0.000]		[0.000]	[0.000]		[0.000]	
FRA	0.062	-0.020	2.608	0.314		0.099		0.084	-0.033
	[0.058]	[0.000]	[0.000]	[0.000]		[0.000]		[0.000]	[0.000]
DEU	0.162	-0.020	2.608	0.188				0.104	-0.033
	[0.001]	[0.000]	[0.000]	[0.000]				[0.000]	[0.000]
GRC	0.102	-0.020	2.608		0.084		0.635	0.020	
	[0.267]	[0.000]	[0.000]		[0.000]		[0.000]	[0.000]	
IRL	-0.079	-0.020	2.608	0.118	0.084		0.212	0.084	
	[0.134]	[0.000]	[0.000]	[0.000]	[0.000]		[0.000]	[0.000]	
ITA	0.107	-0.020	2.608	0.483		0.099		0.061	0.012
	[0.742]	[0.000]	[0.000]	[0.000]		[0.000]		[0.000]	[0.011]
JPN	-0.064	-0.020	2.608		0.084	0.099	0.212	0.020	0.012
	[0.121]	[0.000]	[0.000]		[0.000]	[0.000]	[0.000]	[0.000]	[0.011]
KOR	0.437	-0.020	2.608			0.099		0.061	
	[0.001]	[0.000]	[0.000]			[0.000]		[0.000]	
NLD	0.200	-0.020	2.608	-0.213	0.084		0.212	0.084	0.037
	[0.012]	[0.000]	[0.000]	[0.000]	[0.000]		[0.000]	[0.000]	[0.001]
NOR	0.075	-0.020	2.608		-0.257	0.099		0.020	0.037
	[0.480]	[0.000]	[0.000]		[0.000]	[0.000]		[0.000]	[0.001]
PRT	0.211	-0.020	2.608	0.314	0.084			0.104	-0.033
	[0.001]	[0.000]	[0.000]	[0.000]	[0.000]			[0.000]	[0.000]
ESP	0.191	-0.020	2.608			0.099			0.037
	[0.030]	[0.000]	[0.000]			[0.000]			[0.001]
SWE	-0.055	-0.020	2.608	0.118		0.099	0.212	0.104	
	[0.532]	[0.000]	[0.000]	[0.000]		[0.000]	[0.000]	[0.000]	
CHE	0.065	-0.020	2.608	0.314	0.084			0.061	
	[0.082]	[0.000]	[0.000]	[0.000]	[0.000]			[0.000]	
GBR	0.072	-0.020	2.608			0.099		0.020	
	[0.178]	[0.000]	[0.000]			[0.000]		[0.000]	
USA	0.147	-0.020	2.608	0.118		0.099	0.212	0.104	
	[0.000]	[0.000]	[0.000]	[0.000]		[0.000]	[0.000]	[0.000]	

Note: The numbers in parenthesis are the *p*-values of exclusion restrictions on the coefficients.

γ_2	γ_3	γ_4	δ_0	δ_1	δ_2	δ_3	δ_4	α_3
-0.022			0.059		0.033			0.00029
[0.009]			[0.000]		[0.000]			[0.000]
	0.060	-0.105	0.016	0.027				0.00029
	[0.000]	[0.000]	[0.103]	[0.019]				[0.000]
0.131	-0.046	0.022	0.193	-0.130				0.00011
[0.000]	[0.012]	[0.000]	[0.000]	[0.000]				[0.002]
			0.193		0.077		0.116	0.00008
			[0.000]		[0.000]		[0.000]	[0.001]
			0.016	0.072				0.00008
			[0.103]	[0.000]				[0.001]
	0.021	0.022	0.016	0.027	0.077		0.116	0.00011
	[0.000]	[0.000]	[0.103]	[0.019]	[0.000]		[0.000]	[0.002]
0.028			0.016	0.072				0.00008
[0.000]			[0.103]	[0.000]				[0.001]
	0.060		0.104		0.033			0.00011
	[0.000]		[0.000]		[0.000]			[0.001]
0.028		0.022			0.033		0.116	0.00029
[0.000]		[0.000]			[0.000]		[0.000]	[0.000]
0.131	-0.046	0.111	0.059		0.033			0.00048
[0.000]	[0.000]	[0.000]	[0.000]		[0.000]			[0.000]
			0.016	0.027	0.033			0.00011
			[0.103]	[0.019]	[0.000]			[0.002]
			0.104	0.027				0.00011
			[0.000]	[0.000]				[0.002]
					0.033		0.116	0.00011
					[0.000]		[0.000]	[0.002]
0.028	0.021	0.022	0.193	0.072	0.077			0.00029
[0.000]	[0.016]	[0.000]	[0.000]	[0.000]	[0.000]			[0.000]
			0.016		0.077		0.235	0.00008
			[0.103]		[0.000]		[0.000]	[0.001]
		0.022	0.104	-0.130			0.116	0.00008
		[0.000]	[0.000]	[0.000]			[0.000]	[0.001]
0.028	0.021		0.016	0.180	0.033		0.116	0.00008
[0.000]	[0.000]		[0.103]	[0.001]	[0.000]		[0.000]	[0.001]
		0.022	0.059	0.072	0.033			0.00008
		[0.000]	[0.000]	[0.000]	[0.000]			[0.001]
			0.059	0.027	0.033			0.00011
			[0.000]	[0.019]	[0.000]			[0.002]
0.028		0.022	0.193	0,072	0.077	-0.145	0.116	0.00008
[0.000]		[0.000]	[0.000]	[0.000]	[0.000]	[0.000]	[0.000]	[0.001]
			0.016					0.00011
			[0.103]					[0.002]

import prices.[41] Augmenting the model with an additional world output gap variable and testing the joint significance of the coefficients on this term for all countries suggests that the world output gap does not have a significant additional direct influence on domestic inflation in either of the two sub-periods. Hence the indirect effect through import prices seems to be the only channel through which foreign economic conditions affect consumer price inflation. [42,43] This implies that the importance of foreign economic conditions for domestic inflation will vary across countries, reflecting the different forces that influence international trade prices for each country (Pain *et al.*, 2005), as well as differences in import penetration. The coefficients on the domestic output gap are not affected by the inclusion of the foreign output gap; they remain significant with magnitudes that are close to the base specification.

There is also no strong evidence that the short-run reaction of domestic producers to import price changes varies with the type of import goods. When augmenting the equation with current and lagged changes of commodity import prices, these additional terms were found to be significant for only a small number of countries,[44] suggesting that, in general, changes in commodity import prices have the same impact on consumer price inflation as do changes in non-commodity import prices.

The empirical results also indicate that the inflation process has become less persistent in the majority of the countries over the past decade, although in a small number of countries (Finland, Greece, Ireland and Italy) past inflation appears to have become a more important determinant of current inflation.[45] Given that the model employed in the analysis is equivalent to one in which current inflation is related

---

[41] Import prices of OECD economies depend on world export prices which, in turn, reflect capacity constraints and other cyclical conditions in the exporting economy (Pain *et al.*, 2005).

[42] The coefficient on the world output gap is allowed to differ across countries in both sub-periods.

[43] This finding differs from Borio and Filardo (2007) who demonstrate that measures of global economic slack have a significant influence on the inflation process even after controlling for the indirect impact via import prices. However, the results of the two studies are not directly comparable as Borio and Filardo (2007) use the gap between headline and core inflation as the dependent variable. In contrast, Ihrig *et al.* (2007) also find insignificant or wrongly signed coefficients on the foreign output gap term in Phillips-curve equations.

[44] These are Canada and Germany in the first half of the sample and Canada, France and Ireland in the second half.

[45] These mixed results are consistent with previous research, demonstrating that inflation persistence has risen in some countries but declined in others (Melick and Galati, 2006).

to past inflation and a fixed level of inflation expectations,[46] the change in inflation persistence might be related to a change in the relationship between inflation and inflation expectations.[47]

The error correction coefficients, though small in magnitude, are all highly significant in both sub-samples.[48] For the majority of the countries, the error-correction coefficients become smaller in the second part of the sample period, implying that the speed of adjustment towards the 'desired' price level has slowed. A possible explanation is the more direct focus of monetary policy on inflation objectives over the past decade, with the associated possibility of some degree of price-level drift (Svensson, 1999).

6.6   Quantifying the overall impact of globalisation

On the basis of the preceding results a series of scenario analyses was carried out to obtain illustrative estimates of the possible direct impact of globalisation on consumer price inflation over the past ten years. These incorporate the main findings from the scenario analyses for commodity prices and the estimated 'mechanical' impact on import prices as a result of the higher shares of trade with lower-cost producers discussed in the previous sections. Two alternative starting points for these scenarios are considered, the first quarter of 1995 and the first quarter of 2000.

A baseline scenario was obtained by forecasting consumer price inflation employing the coefficient estimates obtained for the period 1995–2005 and actual values of all exogenous variables. The forecast is dynamic in the sense that projected values of consumer prices are employed for the right-hand-side variables rather than the actual values of the lagged dependent variables. The average annual consumer price inflation rates in the baseline scenario are generally very close to actual annual inflation rates (see Table 6.3).

Then, various scenarios were undertaken by modifying the series on import price inflation, with import price inflation separated into its commodity and non-commodity parts. This requires assumptions about the

---

[46] This can be seen by transforming a simplified version of equation [1] as follows: $\Delta ln\ P_t = \alpha + \beta\Delta\ ln\ P_{t-1} = \beta\Delta\ ln\ P_{t-1} + (1-\beta)\ \Delta\ ln\ P^e + \xi$, where $\xi = \alpha - (1-\beta)\Delta ln\ P^e$.

[47] For this reason, the finding that the sum of the coefficients on the lagged inflation terms is below unity need not imply that a long-run trade-off exists between the level of inflation and the output gap. Inflation expectations, as reflected in the constants, in the estimated equations, also need to be taken into account.

[48] Ihrig and Marquez (2004), who estimate a similar model on a country-by-country basis, obtain error-correction parameters that are in many cases not significantly different from zero or even positive.

Table 6.3 *Average annual consumer price inflation, scenario analysis 1995Q1–2005Q4*

	Average annual inflation (in per cent)		Scenario, difference from baseline (in percentage points)	
	Actual	Baseline	1% point	2% points
Australia	2.0	2.0	0.2	0.4
Austria	1.5	1.5	0.3	0.5
Belgium	1.8	1.8	0.3	0.6
Canada	1.6	1.6	0.1	0.3
Denmark	1.9	1.8	0.3	0.6
Finland	1.7	1.7	0.2	0.3
France	1.2	1.2	0.2	0.4
Germany	1.1	1.1	0.2	0.4
Greece	4.8	4.7	0.3	0.6
Ireland	2.8	2.8	0.5	0.9
Italy	3.0	3.0	0.2	0.5
Japan	-0.5	-0.5	0.1	0.2
Korea	4.6	4.6	0.2	0.4
Netherlands	2.2	2.2	0.3	0.6
Norway	2.0	2.1	0.2	0.4
Portugal	2.9	2.9	0.3	0.5
Spain	3.2	3.1	0.2	0.4
Sweden	1.5	1.6	0.3	0.6
Switzerland	0.8	0.8	0.2	0.4
United Kingdom	2.2	2.2	0.2	0.4
United States	2.0	2.0	0.2	0.4
Euro area	2.0	2.0	0.2	0.5
OECD	1.7	1.7	0.2	0.4

Note: The scenario assumes that import price inflation (total goods and services) was 1 and 2 percentage points per annum above baseline, respectively.

rate of commodity and non-commodity import price inflation had globalisation not taken place.[49] To take account of the uncertainty that surrounds the impact of globalisation on import prices, the scenario analysis derives a range of estimates employing different assumptions about the change in commodity and non-commodity import price inflation.

For commodity import prices, the scenario analysis uses the results discussed above, which derive an alternative path for each commodity

[49] To simplify the analyses, exchange rates are assumed to remain unaffected by globalisation so that they follow their true time paths throughout the simulation exercise.

price under the assumption of slower rates of growth in non-OECD trade and GDP since 2000. These changes are then combined using information on the composition of commodity imports to generate an alternative profile for the price of imported commodities in each OECD economy in the sample.[50] Two alternative profiles are constructed, one for each of the separate oil price estimates.

For the growth rate of non-commodity import prices, the scenario analysis assumes that in the absence of the rising level of imports from low-cost producers, price inflation would have exceeded the actual growth rate by 1 or 2 pp per annum, respectively. This reflects the range of estimates discussed earlier.

Tables 6.3 and 6.4 compare the different scenarios by reporting differences from the baseline in average annual rates of inflation. For the simulation period from 1995 to 2005, only the results of the modification of non-commodity import price inflation are reported in Table 6.3. This provides a longer-term perspective on the influence of globalisation in the absence of any impact on commodity prices. If the prices of non-commodity imports had risen by 1 pp (2 pp) more per annum since 1995, inflation would, on average, have been 0.2 pp (0.4 pp) per annum higher in the OECD economies.[51] Starting the simulation in 2000 reduces the difference in OECD inflation from the baseline to 0.1 and 0.2 pp per annum, respectively.[52]

The impact of the changes in commodity import prices over the period 2000–2005 is reported in Table 6.4 and summarised in Figure 6.10. In the scenario with a 20 per cent decline in oil prices, OECD inflation is found to be reduced by 0.08 pp per annum on average from 2000 onwards. In the scenario with a 40 per cent decline in oil prices, OECD inflation is reduced by 0.15 pp per annum. The impact differs considerably across countries, with the smallest changes found for Norway, Canada and the United Kingdom, and the highest found for Korea.[53]

The final column in Table 6.4 shows the combined effect on consumer inflation from higher non-commodity import price inflation and

[50] The weights of individual commodities in total imports are calculated as described in Pain et al. (2005).

[51] Ireland is an exception, with average annual inflation rates of 0.5 and 0.9 percentage point higher than in the baseline. This reflects both the comparatively high level of import penetration in Ireland and the faster speed at which changes in import prices are reflected in domestic prices.

[52] The calculations do not account for differences in the regional composition of imports. For example, the disinflationary impact may be underestimated for Japan given the comparatively higher share of imports from China in total Japanese imports.

[53] This stems from the comparatively high share of oil in Korea's imports.

Table 6.4 *Average annual consumer price inflation, scenario analysis 2000Q1–2005Q4*

	Average annual inflation (actual, in %)	Difference from baseline (in percentage points)				
		Non-commodity component		Commodity component		Net effect
		1% point	2% points	40% oil 10% metals	20% oil 10% metals	
Australia	2.4	0.1	0.3	0.0	-0.1	0.0–0.2
Austria	1.8	0.2	0.4	-0.1	-0.1	0.1–0.3
Belgium	2.3	0.2	0.4	-0.1	-0.2	0.0–0.3
Canada	1.8	0.1	0.2	0.0	0.0	0.0–0.1
Denmark	2.1	0.2	0.5	0.0	-0.1	0.2–0.4
Finland	1.9	0.1	0.2	-0.1	-0.1	0.0–0.2
France	1.5	0.2	0.3	-0.1	-0.1	0.0–0.3
Germany	1.4	0.2	0.3	-0.1	-0.1	0.0–0.2
Greece	3.4	0.2	0.4	-0.1	-0.2	0.0–0.3
Ireland	2.5	0.4	0.8	0.0	-0.1	0.3–0.7
Italy	2.8	0.2	0.4	-0.1	-0.2	0.0–0.3
Japan	-1.0	0.1	0.1	-0.1	-0.1	0.0–0.1
Korea	3.6	0.1	0.3	-0.1	-0.3	-0.1–0.1
Netherlands	2.7	0.2	0.4	-0.1	-0.2	0.0–0.3
Norway	1.9	0.1	0.2	0.0	0.0	0.1–0.2
Portugal	3.0	0.2	0.4	-0.1	-0.2	0.0–0.3
Spain	3.3	0.1	0.3	-0.1	-0.1	0.0–0.2
Sweden	1.5	0.2	0.5	-0.1	-0.2	0.1–0.4
Switzerland	1.0	0.1	0.3	0.0	-0.1	0.1–0.3
United Kingdom	1.7	0.1	0.2	0.0	-0.1	0.1–0.2
United States	2.2	0.2	0.3	-0.1	-0.2	0.0–0.2
Euro area	2.1	0.2	0.3	-0.1	-0.1	0.0–0.3
OECD	1.8	0.1	0.3	-0.1	-0.1	0.0–0.2

Note: The lower (upper) bound of the total impact is calculated assuming that the prices of non-commodity import price inflation was 1 percentage point (2 percentage points) per annum above baseline and that commodity import prices reflect the 20% (40%) oil price estimate. In both cases the metals price effect is 10%.

lower commodity import price inflation (see also Figure 6.10). The analysis suggests that consumer price inflation could have been up to 0.3 pp higher per annum in the euro area had the estimated effect of globalisation not occurred. For the United States, the estimated impact ranges from 0.04 to 0.21 pp per annum, suggesting that US inflation

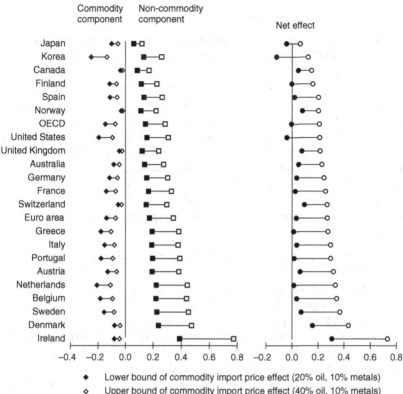

Figure 6.10 The impact on consumer price inflation of removing globalisation effects 2000–2005 – average percentage point difference per annum

might even have been lower in the absence of globalisation.[54] For Japan, the net effect is very small, ranging from 0.04 to 0.06 pp per annum. The uncertainty surrounding the estimates for most countries tends to be quite large as indicated by the difference between the lower and the upper bound which amounts to over 0.2 pp on average.

[54] This requires that globalisation has had a large impact on commodity import prices, but a small impact on non-commodity import prices.

6.7   Concluding remarks

The decline in consumer price inflation observed over the past twenty-five years in all OECD economies has coincided with a marked increase in the level of trade between the OECD and non-OECD economies. Against this background, this study has investigated the contribution of the increasing trade integration of non-OECD economies on the decline in OECD inflation. In doing so, the study has extended the existing literature on this topic in several important respects: a wider allowance is made for possible price-level effects from globalisation, a larger number of countries are included in the analysis and separate impacts of commodity and non-commodity import prices are considered.

The main globalisation-related findings from the new econometric analyses of consumer and commodity prices in this paper are as follows:

- Import prices are found to have become a significantly more important influence on domestic consumer prices since the mid 1990s, coinciding with the growing participation of non-OECD countries in international goods and services trade.
- The impact of import prices on domestic prices in all countries over the past decade is estimated to be significantly larger than the weight of imported goods and services in domestic demand, suggesting that competition from lower-priced imports has placed pressure on domestic producers in import-competing industries to lower the mark-ups of prices over domestic costs.
- The cyclical sensitivity of inflation to domestic economic conditions has declined. At the same time, domestic inflation has become more sensitive to foreign economic conditions, working through import prices. However, there is no evidence of a robust significant impact from global output gaps in addition to that embodied in import prices.
- Strong GDP growth in the non-OECD economies since 2000 is found to be an important factor underlying the growth of real oil prices and real metals prices since 2002. A scenario analysis in which the non-OECD economies are assumed to grow at the same (lower) rate as the OECD economies since 2000 is found to be associated with a decline in real oil prices from baseline by 20–40 per cent by the fourth quarter of 2005, and a decline in real metals prices of just over 10 per cent from their baseline. This removes some, but not all of the strong growth in these commodity prices after 2002.

The econometric findings are also used to quantify the overall impact of particular aspects of globalisation on consumer price inflation in

OECD countries over the period from 2000 to 2005. Two facets of globalisation are considered: the growth in commodity prices that is estimated to have resulted from strong output growth in the non-OECD
economies, and a decline in the average rate of non-commodity import
price inflation that is estimated to have resulted from higher levels of
trade with non-OECD economies. Both of these estimates are uncertain and so a range of possible outcomes is considered in the quantification exercise.

On balance, if such changes had not occurred, it is likely that inflation
would have been higher in all the OECD economies considered, all else
being equal, consistent with the view that globalisation has had a disinflationary effect. For most countries globalisation is estimated to have
been associated with a decline in the rate of consumer price inflation of
between 0 to 0.25 pp per annum since 2000. The impact was found to
be a little larger in many European economies than elsewhere.

Even at the peak of the possible range of net effects the estimated
impact on annual consumer price inflation appears to be modest, and
no greater than the potential change in annual inflation that could result
from a change in indirect taxes or administered prices. However, these
calculations take the behaviour of domestic costs as given. To the extent
that aspects of globalisation may be helping to restrain the cost of capital
or labour costs (Rodrik, 1999; Dumont et al., 2006; IMF, 2007), and
also because of the potential feedback of changes in price inflation to
wages, it is possible that the implicit net disinflationary impact of globalisation on price inflation is understated in this paper. The same holds
for inflation expectations, if globalisation has led to a decline in inflation
expectations or helped expectations to become better anchored.

Globalisation-related developments generate considerable challenges
to monetary policy makers, even if they are continuing to place some
downward pressure on inflation in almost all economies. Identifying
the extent and persistence of structural change in the economy is difficult and could result in policy mistakes. To the extent that globalisation
is changing the price level of imported non-commodity goods and services, the econometric analysis implies that in the long term there will
be an effect only on the domestic price level rather than on domestic
inflation. However, the adjustment to this new steady state is likely to
be a lengthy process that will persist over several years to come, especially if the prices of traded services also begin to decline significantly
relative to the prices of non-traded services.[55]

---

[55] The disinflationary impacts might be weakened by real exchange-rate appreciations
in non-OECD economies.

As regards non-oil commodities, increased supply should eventually lead to a reversal of currently high real metals prices, at least if past behaviour is a guide to the future. As regards oil, continued strong growth in the non-OECD economies can be expected to help keep prices high in real terms. At the margin, however, the effects of this may be attenuated in the longer term as the non-OECD economies begin to attain less energy-intensive stages of development.

The uncertainty about the relative strengths of the various influences on inflation suggests that policy makers should examine developments in headline inflation as well as core inflation (Bean, 2006). The latter is usually regarded as a better signal of ongoing inflationary pressures, but the former will reflect both influences from globalisation.[56] If the favourable external conditions for low inflation begin to wane going forward, higher nominal interest rates may be required to keep inflation low.

REFERENCES

Adams, F.G., and Y. Ichino (1995). 'Commodity prices and inflation: a forward-looking price model', *Journal of Policy Modeling*, 17, 397–426.

Altissimo, F., M. Ehrmann, and F. Smets (2006). *Inflation Persistence and Price-Setting Behavior in the Euro Area – a Summary of the IPN Evidence*, ECB occasional paper No. 46.

Bean, C. (2006). 'Comments on "The impact of globalisation on monetary policy"', presented at the Federal Reserve Bank of Kansas City 30th Annual Economic Symposium, Jackson Hole, Wyoming.

Borio, C., and A. Filardo (2007). *Globalisation and Inflation: New Cross-Country Evidence on the Global Determinants of Domestic Inflation*, Bank for International Settlements working paper No. 227 (May).

Campa, J. M., and L. S. Goldberg (2003). *Exchange Rate Pass-Through into Import Prices: a Macro or Micro Phenomenon?*, NBER working paper No. 8934.

Campa, J. M., L. S. Goldberg, and J.M. Gonzáles-Mínguez (2005). *Exchange Rate Pass-Through to Import Prices in the Euro Area*, Federal Reserve Bank of New York Staff Report No. 219.

CBO (2006). *China's Growing Demand for Oil and Its Impact on U.S. Petroleum Markets*, Congressional Budget Office paper, Congress of the United States.

Cecchetti, S. G., and G. Debelle (2006). 'Has the inflation process changed?', *Economic Policy*, 21, 311–52.

---

[56] Since headline inflation may be rather volatile, short-run changes in headline inflation may not always be very informative. Nonetheless, persistent movements in headline inflation over the medium to long run may contain useful information for monetary policy makers and are taken into account by many central banks when assessing future inflationary pressures.

Chen, N., J. Imbs, and A. Scott (2004). *Competition, Globalization and the Decline of Inflation*, Centre for Economic Policy Research discussion paper No. 4695.

Ciccarelli, M., and B. Mojon (2005). *Global Inflation*, Banco Central de Chile working paper No. 357.

Clark, T. (2003). *Disaggregated Evidence on the Persistence of Consumer Price Inflation*, Federal Reserve Bank of Kansas City working paper No. 03–11.

Cogley, T., and T. Sargent (2001). 'Evolving post-World War II inflation dynamics', *NBER Macroeconomics Annual*, 16, 331–73.

Corrado, C., and J. Mattey (1997). 'Capacity utilization', *Journal of Economic Perspectives*, 11, 151–67.

Debelle, G., and J. Wilkinson (2002). *Inflation Targeting and the Inflation Process: Some Lessons from an Open Economy*, Reserve Bank of Australia research discussion paper No. 2002–01.

Dexter, A. S., M. D. Levi, and B. R. Nault (2005). 'International trade and the connection between excess demand and inflation', *Review of International Economics*, 13, 699–708.

Dumont, M., G. Rayp, and P. Willeme (2006). 'Does internationalisation affect union bargaining power? An empirical study for five EU countries', *Oxford Economic Papers*, 58, 77–102.

ECB (2006). 'Effects of the rising trade integration of low-cost countries on euro area import prices', *European Central Bank Monthly Bulletin*, August 2006, 56–7.

Feyzioğlu, T., and L. Willard (2006). *Does Inflation in China Affect the United States and Japan?*, IMF working paper No. 06/36.

Gagnon, J., and J. Ihrig (2004). 'Monetary policy and exchange rate pass-through', *International Journal of Finance and Economics*, 9, 315–38.

Gamber, E. N., and J. H. Hung (2001). 'Has the rise in globalisation reduced U.S. inflation in the 1990s?', *Economic Inquiry*, 39, 58–73.

Ghosal, V. (2000). 'Product market competition and the industry price-cost markup fluctuations: the role of energy price and monetary changes', *International Journal of Industrial Organization*, 18, 415–44.

Gust, C. J., S. Leduc, and R. J. Vigfusson (2006). *Trade Integration, Competition, and the Decline in Exchange-Rate Pass-Through*, Board of Governors of the Federal Reserve System, international financial discussion paper No. 864.

Haskel, J., C. Martin, and I. Small (1995). 'Price, marginal cost and the business cycle', *Oxford Bulletin of Economics and Statistics*, 57, 25–41.

Hodgetts, B. (2006). 'Changes in the inflation process in New Zealand', *Reserve Bank of New Zealand Bulletin*, 69/1, 18–30.

Hua, P. (1998). 'On primary commodity prices: the impact of macroeconomic/monetary shocks', *Journal of Policy Modeling*, 20, 767–90.

IEA (2006). *Oil Market Report – Annual Statistical Supplement for 2005 and User's Guide*, Paris: International Energy Agency.

Ihrig, J., and J. Marquez (2004). 'An empirical analysis of inflation in OECD countries', *International Finance*, 7, 61–84.

Ihrig, J., S. B. Kamin, D. Lindner, and J. Marquez (2007). *Some Simple Tests of the Globalization and Inflation Hypothesis*, Board of the Governors of the Federal Reserve System, international finance discussion paper No. 891.

IMF (2006a). 'How has globalisation affected inflation?', *IMF World Economic Outlook*, April, Chapter 3.

(2006b). 'The boom in non-fuel commodity prices: can it last?', *IMF World Economic Outlook*, September, Chapter 5.

(2007). 'The globalization of labor', *World Economic Outlook*, April 2007, pp. 161–92.

Kamin, S., M. Marazzi, and J. W. Schindler (2006). 'The impact of Chinese exports on global import prices', *Review of International Economics*, 14, 179–201.

Kaplinsky, R. (2005). 'China, globalisation and neo-liberal dogma', paper prepared for 50th Anniversary Conference, Queen Elizabeth House, Oxford, 4–6 July.

Kohn, D. L. (2006). 'The effects of globalisation on inflation and their implications for monetary policy', paper presented at the Federal Reserve Bank of Boston's 51st *Economic Conference*, Chatham, Massachusetts.

Levin, A., and J. Piger (2004). *Is Inflation Persistence Intrinsic in Industrial Economies?*, ECB working paper No. 343.

Marazzi, M., N. Sheets, and R. Vigfusson (2005). *Exchange Rate Pass-Through to US Import Prices: Some New Evidence*, Board of Governors of the Federal Reserve System, international financial discussion paper No. 833.

Markandya, A., S. Pedroso-Galinato, and D. Streimikiene (2006). 'Energy intensity in transition economies: is there convergence towards the EU average?', *Energy Economics*, 28, 121–45.

Melick, W., and G. Galati (2006). *The Evolving Inflation Process: an Overview*, Bank for International Settlements working paper No. 196.

Molnar, M., N. Pain, and D. Taglioni (2008). 'Globalisation and employment in the OECD', *OECD Economic Studies*, 44 (2008/1), 1–34.

Nickell, S. (2005). 'Why has inflation been so low since 1999?', *Bank of England Quarterly Bulletin*, Spring 2005, 92–107.

OECD (2005). *Economic Survey of China*, Paris: OECD.

(2006). *OECD Economic Outlook*, Vol. 2006/1, Paris: OECD.

Olivei, G. P. (2002). 'Exchange rates and the prices of manufacturing products imported into the United States', *New England Economic Review*, First quarter, 3–18.

O'Reilly, G., and K. Whelan (2005). 'Has euro-area inflation persistence changed over time?', *Review of Economics and Statistics*, 87, 709–20.

Otani, A., S. Shiratsuka, and S. Toyoichiro (2003). *The Decline in the Exchange Rate Pass-Through: Evidence from Japanese Import Prices*, Bank of Japan, Institute for Monetary and Economic Studies.

Pain, N., I. Koske, and M. Sollie (2006). *Globalisation and Inflation in the OECD Economies*, OECD Economics Department working paper No. 524.

Pain, N., A. Mourougane, F. Sédillot, and L. le Fouler (2005). *The New International Trade Model*, OECD Economics Department working paper No. 440.

Rae, D., and D. Turner (2001). *A Small Global Forecasting Model*, OECD Economics Department working papers No. 286.

Rodrik, D. (1999). 'Globalization and labor, or: if globalization is a bowl of cherries, why are there so many glum faces around the table?', in *Market Integration, Regionalism and the Global Economy*, R. E. Baldwin *et al.* (eds.), Cambridge University Press, for CEPR New York.

Rogoff, K. (2006). 'The impact of globalisation on monetary policy', presented at the Federal Reserve Bank of Kansas City 30th Annual Economic Symposium, Jackson Hole, Wyoming.

Rudd, J., and K. Whelan (2005). *Modelling Inflation Dynamics: a Critical Review of Recent Research*, Board of Governors of the Federal Reserve System, finance and economics discussion series No. 2005–66.

Svensson, L. O. (1999). 'Price level targeting vs. inflation targeting: a free lunch?', *Journal of Money, Credit and Banking*, 31, 277–95.

Taylor, J. (2000). 'Low inflation, pass-through, and the pricing power of firms', *European Economic Review*, 44, 1389–408.

Temple, J. (2002). 'Openness and inflation: a new assessment', *Quarterly Journal of Economics*, 113, 641–8.

Tootell, G. M. B. (1998). 'Globalisation and U.S. inflation', *Federal Reserve Bank of Boston, New England Economic Review* (July/August), 21–33.

Vega, M., and D. Winkelried (2004). *How Does Global Disinflation Drag Inflation in Small Open Economies?*, Central Bank of Peru working paper No. 2005–01.

Wu, C.-S., and J.-L. Lin (2006). 'The relationship between openness and inflation in Asian 4 and G7', presented at the NBER 17th Annual East Asian Seminar on Economics, Kohala Coast, Hawaii.

Zellner, A. (1962). 'An efficient method of estimating seemingly unrelated regressions and tests for aggregation bias', *Journal of the American Statistical Association*, 57, 348–68.

7 Globalisation and euro area prices and labour markets: some evidence on the impact of low-cost countries

Gabor Pula and Frauke Skudelny

7.1 Introduction

Globalisation is generally used to describe the increasing global inter-dependence of national economies through trade, production and financial market linkages.[1] At the current juncture, one aspect of intensifying trade relations is the increasing importance of low-cost countries in international trade, with an impact on the domestic economies of developed countries, basically through an effect on the competitiveness, import prices and labour markets of these countries. The impact on import prices is ambiguous. While import prices have moderated due to increased trade integration with low-cost emerging economies, the combined effect of rising global demand and the existence of important supply bottlenecks have boosted prices of commodities, particularly energy. As regards labour markets, the trade integration with low-cost countries has shifted relative labour demand in developed countries towards high-skilled workers, but the impact on aggregate labour demand is less obvious. Globalisation has also resulted in an increase in the effective labour supply, i.e. domestic firms – via offshoring – now have easier access to global labour markets.

This paper will quantify some of the consequences of globalisation for the domestic euro area economy. A comprehensive survey of the transmission channels and the literature on globalisation effects can be found in chapter 2. Given the number of channels via which globalisation affects the domestic euro area economy and the variables on which

We gratefully acknowledge helpful input and comments by B. Anderton, R. Bems, L. Dedola, E. Gnan, N. Kennedy, G. Kenny, H.-J. Klöckers, G. Korteweg, B. Landau, L. Maurin, R. Rodzko, R. Rüffer, D. Taglioni, an anonymous referee and participants of internal ESCB seminars and participants at the ECB conference on 'Globalisation and the macroeconomy' held at Frankfurt in July 2007. The views expressed are those of the authors only and do not necessarily reflect those of the European Central Bank or the ESCB.

[1] See also the article 'Globalisation, Trade and the Euro Area Macroeconomy' in the January 2008 edition of the *ECB Monthly Bulletin*.

globalisation is expected to have an impact, we limit the analysis in the current paper to a narrow range of channels and impacts of globalisation. Primarily this paper aims to look at the impact of rising non-energy imports from low-cost countries on euro area price developments and labour demand. Hence, the wider impacts on exports and output are not considered. The analysis is constrained to two major channels of price effects: import prices and labour markets. As regards import prices we focus on the impact of lower non-energy import prices on producer and consumer prices, leaving the channel from higher commodity prices through global supply bottlenecks uncovered. In addition, the impact of exchange-rate fluctuations resulting from globalisation on euro area prices is also not taken into account as there is an ample literature on the effects of exchange rates on price developments. As regards the labour market we investigate the impact of increasing import penetration on aggregate labour demand in the euro area, with no deeper analysis of changes in labour demand by skill intensity.

The paper provides an overview of how the above described transmission channels work, and tries to give a preliminary quantification of the impact of rising imports from low-cost countries on the euro area economy through these channels. Section 7.2 describes the main transmission channels through which lower import prices are expected to have an impact on the euro area economy. Section 7.3 analyses this impact on euro area prices. Finally, Section 7.4 covers the impact on the euro area labour market and Section 7.5 concludes.

7.2   Main transmission channels

Increased trade with low-cost countries has a downward impact on non-energy import prices of developed economies. The pass-through of lower import prices on domestic prices has two main channels of transmission. First, import prices feed into domestic prices through the import content of production and consumption. Second, the growing integration of low-cost countries may increase worldwide competition, with effects on domestic and foreign labour markets, profits, innovation and, thereby, on prices (see Figure 7.1). While the first channel focuses on trade openness in the sense that more import-dependent economies may have greater effects, the second channel encompasses the impact of rising imports from low-cost countries in a broader and more inter-linked sense, as the different variables concerned have repercussions for each other.

Under the first channel, opening up to international trade may contribute to import price moderation, notably through imports from low-

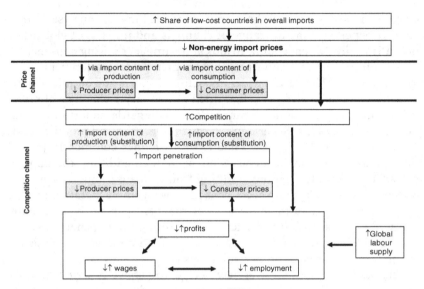

* Thick arrows indicate the direction of the impact, thin arrows indicate the direction of change

Figure 7.1 Transmission mechanism of the impact of rising non-energy imports from low-cost countries to euro area domestic prices

cost countries. Lower import costs should have a downward impact directly on producer and consumer prices via the import content of production (intermediate and final goods) and consumption (final goods). The decline in input prices may then – at least partly – be passed on to final prices of domestically produced goods (see the 'price channel' on Figure 7.1). As most high-cost countries are affected by this channel, there are spillover effects between high-income countries as well.

Under the second channel, increased competition may affect the import content of production and consumption, as well as challenge domestic labour markets and profits (see the lower panel of Figure 7.1). As a result of growing competitive pressures firms need to adjust either by cutting costs or squeezing their profits. One way of reducing costs is to shift input demand towards cheaper inputs from low-cost countries. Another way is to cut labour costs, which has a direct impact on domestic labour markets. However, the opening up of low-cost countries provides an additional tool of labour-demand adjustment for some firms, namely offshoring. Because of transitory adjustment costs labour demand is expected to decline in the short run, but to increase in the longer term due to the increase in the scale of production (Terfous, 2006).

The impact of increased imports from low-cost countries on profits and mark-ups is again far from clear-cut. Indeed, firms could be obliged to squeeze their profits due to the increase in competition. At the same time, however, a possible downward impact of increased import penetration on both input and labour costs could be associated with increased profits if this reduction in costs is not fully passed on to output prices. This is, however, less likely the more firms are exposed to competition.

The above described scheme of transmission channels does not take monetary policy reaction into account, which would alter the medium-term impact on prices, profits and labour demand. Given that we focus on non-energy imports we exclude from the analysis both the upward pressure on domestic inflation due to higher oil prices and the positive impact on labour demand (and wages) due to expanding export markets. Thus, our analysis is of a partial nature and the overall net effects on domestic prices are expected to be smaller in absolute terms than depicted by our analysis.

7.3 Rising imports from low-cost countries and euro area domestic prices

In this section we focus on the impact of import prices and rising import penetration on euro area producer and consumer prices. In particular, we will present evidence from the literature (Section 7.3.1), an estimation of the effect of low-cost countries on euro area producer and consumer prices based on an input–output table analysis (Section 7.3.2) and on a production chain VAR (Section 7.3.3) and some empirical results using panel estimations with a sectoral dimension (Section 7.3.4).

7.3.1 Literature

A couple of studies have analysed empirically whether rising import penetration has affected inflation, although none of them has focused on the euro area. The main difference between the studies is whether they analyse the question at the aggregate or sectoral level. Important studies working with aggregate data are Romer (1993), Atkeson and Burstein (2005), Kim and Beladi (2005), the IMF (2006) and Borio and Filardo (2007).

Romer (1993) shows that average rates of inflation are negatively correlated with openness. The intuition behind this is that monetary authorities benefit less from expansionary monetary policy in an open economy, as a monetary expansion which leads to real exchange-rate depreciation harms the economy more than in a less open economy.

Thereby, monetary expansion would entail a relatively larger increase in domestic prices for a given increase in output. This is empirically tested in a cross-sectional study of 114 countries. The results show that average inflation since 1973 is significantly and negatively affected by average import penetration over the same time horizon. The main conclusion that can be drawn from this paper is that a further increase in openness due to globalisation may make expansionary monetary policy even more difficult and therefore have a downward impact on inflation.

Kim and Beladi (2005) analyse empirically whether trade openness has an impact on price levels, and whether this relationship is stronger in countries with less independent central banks. Their evidence is mixed, with the impact of openness on prices sometimes positive and sometimes negative, while the study does not confirm an impact of monetary policy on the relationship.

Atkeson and Burstein (2005) propose a model parameterised to match some of the main features of trade volumes both at the aggregate and firm level and to reflect the fluctuations in the relative producer and consumer prices of tradable goods. This model is used to assess the extent to which international trade costs and imperfect competition with pricing-to-market play essential roles in accounting for producer and consumer price data. They find that international trade costs are a major determinant in the behaviour of both producer and consumer prices for tradable goods. They also find that imperfect competition with pricing-to-market plays an essential role in accounting for the behaviour of producer prices, but it plays only a minor role in accounting for the behaviour of consumer prices of tradable goods.

A number of studies have used a Phillips-curve framework to analyse the impact of globalisation on prices at the aggregate level. Rogoff (2003) has argued that theoretically, globalisation should lead to an increase in competition, which in turn would imply faster response to changes in the cost structure due to lower profit margins and thereby make the Phillips curve steeper. However, empirical studies instead found evidence that the Phillips curve became flatter (see, for example, Borio and Filardo, 2007). Besides increased credibility and the effect of structural reforms, one possible reason is the lower volatility of domestic production due to the increased role of net exports in buffering fluctuations in domestic demand.

The IMF (2006) addresses the question whether increasing openness has affected producer price inflation over the past fifteen years. The study argues that the impact of openness on inflation will be temporary as long as there is no change in the objectives of monetary policy. Indeed, openness should only involve relative price effects and therefore affect inflation only temporarily as the long-run development in prices is expected to be mainly determined by monetary policy. Therefore, price decreases due to lower import prices from low-cost countries should be offset by price increases elsewhere, for example energy prices, which are also affected by globalisation. Indeed, the strong increase in world demand for oil is to a large extent due to emerging economies, which thereby puts upward pressure on oil prices. The IMF introduces a term capturing the openness of the country into a Phillips-curve-type model for inflation, defined as the non-oil trade share in GDP. Panel estimation results suggest a significant negative impact of openness on relative prices. They also estimate a version of the model including import prices. Their simulation results starting in 1997 show that for advanced economies, import prices brought down inflation from 1997 to 2002 but had no impact thereafter. Their conclusion from this simulation exercise is that during 2003–2005, 'there was almost no globalization-related impact on inflation'. It should, however, be noted that this result may be due to the fact that the authors do not separate the impact of oil price and exchange-rate changes from any globalisation impact.

Finally, Borio and Filardo (2007) estimate an extended Phillips-curve equation explaining inflation by the domestic output gap, a global trade weighted output gap, import prices, exchange rates and oil prices. They find that the global output gap is statistically significant and reduces the coefficient on the domestic output gap, in particular since the 1990s in many euro area countries. At the aggregate euro area level, however, the results are more ambiguous. They find no significant decline in the sensitivity of inflation to the domestic output gap, and the significance of the global output gap disappears when supply shock variables (import prices, oil prices) are included in the Phillips-curve specification. On a data set of fourteen industrial countries Ihrig et al. (2007) find that the coefficient on the global output gap is generally insignificant or even of the wrong sign when changing country weights and idiosyncratic shocks are included in the specification. Using the same data set Ball (2006) also finds either insignificant or very small effects of the global output gap.

Although aggregate studies help to get a general flavour of the impact of openness on inflation, the effect can differ a lot across sectors. However, only a few studies have conducted a sectoral analysis.

As regards the impact of rising trade integration on import prices, ECB (2006) estimated that the higher level of imports from low-cost countries had a sizeable dampening impact on overall euro area manufacturing import prices of approximately 2 percentage points (pp) per annum on average over the period 1996–2005.

Chen et al. (2004) use a disaggregated data set to analyse the effect of globalisation (defined as trade openness, or imports divided by the turnover on current prices). They distinguish between the direct impact on domestic prices and the indirect impact via productivity and mark-ups on prices. Their finding is that both channels have a significant and similar impact in the short run, while the productivity channel is predominant in the long run.

IMF (2006) also includes a sectoral analysis and finds the direct effect on producer price inflation via import prices to be generally small in industrial economies. In a panel study with sectoral data (using a similar approach to Chen *et al.* (2004)), import penetration and productivity growth are found to have been important in explaining relative price changes between sectors. According to the results, increased trade openness has reduced relative producer prices in manufacturing by about 0.3 pp on average per year over the past fifteen years in their sample of industrialised countries.

Overall, the literature has used different methods to assess whether globalisation in the form of increased openness to international trade has reduced domestic prices. Most studies found a negative, although mostly small, effect. One shortcoming of all studies is that they cannot capture the impact of the increasing importance of low-cost countries on import prices in high-cost countries. The studies are not focused on the euro area, which is of clear interest for the ECB. Therefore, in the following section we will focus explicitly on the effect of lower euro area import prices due to the growing importance of low-cost countries on euro area producer and consumer prices. We thereby neglect the effect of low-cost countries on oil prices and exchange rates, as the impact of these on the euro area has already been analysed in a large number of studies.[2] These studies, however, often do not take into account where oil price and exchange-rate movements come from and that they might be accompanied by cost-lowering effects such as the one described below.

7.3.2   *Effect on prices through the import content of domestic production and consumption*

In this section, we attempt to quantify the effect of rising imports from low-cost countries on euro area domestic prices, using information on the import content of production from input–output tables. The advantage of this approach is that it enables us to analyse the impact at a sectoral level and that it takes into account sectoral effects through the production chain.

As a major input to the analysis we use estimated impacts of higher levels of imports from low-cost countries on euro area manufacturing import

[2] See ECB Occasional Paper No. 113, 'Emerging markets and the euro area macroeconomy', June 2010.

prices by sectors. On the basis of sectoral data on extra-euro area import unit values,[3] ECB (2006) estimated that rising imports from low-cost countries have dampened euro area import price inflation of manufactured goods by approximately 2 pp on average each year during 1996–2005, an effect almost equally accounted for by China and the New Member States. This effect is disentangled into a share and a price effect.[4] The *share effect* is defined as the change in euro area import prices due to the change in the import share of low-cost countries, while the *price effect* designates the contribution to total import prices due to import price inflation differentials between low-cost countries compared to that of high cost countries. To measure the impact of import penetration, the share effect is the relevant measure as it mainly reflects the effect of a rising share in euro area imports from low-cost countries through their impact on the total import prices of the euro area. Therefore, it can also be thought of as a price-level effect. The price effect is due to changes in the import prices of these countries and is therefore strongly influenced by exchange-rate movements. For this reason, in what follows we will focus on the share effect, which is estimated to account for an approximately 1.5 pp per annum, while the remaining 0.5 pp is mainly due to the import price effect. Indeed, the current contribution focuses on the impact of the increasing importance of low-cost countries on import prices in high-cost countries.

Using this information, the effect of low-cost countries on euro area domestic prices can be quantified by linking the share effects on import prices estimated at a sectoral level to the use of imports in production and consumption in this sector using input–output tables.

---

[3] Import unit values are used as a proxy for import prices as "for the euro area" import values and volumes are available at a disaggregated level, thereby enabling a detailed analysis of euro area import unit values. These differ from import prices in the national accounts as they do not correct for changes in the quality of the product traded. As a result, unit values may be upward biased compared to import deflators. Therefore, the effect could be overestimated.

[4] The calculation is similar to the one used by Kamin *et al.* (2004):

$$\frac{\Delta p_t}{p_{t-n}} = \sum_j \left[\frac{p_{j,t} - p_{HC,t}}{p_{t-n}} \Delta \alpha_{j,t} \right] + \sum_j \alpha_{j,t-n} \left[\frac{\Delta p_{j,t}}{p_{j,t-n}} \frac{p_{j,t-n}}{p_{t-n}} - \frac{\Delta p_{HC,t}}{p_{HC,t-n}} \frac{p_{HC,t-n}}{p_{t-n}} \right] + \frac{\Delta p_{HC,t}}{p_{HC,t-n}} \frac{p_{HC,t-n}}{p_{t-n}}$$

where:
the first term is the share effect – that is, the effect of a change in the import share from a particular country *j* given its price differential against the reference (high-cost) group of countries. The size of the share effect depends on both the magnitude of the change in the share, and the import price differential of country *j* against the reference country;
the second term represents the price effect. It captures the change in the euro area import price due to different import price inflation rates for country *j* and the reference country. This impact increases with the import share of country *j*;
the third term in the decomposition represents the residual effect due to price developments in the high-cost countries.

To calculate the effect on producer prices, we have to take into account not only the direct effect of lower import prices on one specific sector, but also the effect of lower costs in this domestic sector on other domestic sectors. Therefore, the Leontieff coefficients of the input–output tables are used to obtain the total import content of production. Summing up this effect over the different input sectors gives the effect on a specific production sector:

$$\Delta PPI_{S1} = \sum_i \left(McontP_{S1,i} {}^* MShare\_effect_i \right) \tag{1}$$

where $McontP_{S1,i}$ is the import content of production of sector i used in sector $S1$ and $MShare\_effect_i$ is the import share effect in sector i, i.e. the average annual percentage point impact of the relatively lower price level in low-cost countries on euro area import price inflation due to an increase in the import share of these countries. For example, considering the textile sector as the main sector ($S1$ = textile), $McontP_{S1,i}$ are the imported inputs of products from sector i used for the production of textiles. We have multiplied the share effect on extra-euro area import prices as calculated in ECB (2006) with the share of extra-euro area imports in total euro area imports for each sector because the input–output tables provide information on total trade only. That means that the variable $McontP_{S1,i}$ considers the import content for both imports from the euro area and from outside the euro area, and we transform the share effect from ECB (2006), which was based on imports from outside the euro area only, into a share effect including intra-euro area imports ($MShare\_effect_i$). The effect on total manufacturing producer price inflation (PPI) is then obtained by calculating the contributions of each individual sector to PPI (using the weights from the input–output tables) and adding them up over all manufacturing sectors.[5] Table 7.1 shows the results in columns (2) and (3).[6]

The table shows that the impact of lower import prices due to the increasing share of low-cost countries in total imports on sectoral PPI is strongest in 'office machinery and computers' and 'radio, TV, communication equipment', where rising import penetration has brought down producer price inflation by about 1.2 and 0.6 pp annually on average over the period 1996 to 2004, respectively. This means that without the

---

[5] Information on the data sources and the matching of sectors between producer and import prices can be found in Appendix A1.

[6] The sectors 'food products and beverages', 'tobacco products', 'coke, refined petroleum products and nuclear fuel day' and 'Electricity, gas, steam and hot water supply' have been excluded due to data shortages. Although their combined weight in the PPI amounts to about 30 per cent, with the exception of tobacco, the import penetration effect is probably not relevant in these sectors.

Table 7.1 *Low-cost country share effect on euro area prices (percentage points; average annual effect from 1996 to 2004)*

	Effect of low-cost country share effect on:				
	(1) Sectoral import price inflation	(2) Sectoral PPI	(3) Contribution to total manuf. PPI	(4) Sectoral consumer price inflation	(5) Contribution to total CPI
Textiles	-0.35	-0.07	-0.002	-0.197	-0.002
Wearing apparel; dressing and dyeing of fur	-0.43	-0.08	-0.001	-0.244	-0.005
Tanning, leather; luggage, handbags, saddle, harness, footwear	-0.28	-0.05	-0.000	-0.167	-0.001
Wood, prods, cork, exc. furn; manuf. Artic.straw, plait. mats.	-0.87	-0.09	-0.002	-0.302	0.000
Pulp, paper and paper products	-0.03	-0.03	-0.001	-0.030	0.000
Publishing, printing and reproduction of recorded media day	-0.03	-0.02	-0.001	-0.022	0.000
Chemicals and chemical products	-0.17	-0.06	-0.006	-0.098	-0.002
Rubber and plastic products	-0.30	-0.06	-0.002	-0.149	-0.001
Other non-metallic mineral products	0.66	-0.00	-0.000	0.166	0.001
Basic metals	-0.48	-0.15	-0.008	-0.306	0.000
Fabricated metal products, except machinery and equipment	-0.48	-0.08	-0.005	-0.209	-0.001
Machinery and equipment n.e.c.	-1.11	-0.20	-0.018	-0.529	-0.004
Office machinery and computers	-2.21	-1.22	-0.013	-1.922	-0.003
Electrical machinery and apparatus n.e.c. day	-1.67	-0.21	-0.008	-0.888	-0.002
Radio, TV, communication equipment/apparatus	-2.60	-0.59	-0.025	-1.811	-0.013
Medical, precision and optical instruments, watches/clocks day	-0.77	-0.19	-0.004	-0.489	-0.002
Motor vehicles, trailers and semi-trailers day	-0.28	-0.12	-0.016	-0.197	-0.007
Other transport equipment	-0.26	-0.19	-0.006	-0.235	-0.001
Furniture; manufacturing n.e.c.	-0.59	-0.09	-0.003	-0.259	-0.005
Sum contributions			-0.121		-0.047

Source: Eurostat, OECD and ECB calculations, using information from input–output tables for 2000. Please note that the effect on sectoral import price inflation is calculated on the basis of intra- plus extra-euro area.

increasing importance of low-cost countries, annual price increases in these two sectors would have been 1.2 pp and 0.6 pp higher on average, respectively. In the textile sectors, the corresponding effect was about 0.07 pp. This significantly smaller effect can be partly explained by the relatively small increase in the import shares of low-costs countries in the textile sector. This is due to the fact that the increase of textile imports from China was to a large extent at the expense of the market share of the NMS, leaving the overall low-cost import penetration unaltered. Also, branding plays an important role in this sector, thereby reducing the competition and, as a result, the import share effect in this sector. Weighting together the effect of the individual sectors gives an estimate of the total low-cost country share effect on euro area manufacturing PPI of about 0.12 pp per annum on average.

Turning to the impact on consumer prices, we use information from input–output tables on the import content of consumption in specific sectors and multiply it with the import share effect. As this provides us only with an estimate of the direct effect on consumer prices via imports of final goods, we have to add the domestic production content in consumption of each sector multiplied with the low-cost countries' effect on producer prices calculated above:

$$\Delta CPI_{S1} = McontC_{S1} {}^{\star} MShare\_effect_{S1} + \Delta PPI_{S1} {}^{\star} (1 - McontC_{S1}) \qquad (2)$$

where $McontC_{S1}$ is the import content of consumption in sector $S1$ and $MShare\_effect_{S1}$ is the import share effect in sector $S1$ and ΔPPI is the effect of low-cost countries' increasing import share on euro area producer prices, as defined above. Again, the total effect is obtained by calculating the contribution of each sector to total consumption of manufactured goods (using weights from the input–output tables) and adding them up over all manufacturing sectors. The results are shown in columns (4) and (5) of Table 7.1. Overall, the impact on the CPI is larger than the one on PPI in all sectors as a result of the additional direct impact via cheaper final goods imports. Again, the low-cost country share effect on sectoral consumer price inflation is strongest in 'office machinery and computers' and 'radio, TV, communication equipment', where rising import penetration has brought down consumer price inflation by about 1.9 pp and 1.8 pp annually on average over the period 1996 to 2004, respectively. (In the textile sectors, the corresponding effect was small, about 0.2 pp.) The weighted effect on overall consumer price inflation is relatively small, at 0.05 pp. It should, however, be noted that the calculation includes only those sectors for which we have data on the import share effect, i.e. most of the manufacturing sector, while services, food and tobacco are not included. Therefore, the overall coverage of consumer prices in our calculation amounts to only about 18 per cent.

A number of further caveats regarding our input–output analysis need to be borne in mind. First, we focus on the share effect on import prices from China and the New Member States only. This means that we do not consider the import penetration effect from other low-cost[7] and high-cost competitors on the euro area, which is expected to be particularly strong in high technology sectors, such as IT. Second, the calculations above do not include the impact of rising import penetration on competition in the euro area, with the expected effects on prices, profits and the labour market and thereby indirectly again on prices. Third, the calculation of the effect on producer prices would be more precise if we could use a more detailed sectoral breakdown, as the sectors used above contain still relatively heterogeneous goods so that the goods within one sector are not always competing goods. This also introduces a downward bias into the estimations above. The current limits to the breakdown stem from the number of sectors included in the input–output tables. Fourth, the estimates on the sectoral effects are based on import unit values instead of import prices with the standard caveats that this implies.

Finally, the calculation is done in a static accounting framework, without taking into account dynamic adjustment mechanisms, as input–output tables are not available on an annual frequency and are published with substantial delay and the country coverage for the euro area tends to change over time.[8] For this reason, the next section quantifies the effect using a VAR model on the production chain for the euro area.

7.3.3 Passing import price-level effects through the pricing chain: results from a VAR model

We also calculated the overall effect using results from an updated version of a VAR on the euro area production chain as presented in Hahn (2003). This VAR is based on a set of seven variables (oil prices, interest rate, GDP, exchange rate, import prices, producer prices and the HICP). The identification is given by a basic Cholesky-decomposition

---

[7] China and the New Member States had a somewhat lower than 30 per cent market share in the euro area external trade in 2004. All the other members of the low-cost group (India, ASEAN countries, CIS, MEDA, Central and South America, etc.) had another 20 per cent market share, which the I-O and VAR analysis did not take into account.

[8] We have compared the results for the euro area countries for which input–output tables are available for both 1995 and 2000 (D, ITA, NL, BE, FIN, AUT). In 2000, the total producer price effect was 0.024 pp higher than in 1995, and the consumer price effect was 0.002 pp higher.

with the ordering as indicated above. The intuition behind the VAR is that there is a chain reaction to a shock which goes through different steps. In the above-mentioned VAR, an oil-price shock has an impact on all variables, while an interest-rate shock has an impact on all variables except oil prices, GDP has an impact on all variables except oil prices and interest rates, and so on. Impulse responses are calculated for each of these shocks, which represent the impact of, say, oil prices on the HICP directly and via other variables included in the VAR. The VAR also allows the impact of a shock to import prices on manufacturing producer prices and on the overall HICP to be quantified.

Using the VAR we assume that the average annual share effect on extra-euro area import prices will be passed on to the consumer as any other import price shock observed over the estimation sample. In order to calculate the effect, we simply multiply the impulse responses of producer prices and the HICP from a 1 per cent increase in non-oil import prices with the above-mentioned share effect on import prices.[9] That means that instead of assuming a 1 per cent shock on import prices as in the standard impulse response, we assume a shock on import prices corresponding to the impact of low-cost countries on euro area import prices. The results (see Table 7.2) point to an average annual impact over the period 1995 to 2004 on PPI inflation of about −0.3 pp and on HICP inflation of about −0.07 pp when using impulse responses for the first year. The effect for HICP inflation increases to about −0.2 pp when using impulse responses cumulated over three years. The results confirm that when taking into account dynamic adjustments between different price variables, the effect is somewhat larger than what we found in the static input–output analysis above. It is, however, difficult to disentangle whether the stronger effect compared with the input–output analysis is due to the adjustment in import shares, which is not taken into account in the input–output table analysis, or to some other effects, such as wage adjustment, adjustment in foreign prices or other variables, which are implicitly included in the VAR. It should be noted that these results are probably higher than in reality, as the impulse responses of the VAR are identified unexpected shocks, while the estimated import price effect is an average effect, i.e. includes more than the unexpected component.

[9] In order to calculate the impact of low-cost countries, we use the total average annual share effect on extra-euro area manufacturing import prices as calculated in ECB (2006) and convert it into an effect on intra- plus extra-euro area non-oil import prices as the VAR uses non-oil intra- plus extra-euro area import prices. The total effect on intra- plus extra-euro area import prices (−0.65 pp) is calculated as the effect on extra-euro area manufacturing import prices (−1.6 pp) times the weight of manufacturing in extra-imports (0.72) times the weight of extra- in total euro area imports (0.5 pp) divided by the weight of non-oil in total intra- plus extra-euro area imports (0.9).

Table 7.2 *Impact of low-cost country share effect on euro area prices using VAR results (cumulated percentage points)*

	Year 1	Year 2	Year 3
PPI	-0.30	-0.30	-0.31
HICP	-0.07	-0.15	-0.18

Note: Annual averages over quarters.

The VAR analysis still has two of the above mentioned caveats: we focus on the share effect on import prices from the low-cost countries China and the New Member States only, and the estimates on the sectoral effects are based on import unit values instead of import prices. Therefore, we also estimate the overall effect of rising import penetration on PPI, which includes import penetration effects from high-cost and other low-cost countries and the effect of import penetration on domestic market competition.

7.3.4   A broader view: price effects using panel estimation models

In this section, we measure the impact of rising import penetration on euro area domestic prices in an econometric analysis using a sectoral data set for euro area countries. Chen *et al.* (2004) derive a two-country general equilibrium model, extending the model of Melitz and Ottaviano (2005) to introduce cross-country heterogeneity in costs. Although they solve the model to obtain equations for prices, productivity and mark-ups of firms, we will focus here only on the price equation. Chen *et al.* (2004) estimate a reduced form of their equations, taking some simplifying assumptions to allow for an econometric estimation of the equation. The estimation equations of IMF (2006) are a variant of Chen *et al.* (2004), specifying producer prices in relative form, i.e. estimating the impact of openness on prices in a specific sector relative to the average price in that sector. This allows them to get rid of the monetary variable included in Chen *et al.* (2004) to account for the impact of monetary policy. We use the same data set as IMF (2006)[10] but modify somewhat the regression as we want to obtain the effect on producer prices rather than on the sectoral price differentials. Indeed, as argued by Ball (2006), using relative specifications does not allow us to find an overall price effect of increased import penetration,

---

[10] Kindly put at our disposal by F. Jaumotte from the IMF.

since for each relative price fall in one sector there is a relative price increase in another sector. As we do not use a relative specification, we also include, like Chen *et al.* (2004), a monetary policy variable, namely interest rates. In addition, we restrict the sample to euro area countries. The data set stems from the OECD STAN database and comprises six euro area countries[11] and fifteen manufacturing sectors over a period from 1978 to 2003, which is currently the latest available year from the STAN data set.

The estimated equation is:

$$\Delta \ln p_{ijt} = c_{ij} + \alpha \Delta \ln \mathit{impsh}_{ijt} + \beta \Delta \ln \mathit{prod}_{ijt} + \gamma \Delta ir_{it} + \varepsilon_{ijt} \tag{3}$$

where p is the producer price, *impsh* the import share (nominal imports divided by value added), *prod* is labour productivity and *ir* is the interest rate. The subscript i stands for the country, and the subscript j for the sector. The variable *impsh* should capture the import penetration effect including also competition effects and spillover effects between high-cost countries. In addition, it also includes the effect of import price changes which are, to a large extent, due to exchange-rate movements. We have also tested the equation with different versions of country and sector specific time trends but they were dropped from the estimation as they were not significant.

Analogously to the IMF (2006), we use a two-step feasible generalised method of moments estimator, instrumenting for changes in the import ratio given the possibility of endogeneity.[12] The instruments are the weighted sum of the shares of the other countries in the world production of a sector and the nominal effective exchange rate. Since the nominal effective exchange rate for the euro area countries is strongly correlated with the US dollar exchange rate, we do not include the latter in our regression, unlike the IMF (2006). In addition to the full sample from 1978 to 2003, we also use a reduced sample from 1995 onwards, mainly for two reasons: first, the sub-sample covers a period over which the output gap is, on average, close to zero, so that we reduce the impact of the business cycle on our estimation results. And second, the results are therefore better comparable to the input–output analysis above. The estimation results are shown in Table 7.3.

For the long sample, a lag of the dependent variable had to be introduced to correct for autocorrelation.[13] All estimates have robust

---

[11] Germany, Ireland, the Netherlands, Portugal and Spain have been excluded from the sample because of missing observations.

[12] We have also experimented without instrumental variables. In most static versions of the model, we then found no significant effect of the import share.

[13] Although it is recommended to use the Arellano-Bond estimator in panel data with fixed effects when introducing a lagged dependent variable, we have used the

Table 7.3 *Estimation results – producer prices*

	Coef	Std error	T-stat	Prob	Long-term coefficient[1]	Contribution of the import share (pp)[2]
1978–2003						
producer prices (-1)	0.420	0.166	2.540	0.011		
change in import share	-0.214	0.137	-1.560	0.119	-0.370	-0.78
change in labour productivity	-0.083	0.049	-1.690	0.091	-0.142	
interest rate (-1)	-0.006	0.002	-2.930	0.003	-0.011	
1995–2003						
change in import share	-0.433	0.145	-2.980	0.003		-1.01
change in labour productivity	-0.175	0.067	-2.600	0.010		
interest rate (-1)	-0.009	0.002	-4.680	0.000		

All variables are estimated in first log-differences.
[1] This effect is calculated by dividing the coefficient of each variable by 1 minus the coefficient of the lagged dependent variable.
[2] This effect is calculated by multiplying the (long-term) coefficients with the average annual growth in the import share.

standard errors. Most variables enter with the expected sign and are significant: interest rates have a negative and significant impact on producer prices in all specifications and productivity has a positive significant impact. Most importantly, the import share is negative and significant, although only at 12 per cent for the long sample.

Overall, the average annual import share effect (calculated as the coefficient multiplied with the average annual growth in the import share, at 2.1 per cent according to the full sample and 2.3 per cent according to the short sample) is estimated to be around 0.8–1.0 pp. This effect is substantially higher than the effect obtained from the VAR. A possible reason for this difference is that the VAR estimates only the impact from a lower import price level due to a higher share of imports from low-cost countries, while the panel estimation has a broader concept

correction proposed by Anderson and Hsiao (1981) as the first method does not allow the instruments for the other explanatory variables to be kept.

of openness, using the change in the total import share. However, the estimated impact is also large compared with the estimate of the IMF (2006) which could be due to the fact that the IMF estimates changes in sectoral producer prices relative to the manufacturing average while our estimates are not specified in relative terms. Taking only the short-term reaction, which is possible in the estimation with the full sample due to the dynamic specification, the effect would be somewhat lower, at 0.45 pp, which is similar to a relative specification as used in the IMF (2006) where the effect amounts to 0.4–0.5 pp. Nevertheless, it should be noted that the quality of the data used for the panel analysis is rather poor, which suggests that the relatively high numbers should be interpreted with caution. Therefore, our best guess would still suggest that the impact of globalisation on prices is closer to the results of the VAR than to those of the panel estimation, with the latter representing something like an upper band of the impact. The effect on consumer prices can, however, not be assessed due to data limitations at this dis-aggregation level.

It should be emphasised that the quantification in this section is of a partial nature. Globalisation affects domestic prices in a very complex way. However, the input–output analysis is of a partial nature, as it does not include dynamic effects and is more an accounting exercise, while the sectoral panel estimation is more encompassing but does not enable us to disentangle the impact of globalisation from other shocks hitting the economy. Therefore, the results should be interpreted with caution.

It should be also noted that all of the above estimates are based on observations in the recent past and cannot easily be extrapolated to the future. In particular, for the results using data on low-cost countries, the effect of China and the New Member States might decline in the future as these countries catch up with associated higher prices. Although other countries might then take over the role of China and the New Member States as main low-cost exporters to the euro area, their impact may be different from what we have presented in this section.

7.4.   The impact of increasing import penetration on the euro area labour markets

7.4.1   Literature

Theoretically, globalisation affects domestic labour markets through two main mechanisms: it enhances product market competition through the increased volume of trade and gives easier access to global labour supply via immigration and increased capital mobility. These two mechanisms are, however, strongly interrelated. On the one hand, stronger product market competition squeezes profits and enforces an adjustment mostly by innovation and cost reduction through lower employment and/or lower wages. On the other hand, fostered by higher capital mobility, corporate adjustment has taken the form of production segmentation (offshoring, delocalisation) in recent decades, in relation to both developed and emerging economies. Regarding the effect of production segmentation on the domestic labour market, possible efficiency gains can in the long term counterbalance the initial decline of labour demand. Above that, even just the threat of offshoring, without any actual action may be sufficient to decrease wage pressures of employees.

Empirical evidence on the impact of globalisation on labour market developments is limited. Traditional trade theory focuses on what effects trade in final goods may have on the domestic economy. Based on the Stolper-Samuelson theorem[14] the main effect in advanced economies is a shift in the labour demand towards skilled relative to unskilled workers rather than changes in aggregate employment and wage levels. In addition, the literature indicates that international trade explains only a modest 10 to 20 per cent in rising income inequalities during the 1980s in the USA and claims that labour market developments have been driven by other factors than trade, mainly technology (Borjas *et al.*, 1992; Lawrence and Slaughter, 1993). Evidence for Europe also suggests no or only small impacts of international trade on relative wages, but possibly a larger effect on employment (Cuyvers *et al.* (2002)). This is in line with the supposedly more rigid nature of wages in Europe. Machin and van Reenen (1998) investigated seven OECD countries and revealed that – although import competition and skill upgrading took place mostly in the same industries – changing skill structure was driven by technological changes and trade had no significant effect.

There are several explanations for the weak empirical findings on the impact of trade on domestic labour markets. One is the endogeneity

---

[14] According to the Stolper-Samuelson theorem if trade opens up between advanced and developing countries, advanced countries start to import low-skilled-labour-intensive products from developing countries, where these products can be produced with a comparative advantage due to a relative abundance of low-skilled labour. As a consequence of trade, relative prices of low-skilled products and the demand for low-skilled workers will fall in the developed countries, deteriorating the relative labour market position of low-skilled workers (lower wages and/or employment). On the other hand, the demand for high-skilled labour will increase as the advanced economy specialises in high-skilled-intensive products, and so the wages and/or employment of the high-skilled workers should rise.

of technological change. Wood (1994) argues that a significant part of labour-saving innovations are induced by trade and claims that a plausible magnitude would be to simply double the previously estimated direct impact coming from trade. Another important aspect is given by Feenstra and Hanson (2003), who point to the relevance of offshoring.[15] Offshoring to low-cost countries is mainly concentrated in labour-intensive production segments (Braconier *et al.*, 2002), and shifts labour demand from unskilled towards skilled labour within the same industry (Feenstra and Hanson, 1999; Gorg *et al.*, 2005) rather than across industries as assumed by the 'final goods trade' literature.

The impact of offshoring on aggregate levels of domestic wages and employment depends on how the parent company and its affiliate (in low-cost countries) specialise. One possibility is when offshoring follows the pattern of comparative advantages and the outsourced (low-skilled) activities are complementary to those left in the parent company. In this case the shift of labour demand for skilled labour is likely to push average wage levels up within the parent company, while the employment of the low-skilled should decrease. However, the initial employment loss may be counterbalanced by the increase in overall activity due to efficiency gains. An important argument of the literature is that these efficiency gains most likely need time to develop. Therefore, in the short run negative temporary adjustment effects may be dominant and their persistence will depend upon the flexibility of product and labour market structures (Terfous, 2006).[16]

Another line of the literature claims that the impact of globalisation occurs via elasticities and, in particular, via the real wage elasticity of labour demand. The main argument behind this idea is that while pressure on prices (wages) shows up only via trade between countries with dissimilar relative endowments, elasticities are affected even when trade intensifies between countries with quite similar endowments (Rodrik, 1999).[17] Based on the fundamental law of labour demand (Hamermesh, 1993)

[15] In a broad sense offshoring is a term for imports of intra-industry intermediate inputs, in a more strict sense it means the geographic separation of producing activities, and so it is more of a synonym of delocalisation.

[16] The newly emerging trade in tasks theory claims that offshoring is increasingly focused on tasks rather than intermediate goods. Tasks refer to a much finer disaggregation level than intermediates and cover service types of activities rather than goods. But most importantly, the extent to which tasks are exposed to offshoring does not necessarily depend on skill intensity any more, but is much more affected by how easily these tasks can be delivered down a fibre optic cable to remote locations (Baldwin, 2006). Consequently, skill intensity is no longer a useful category to describe shifts in the labour demand.

[17] For example, in a Heckscher-Ohlin trade model if an economy's autarkic relative endowment equals that of the rest of the world then when the country opens to trade it experiences no change in product prices and thus (via the Stolper-Samuelson

globalisation may raise the elasticity of real wages via two channels: (1) increased competition exerts downward pressure on domestic product prices (higher price elasticity on product markets) so that companies have to limit increases in labour costs and (2) easier access to capital and foreign labour makes it less difficult to substitute away from domestic labour in case its price increases.[18] However, this theoretical relationship has so far seen only weak empirical grounding. For the USA Slaughter (2001) finds that openness explains only a small part of changing labour demand elasticities. Bruno et al. (2004) obtain a significant impact of changes of import penetration on the price elasticity of demand for labour in the UK, and to a lesser extent in France and Italy. In a recent study, Molnar et al. (2006) use the ratio of outward FDI stock to nominal output as a proxy for an impact of globalisation. They find an overall negative effect on employment growth and a significant positive impact on labour demand elasticities in the OECD countries – in at least the group of those industries that have strong trade relations with emerging economies and supposedly have low cost of delocalisation (textiles, transport equipment, electrical and optical equipment and food).

The increased pressure on employers to keep labour costs low and the possibility for them to use non-domestic factors of production more extensively results in a weakening of the position of workers in the wage-bargaining process. This line of argumentation is in line with the anecdotal evidence that even the threat of offshoring, without any actual action may be sufficient to decrease wage pressures in several industries. Some recent empirical studies seem to confirm that indicators of globalisation are negatively correlated with both union bargaining power (Dumont et al. (2006)) and with union membership (Dreher and Gaston, 2005) in a number of OECD countries. Boulhol et al. (2006) finds that imports from developed countries have contributed significantly to the decrease in both mark-ups and workers' bargaining power in the UK manufacturing sectors in the 1988–2003 period.

The number of studies that try to quantify the aggregate impact of globalisation on labour markets is limited. The IMF (2006) estimates a panel regression across manufacturing industries of major developed

---

theorem) no change in wages. But opening may make foreign factors more substitutable with domestic ones and may make product markets more competitive, resulting in higher labour demand own-price elasticities.

[18] According to the fundamental law of labour demand the own-price labour demand elasticity is determined by two factors: $\eta_{LL} = -(1-s)\sigma - s\eta$. The first term (substitution effect) shows how much labour is substituted by other factors of production when wages increase and so this term is basically determined by the elasticity of substitution (σ). The second term (scale effect) indicates by what extent output falls due to an increase in production costs implied by higher wages. This is determined by the price elasticity of product demand (η), which is related to product market competition.

countries over the period 1978 to 2003. The study quantifies the impact of openness on wages and productivity separately. According to their findings, a 1 per cent increase in relative trade openness would increase relative productivity by 0.12 per cent and – although the higher productivity induces higher wages – relative unit labour costs would still decrease by 0.09 per cent.

Pain *et al.* (2006) found a significant negative impact of increased import penetration on manufacturing sectoral employment of −0.006 pp in the 1987–2003 period by estimating a labour demand equation with variables of five-year differences. The estimated impact was higher in the case of imports from low-cost countries (−0.05) and using the 'narrow' offshoring measure (−0.09). According to their estimates of a translog cost function, import penetration has a negative effect on the relative demand for low- and high-skilled workers – albeit, more strongly for low-skilled workers – and no effect on the demand for medium-skilled workers.

It has to be mentioned that although our analysis is limited to manufacturing developments, a significant increase has occurred in the offshoring of services since the mid 1990s. The service sector's offshoring affects high-skilled rather than low-skilled workers, which means that it has the opposite impact on changes in relative labour demand to that of offshoring in manufacturing. Looking forward, offshoring is expected to be an increasingly important factor affecting labour market developments: about 15–20 per cent of total employment could be subject to international offshoring in the OECD countries in the upcoming years (van Welsum and Vickery, 2005).

7.4.2   Stylised facts

Based on the literature survey in the previous section we may conclude the following. According to traditional trade theory, the opening up of trade with low-cost countries shifts the labour demand from low-skilled to high-skilled workers. Sluggishness of the reallocation of resources may result in temporary losses in output and employment at the aggregate level. In the long run, however, we expect efficiency gains to enhance activity, employment and productivity. Globalisation also weakens the bargaining power of employees and increases the real wage elasticity of labour demand due to increased product market competition and easier substitution among the various inputs of production. This impact moderates real wage developments. In addition, even the threat of offshoring, without any actual action may be sufficient to decrease wage pressures of employees.

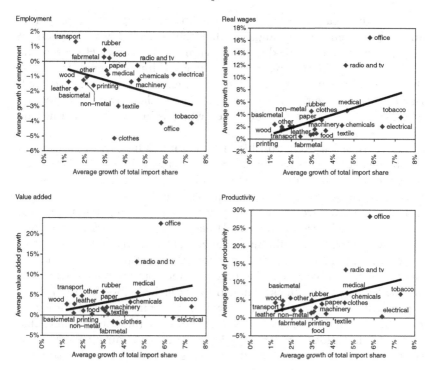

Figure 7.2 Labour market developments and import shares across manufacturing industries

Source: OECD STAN; data for aggregate EU6 (AUT, FIN, FRA, GER, NL, ESP).

As a first step of the analysis we investigate how much the stylised facts are in line with the above implications of the theory. Figure 7.2 plots annual average changes in import penetration[19] with changes in employment, real wages, value added and productivity in the 1995–2003 period, in the manufacturing sector at an aggregated euro area level.[20]

---

[19] Openness is measured by the share of (intra+extra euro area) imports in nominal domestic use (output+imports-exports). The data set used in this section is slightly different from the one used in the previous section on PPI and combines data from the EUKLEMS (employment, compensation per employee, output, producer prices) and the OECD STAN (trade data, R&D expenditures) at a 2-digit level (twenty-one manufacturing industries) and for nine EU countries (euro area with the exception of Ireland, Luxembourg and Greece). The time period used in the analysis is 1995–2003.

[20] The euro area aggregate is calculated as a weighted average of six euro area countries (Austria, Finland, France, Germany, the Netherlands and Spain). The other euro area countries have been excluded because of severe data limitations.

The clear negative relationship between the changes in employment and import penetration suggests that short-run negative impacts of rising import shares are dominant within our sample. However, the positive relationship between the changes in import penetration and the value added indicate that other mechanisms are present as well. In addition, we see that real wages increased relatively more in sectors where import penetration grew faster, which is in some way against the implications of the theory.

There are at least two possible factors that can help us to understand the somewhat contradictory picture indicated by the Figure 7.2. One is the impact of technological development. The positive relationship between the import penetration and both real wages and value added is strongly influenced by two sectors, i.e. the office and accounting machinery and the radio and television industries. When these two sectors are excluded from the analysis one would find a horizontal trend line in the case of real wages and a negative relationship between import penetration and the value added.[21] Office and accounting machinery and radio and television are the leading IT producing industries, with the highest share of R&D expenditure in output among the manufacturing industries (Figure 7.3). Benefiting from the use of advanced technologies, these sectors were able to reach value-added growth well above the manufacturing average and strong productivity gains allowed real wages to grow at around 10 per cent in these sectors during the 1995–2003 period.

Another possible explanation of the positive relationship between changes in import penetration and changes in value added, productivity and real wages is the realisation of efficiency gains due to offshoring of various stages of production. Figure 7.4 plots the average growth rate of the ratio of own imported inputs to production (a change in the so-called narrow offshoring measure) across industries. In the office and accounting machinery and radio and television sectors offshoring increased strongly in recent years, and as a result, efficiency gains from the reallocation of resources are anticipated to emerge. It is also worth mentioning, however, that offshoring activity rose relatively strongly in the tobacco, textile, clothes and leather industries, in which value added declined, and productivity and real wage dynamics remained modest.

Overall, the stylised facts indicate no clear patterns across sectors. Import penetration increased similarly in a group of high-skill sectors with strong productivity and in a group of low-skill sectors with negative

[21] The horizontal trend line in the context of real wages and the negative relationship between changes in import penetration and employment supports the idea that the bulk of the labour-demand adjustment materialises in the decline in employment rather than wages due to the existing nominal wage rigidities in the euro area.

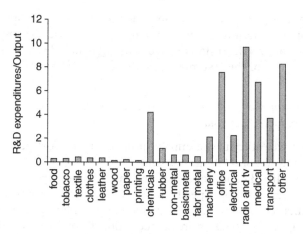

Figure 7.3 R&D expenditures (1995–2003 average)
Source: OECD STAN; data for aggregate EU6 (AUT, FIN, FRA, GER, NL, ESP).

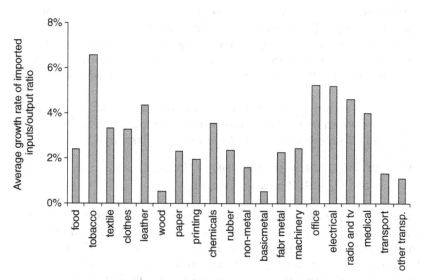

Figure 7.4 Narrow offshoring (annual average growth 1995–2003)
Source: OECD STAN; data for aggregate EU6 (AUT, FIN, FRA, Ger, NL, ESP).

output growth. This phenomenon may possibly be explained by strong technological developments in the high-skill sectors. However, it is also possible that efficiency gains from resource reallocation are strong in the leading high-skilled industries, while in the low-skilled sectors of textile, clothes and leather the negative temporary impacts remained dominant.

This dualism may justify a sectoral approach in analysing the impact of increased import penetration on labour markets in case the impact is allowed to vary across the different groups of high-skilled vs. low-skilled sectors. This is one of the assumptions we test in the following section.

7.4.3   Estimating the effects of import penetration on sectoral labour demand

In this section we estimate the impact of increased import penetration on the euro area sectoral labour demand.

We use a simplified conditional labour demand model specification,[22] where we augment the core specification by measures of import penetration as demand shifters. We also include an interactive term of real wages and import penetration in our equation in order to be able to incorporate the impact of globalisation on real wage elasticity of labour demand. Our specification is similar to that of Bruno *et al.* (2004), whose model is based on an economy with a representative firm for each sector of the economy which works with two inputs, labour and capital, producing one output. Trade openness (or international exposure) enters the model through its role in the production function of the domestic firms. The labour demand function is then derived from the minimisation of the firms' costs. Although the theoretical model is somewhat simplistic, it has the advantage of being easy to estimate without major transformations. The resulting labour demand equation assumes that globalisation may have an impact on labour demand through both a direct effect (β_{imp}) and via an impact on the labour demand elasticity (β_{wimp}):

$$
\begin{aligned}
\ln l_{i,j,t} = \gamma * \ln l_{i,j,t} + (\beta_w + \beta_{wimp} * \ln impsh_{i,j,t}) * \ln wp_{i,j,t} \\
+ \beta_y * y_{i,j,t} + \beta_{imp} * \ln impsh_{i,j,t} + \mu_t + \varepsilon_{i,j,t}
\end{aligned}
\tag{4}
$$

where l is employment, wp is the real wage, *impsh* is the import penetration measure, y is output, μ_t is a time dummy and all variables are in logs. β_{wimp} is a coefficient of the interactive term for the impact of increased import penetration on the real wages elasticity. As discussed previously, globalisation should have raised the elasticity of real wage of the labour demand via two channels: (1) increased competition exerts downward pressure on domestic product prices (higher price elasticity on product markets) so that companies have to limit increases in

---

[22] In the conditional model, the profit-maximising level of labour demand is determined by minimising the cost of production at a given level of output, contrary to the unconditional labour-demand model where firms maximise profits by choosing the optimal mix of input quantities and the level of output for given input and output prices.

labour costs and (2) easier access to capital and foreign labour makes it less difficult to substitute away from domestic labour in case its price increases.

The data set used in the analysis consists of nine euro area countries, twenty-one manufacturing sectors (at the 2-digit NACE level) and covers the period of 1995–2003. (A detailed description of the countries and sectors is given in Appendix A2.) Trade data are extracted from OECD STAN in order to compile the import-penetration measures. The employment, output and real wages variables were constructed on the basis of the EUKLEMS data set.

We use two measures of import penetration to estimate the impact of globalisation on labour demand: the import share and the 'narrow' offshoring measure. The import share is defined as the ratio of imports over domestic absorption:

$$impsh_{i,j,t} = M_{i,j,t}/(Y_{i,j,t} + M_{i,j,t} - X_{i,j,t})$$

where Mij and Xij are values of imports and exports in industry i and country j and Yij is output at current prices. 'Narrow' offshoring is defined as the ratio of own imported inputs over domestic absorption:

$$narrow_{i,j,t} = M^{INP}{}_{ii,j,t}/(Y_{i,j,t} + M_{i,j,t} - X_{i,j,t}) = \alpha^{INP}_{ii,j,2000}$$
$$\star\, M_{i,j,t}/(Y_{i,j,t} + M_{i,j,t} - X_{i,j,t})$$

where $\alpha^{INP}_{ii,j,2000}$ is the share of imported inputs of industry i in total imports of the same industry in the year 2000. The source of the coefficient is the OECD Input–output database.[23] Given that our $\alpha^{INP}_{ii,j,2000}$ coefficient has no time dimension, the 'narrow' measure of offshoring differs from the import share only at the cross-sectional level.[24]

To control for the possibly different impact of increased import penetration on high-skilled and low-skilled sectors we classify the sectors into two groups. (The classification is based on Jean and Nicoletti (2002), for more info see the Appendix A.3.) Our augmented labour

---

[23] We also created a 'broad' offshoring measure, which is defined as the ratio of all imported inputs over domestic absorption:

$$broad_{i,j,t} = (\sum_m M^{INP}_{im,j,t})/(Y_{i,j,t} - X_{i,j,t}) = (\sum_m a^{INP}_{im,j,2000} \star M_{m,j,t}))/(Y_{i,j,t} + M_{i,j,t} - X_{i,j,t})$$

where $\alpha_{im,j,2000}{}^{INP}$ is the share of imported inputs of industry i in country j in total imports of industry m in country j in the year 2000, taken from the OECD Input–output database. However, estimates were insignificant and therefore we do not report the results.

[24] Given that data on imported input shares are available for the year 1995 it is possible to give a time dimension to this factor as well.

demand equation is first estimated on the sample of all sectors and then independently on each of the sub-samples of the high-skilled and low-skilled sector groups.

The equation contains a lagged dependent variable. In order to get unbiased and consistent estimates of the regression coefficients we use the Arellano-Bond estimator. To test that there is no serial autocorrelation in the levels, we present the second-order serial correlation of the differenced equation. We consider all the explanatory variables as endogenous and instrument them with their own second, third and fourth lagged values. In order to check the validity of the instruments the Hansen J-test of over-identifying restrictions is used. When the equation is estimated on the sub-sample of high-skilled/low-skilled sector groups the number of instruments is cut in order to keep the power of the test.

The results of the estimations using the import share and the 'narrow' offshoring measure are presented in Table 7.4. The table consists of three blocks: basic labour demand specification (columns 1–3), the augmented labour demand specification using the import share (columns 4–6), and the augmented labour demand specification using the 'narrow' offshoring measure (columns 7–9). Each of the estimations has been done on three different samples: including all sectors, and restricting the sample to the high-skilled sectors and low-skilled sectors.

The test statistics on the second-order autocorrelation and on the over-identifying restrictions indicate that our estimates are consistent and unbiased and the instruments are valid. The relatively small changes in the major parameters of the basic labour demand equation in the different specifications show that these estimates are robust. As regards the import penetration measures the picture is somewhat mixed. When estimated on the sample of all sectors and the sub-sample of high-skilled sectors their coefficients are insignificant. However, in the sub-sample of low-skilled sectors both the direct impact and the impact on the real wage elasticity are negative and significant at the 10 per cent level. This may imply that the import share and offshoring indeed has a different impact on high-skilled and low-skilled sectors: the impact is significant and negative on both employment and real wage elasticity in the low-skilled sectors, but insignificant in the high-skilled ones. This finding is in line with the conclusions drawn from the stylised facts exercise at the end of Section 7.4.2.

As regards the magnitude, the derived long-term coefficients of the direct effects of import penetration measures are in the range of -0.08–-0.12 (Table 7.5). The 2.1 per cent actual annual growth rate of the import share would imply that the increase of the import share had a -0.17 pp contribution to the annual average low-skilled employment

Table 7.4 *The effects of import penetration on sectoral employment – estimation results*

	Basic labour demand specification			Augmented by import share			Augmented by 'narrow' outsourcing		
	(1)	(2)	(3)	(4)	(5)	(6)	(7)	(8)	(9)
Dependent var. Employment	All sectors	High skilled	Low skilled	All sectors	High skilled	Low skilled	All sectors	High skilled	Low skilled
Employment (-1)	0.6603***	0.6347***	0.6858***	0.5816***	0.4929***	0.6038***	0.5829***	0.4941***	0.6883***
	[7.55]	[4.33]	[10.2]	[10.7]	[6.42]	[9.65]	[11.0]	[6.01]	[13.5]
Output	0.1640**	0.1983*	0.3890***	0.2149***	0.2978***	0.3288***	0.2044***	0.3057***	0.3183***
	[2.50]	[1.81]	[4.65]	[3.47]	[3.33]	[4.51]	[3.10]	[3.42]	[5.27]
Real wages	-0.1556***	-0.1242**	-0.2572***	-0.1033***	-0.0788*	-0.1890***	-0.1078***	-0.1890*	-0.2394***
	[-3.01]	[-2.06]	[-3.27]	[-2.06]	[-1.93]	[-3.70]	[-3.10]	[-1.93]	[-3.10]
Real wages * Import share				-0.0087	-0.0036	-0.0619*			
				[-0.56]	[-0.25]	[-1.93]			
Import share				-0.0067	0.0054	-0.0314*			
				[-0.70]	[0.58]	[-1.90]			
Real wages * Narrow Offshoring							-0.0058	-0.0002	-0.0612*
							[-0.42]	[-0.012]	[-1.68]
Narrow Offshoring							-0.004	0.0092	-0.0369*
							[-0.44]	[1.06]	[-1.84]
Observations	1444	704	740	1350	649	701	1350	649	701
Number of id3	162	79	83	155	75	80	155	75	80
# instruments	90	54	54	144	99	99	144	99	99
Hansen p-value	0.229	0.440	0.274	0.198	0.927	0.984	0.229	0.962	0.893
AR1 p-value	0.000	0.005	0.013	0.000	0.003	0.000	0.000	0.002	0.000
AR2 p-value	0.371	0.299	0.697	0.936	0.972	0.859	0.953	0.972	0.784

All variables are in logarithms. All equations include time dummies. The reported coefficients are results of a one-step robust Arellano–Bond estimation, i.e. the standard error estimates are consistent in the presence of any pattern of heteroskedasticity and autocorrelation within panels.
Robust *t* statistics in brackets.
***p<0.01, **p<0.05, *p<0.1.

Table 7.5 *Long-term elasticities and calculated actual impacts in the low-cost manufacturing sectors*

Variables	Coeff Import share	Long-term elasticities	Annual average growth of openness measure (%)	Actual impact annual average
Emp(-1)	0.603***			
Output	0.328***	0.83		
Real wages	-0.189***	-0.48		
Real wages * Import share	-0.061*	-0.16		-0.33
Import share 'Narrow' offshoring	-0.031*	-0.08	2.1	-0.17
Emp(-1)	0.688***			
Output	0.318***	1.02		
Real wages	-0.239***	-0.77		
Real wages * Narrow offsh.	-0.061*	-0.20		-0.41
Narrow offsh.	-0.036*	-0.12	2.1	-0.24

growth over the period the 1995–2003. The contribution of the 'narrow' offshoring is somewhat higher (−0.24 pp). Given the −0.3 per cent annual average growth rate of low-skilled employment, the contributions from increased import penetration explain 50–75 per cent of the total annual decline. According to the calculations, import penetration increased the real wage elasticity of labour demand by 0.3 pp on an annual average, which compared to an estimated long-term elasticity of real wages of −0.5 to −0.8. However, given the high uncertainty around the real wage elasticity estimates in the empirical literature the impact is in an acceptable range.

As regards the robustness of our estimates the picture is somewhat mixed. We tried three alternative specifications by excluding either the direct impact or the interactive term and also by including the export share into our augmented labour demand specification. Although the signs and value of the coefficients of the import penetration measures remained mostly unchanged, in the new specifications they lost their significance. We also experimented with the inclusion of capital stock and technology proxies into the equations, but these proved to be insignificant.[25]

The theory offers various possible explanations as to why it is difficult to obtain robust and significant estimates for the impact of rising import

[25] One possible explanation for that is the serious data limitation at the 2-digit industry level both in the context of capital stock and R&D expenditure data.

penetration on labour demand at the sectoral level. First, it is hard to disentangle the temporary negative effects from the positive impact of the long-term efficiency gains. Second, it is hard to find an appropriate proxy for technology and, given the strong endogeneity of technology and trade, it is almost impossible to separate these two effects from each other. Third, due to increased production segmentation substitution of low-skilled workers with high-skilled workers takes place within sectors rather than between them. Thus, a measure that describes the changes in skilled/unskilled ratios within sectors would probably improve the results. Fourth, the import penetration measures used in our analysis are not disaggregated enough, i.e. a possible distinction by imports of origin could reveal more direct impacts. Finally, according to the theory, one of the new characteristics of the recent phase of globalisation is its relatively strong indirect impact on domestic labour markets, the so-called 'threat' effect. As this effect goes beyond actual import penetration numbers, regressing actual trade data on labour market indicators cannot identify this potentially significant impact of globalisation.

7.5   Conclusions

This paper tries to give a preliminary quantification of the impact of increasing import penetration on euro area prices and labour markets. Given that we focus on non-energy imports, we exclude from the analysis both the upward pressure on domestic inflation due to higher oil prices and the positive impact on labour demand (and wages) due to expanding export markets. Thus, our analysis is of a partial nature and the overall net effects on domestic prices are expected to be smaller in absolute terms than depicted by our analysis.

Different methods are used to try to quantify the effect of rising imports on euro area domestic prices. First, we measure the low-cost-country effect on euro area producer and consumer prices using information from input–output tables. The main finding is that imports from low-cost countries reduced euro area PPI by about 0.12 pp and consumer price inflation by about 0.05 pp per year on average over the period 1996 to 2004. As this method allows only a static analysis, we also use a VAR of the production chain to estimate the effect of lower import prices on euro area producer prices and the HICP. These estimates point to an average annual downward impact of about 0.3 pp on producer price inflation and 0.1–0.2 pp on headline HICP inflation over the period 1995 to 2004.

Both the approaches using the input–output tables and the VAR do, however, only include the effect of China and the New Member States on euro area import prices. Therefore, we also estimate the import penetration effect using a panel with sectoral data for euro area countries and introducing a more encompassing variable for the import penetration, namely the import share in production of each sector. This variable includes not only the more recently observed effect of low-cost countries but more generally the effect of stronger trade integration. The results indicate that increased imports have reduced euro area producer prices at the sectoral level (including both competition and input cost effects and all trading partners) by about 0.8–1.0 pp per year on average over the two estimation periods, namely 1978–2003 and 1995–2003. This effect is, as expected, higher than the one obtained from the VAR. In addition, it also exceeds the estimates in IMF (2006) as our estimates are based on long-term elasticities, controlling, for example, for the effects of monetary policy. Taking a more short-term perspective would reduce the estimated impact to about 0.4–0.5 pp. The effect on consumer prices cannot, however, be assessed due to data limitations at this disaggregation level of disaggregation.

It should be noted that all of the above estimates are based on observations in the recent past and cannot easily be extrapolated to the future. In particular, for the results using data on low-cost countries, the effect of China and the New Member States might decline in the future as these countries catch up with higher price standards. It is important to emphasise that the analysis does not consider the monetary policy reaction, which would alter the medium-term impact on prices, profits and labour demand. Given that monetary policy controls inflation in the medium term, the assumption of unaltered monetary policy reaction means that a one-time opening up of trade is seen to have an impact on changes in relative prices, with only temporary effects on inflation.

Turning to the impact of globalisation on labour markets, an opening up of trade with low-cost countries would imply an increased import penetration in low-skilled sectors and a shift in labour demand from unskilled towards skilled workers in the euro area. According to the traditional trade theory this shift should occur between sectors, i.e. employment/wages in the low-skilled industries with strong import competition should decline relative to the high-skilled sector employment/wages. However, actual data indicate that import penetration increased to a similar strong degree both in high-skilled and low-skilled industries in the euro area during the 1995–2003 period. Moreover, while employment declined at the same rate, output, productivity and real wage developments showed a different pattern in the two groups: they increased strongly in the high-skilled sectors but remained contained in the low-skilled group. There are two possible explanations for this dualism. One is the strong technological development in high-tech sectors (especially office and accounting and radio and television), which boosted productivity growth. Given the strong increase of offshoring activities in some of the high-skill sectors, another possible explanation is that in these industries the positive efficiency gains from resource reallocation are relatively strong, while in the low-skilled sectors of textile, clothes and leather the negative temporary impacts remained dominant.

We tried to quantify the impact of increased import penetration on employment and wages by estimating sectoral labour demand equations for the euro area. We found no significant effects either in the sample of all sectors or in the sub-sample of high-skilled industries. In the low-skilled sectors the estimates showed a direct negative impact of import penetration on employment and also a positive impact on the real wage elasticity of labour demand. According to the estimates, actual import penetration contributed -0.2 pp annually directly to the decline in employment, and increased the real wage elasticity by $0.3–0.4$ pp in the low-cost sectors. Given that technology and the capital stock are not included in our specification (mainly due to data problems) these estimates are somewhat uncertain and should be interpreted with caution. The main message from the analysis of labour markets is that there is some evidence that globalisation has helped to keep wage developments contained in the 1995–2003 period. However, given the complexity of the globalisation effect and the presence of a number of simultaneous shocks (technology, structural reforms, etc.), the actual impact is hard to quantify.

Appendix A.1 Data used for the input–output analysis

As the classification of producer prices differs from that for import prices, the following matching was done between different sectors, taking the weighted average where several import price sectors have an impact on producer prices:

Table 7A.1 *Data used for the input–output analysis*

Producer price sector	Corresponding import price sector(s)
Textiles	Textile yarn, fabrics
Wearing apparel; furs	Dyeing, tanning and colouring materials; Textile yarn, fabrics; Articles of apparel and clothing;
Leather and leather products	Dyeing, tanning and colouring materials; Leather manufacture, n.e.s.; Travel goods; Footwear;

Table 7A.1 (*cont.*)

Producer price sector	Corresponding import price sector(s)
Wood and products of wood and cork (except furniture)	Cork and wood manufacture (excl. furniture)
Pulp, paper and paper products	Paper, paperboard and their articles
Printed matter and recorded media	Paper, paperboard and their articles
Chemicals, chemical products and man-made fibres	Organic chemicals; Inorganic chemicals; Medicinal and pharmaceutical products; Fertilisers; Chemical materials and products, n.e.s.
Rubber and plastic products	Plastics in primary forms; Plastics in non-primary forms; Rubber manufacture, n.e.s.
Other non-metallic mineral products	Non-metallic mineral manufacture, n.e.s.
Basic metals	Iron and steel; Non-ferrous metals; manufacture of metals, n.e.s.
Fabricated metal products, except machinery and equipment	Iron and steel; Non-ferrous metals; manufacture of metals, n.e.s.
Machinery and equipment n.e.c.	Power-generating machinery; Specialised industrial machinery; Metalworking machinery; General industrial machinery, n.e.s.
Office machinery and computers	Office and data processing equipment
Electrical machinery and apparatus n.e.c.	Electrical machinery, n.e.s.
Radio, television and communication equipment and apparatus	Telecommunications and sound recording equipment
Medical, precision and optical instruments, watches and clocks	Professional and scientific instruments, n.e.s.; Optical and photographic goods and equipment
Motor vehicles, trailers and semi-trailers	Road vehicles
Other transport equipment	Other transport equipment
Furniture; other manufactured goods, n.e.c.	Furniture, and parts thereof

All data are from Eurostat, with the import data from the COMEXT database using extra-euro area trade data.

Appendix A.2 Data used for the regression analysis

For the regression analysis, sectoral data from the STAN database of the OECD are used. In the estimations of producer prices, we have used the same data set as IMF (2006), while we have constructed our own somewhat more extensive data set for the labour market regressions based on the EUKLEMS and the OECD STAN. The IMF data set and the EUKLEMS – OECD STAN cover the time periods of 1978–2003 and 1995–2003, respectively. The sectors included are the following:

Table 7A.2 *Data used for the regression analysis*

	STAN class	IMF data set	EUKLEMS -STAN OECD data set
Food products, beverages and tobacco	15–16	x	
Food products and beverages	15		x
Tobacco products	16		x
Textiles, textile products, leather and footwear	17–19		
Textiles and textile products	17+18	x	
Textiles	17		x
Wearing apparel, dressing and dying of fur	18		x
Leather, leather products and footwear	19	x	x
Wood and products of wood and cork	20	x	x
Pulp, paper, paper products, printing and publishing	21–22		
Pulp, paper and paper products	21	x	x
Printing and publishing	22	x	x
Chemical, rubber, plastics and fuel products	23–25		
Coke, refined petroleum products and nuclear fuel	23		
Chemicals and chemical products	24	x	x
Rubber and plastics products	25	x	x
Other non-metallic mineral products	26	x	x
Basic metals and fabricated metal products	27–28		
Basic metals	27	x	x
Fabricated metal products, except machinery and equipment	28	x	x
Machinery and equipment	29–33		
Machinery and equipment, n.e.c.	29	x	x
Electrical and optical equipment	30–33	x	
Office, accounting and computing machinery	30		x
Electrical machinery and apparatus, n.e.c.	31		x
Radio, television and communication equipment	32		x
Medical, precision and optical instruments	33		x
Transport equipment	34–35		
Motor vehicles, trailers and semi-trailers	34	x	x
Other transport equipment	35	x	x
Manufacturing n.e.c.; recycling	36+37	x	

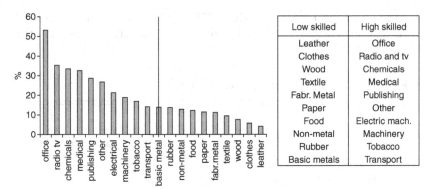

Figure 7A.1 Share of skilled workers in sectoral employment
Source: Jean and Nicoletti (2002).

In addition, the following euro area countries were included in the two data sets:

	AUT	BEL	DEH	ESP	FIN	FRA	GRE	IRL	ITA	NDL	LUX	PRT
IMF data set	x	x			x	x	x		x			
EUKLEMS – STAN OECD data set	x	x	x	x	x	x			x	x		x

Appendix A.3 Classification of sectors by skill intensity

Jean and Nicoletti (2002) presents data on the share of skilled workers in sector employment for eighteen OECD countries for the year 1995 (see p. 26, Table 1). We use this data to classify the sectors into groups of high-skilled and low-skilled sectors.

REFERENCES

Anderson, T. W., and C. Hsiao (1981). 'Estimation of dynamic models with error components', *Journal of the American Statistical Association*, 76, 598–606.

Atkeson, A., and A. Burstein (2005). 'Pricing-to-market, trade costs and international relative prices', *American Economic Review*, 98(5), 1998–2031.

Baldwin, R. (2006). 'Globalisation: the great unbundling(s)', in *Globalisation Challenges for Europe*, Secretariat of the Economic Council, Helsinki: Finnish Prime Minister's Office, Chapter 1.

Ball, L. (2006). *Has Globalization Changed Inflation?*, NBER working papers No. 12687.

Borio, C., and A. Filardo (2007). *Globalisation and Inflation*, BIS working paper series No. 277 (May).

Borjas, G. J., R. B. Freeman, and F. Katz (1992). 'On the labour market effects of immigration and trade', in *Immigration and the Work Force*, G. Borjas and R. Freeman (eds.), University of Chicago and NBER, pp. 213–44.

Boulhol, H., S. Dobbelaere, and S. Maioli (2006). *Imports as Product and Labor Market Discipline*, Institute for the Study of Labor, discussion paper series No. 2178 (June).

Braconier, H. *et al.* (2002). *Vertical FDI Revisited*, The Research Institute of Industrial Organization, working paper No. 579.

Bruno, G., A. M. Falzoni, and R. Helg (2004). *Measuring the Effect of Globalization on Labour Demand Elasticity: an Empirical Approach to OECD Countries*, CESPRI working paper No. 153.

Chen, N., J. Imbs, and A. Scott (2004). *Competition, Globalization and the Decline of Inflation*, CEPR discussion paper series, No. 4695.

Cuyvers, L., M. Dumont, G. Rayp, and K. Stevens (2002). *Wage and Employment Effects in the EU of International Trade with the Emerging Economies*, University of Gent working paper No. 2002/142.

Dreher, A., and N. Gaston (2005). *Has Globalization Really Had an Effect on Unions?*, Swiss Institute for Business Cycle Research working paper No. 110.

Dumont, M., G. Rayp, and P. Willeme (2006). 'Does internationalization affect union bargaining power? An empirical study for five EU countries', *Oxford Economic Papers*, 58, 77–102.

ECB (2006). 'Effects of the Rising Trade Integration of Low-Cost Countries on Euro Area Import Prices', *Monthly Bulletin*, Box No. 6, August 2006.

Feenstra, R. C., and G. H. Hanson (1999). 'The impact of offshoring and high-technology capital on wages: estimates for the US, 1979–1990', *The Quarterly Journal of Economics*, 114(3), 907–40.

(2003). 'Global production and inequality: a survey of trade and wages', in *Handbook of International Trade*, E. K. Choi and J. Harrigan (eds.), Oxford: Basil and Blackwell.

Gorg, H. *et al.* (2005). 'Labour demand effects of international offshoring: evidence from plant-level data', *International Review of Economics and Finance*, 14(3), 365–77.

Hahn, E. (2003). *Pass-Through of External Shocks to Euro Area Inflation*, ECB working paper No. 573.

Hamermesh, D. S. (1993). *Labor Demand*, Princeton University Press.

Ihrig J., S. B. Kamin, D. Lindner, and J. Marquez (2007). *Some Simple Tests of the Globalisation and Inflation Hypothesis*, Board of Governors of the Federal Reserve System (U.S.), international finance discussion papers No. 891.

IMF (2006). 'Globalization and inflation', *World Economic Outlook*, April.

Jean, S., and G. Nicoletti (2002). *Product Market Regulation and Wage Premia in Europe and North America: An Empirical Investigation*, OECD Economics Department working papers No. 318.

234   G. Pula and F. Skudelny

5

Kamin, B., M. Marazzi, and J. W. Schindler (2004). *Is China Exporting Deflation?*, Board of Governors of the Federal Reserve System, international financial discussion papers No. 791.

Kim, M. K., and H. Beladi (2005). 'Is free trade deflationary?', *Economics Letters*, 89, 343–9.

Lawrence, R. Z., and M. J. Slaughter (1993). 'International trade and american wages in the 1980's: giant sucking sound or a small hickup?' in *Brookings Papers on Economic Activity: Microeconomics 2*, Martin Neil Baily and Clifford Winston (eds.), pp. 161–211.

Machin, S., and J. van Reenen (1998). 'Technology and changes in skill structure: evidence from seven OECD countries', *The Quarterly Journal of Economics*, 113(4), 1215–44.

Melitz, M. J., and G. I. P. Ottaviano (2005). *Market Size, Trade and Productivity*, NBER working paper No. 11393.

Molnar, M., N. Pain, and D. Taglioni (2006). *The Internationalisation of Production, International Offshoring and OECD Labour Markets*, Paris: OECD.

Pain, N., I. Koske, and M. Sollie (2006). *Globalisation and Inflation in the OECD Economies*, OECD Economics Department working papers No. 524.

Rodrik, D. (1999). 'Globalisation and labour, or: if globalisation is a bowl of cherries, why are there so many glum faces around the table?', in *Market Integration, Regionalism and the Global Economy*, R. E. Baldwin et al. (eds.), Cambridge University Press, pp. 117–48.

Rogoff, K. (2003). 'Globalization and global disinflation', paper prepared for the Federal Reserve Bank of Kansas City conference on *Monetary Policy and Uncertainty: Adapting to a Changing Economy*, Jackson Hole, WY, 28–30 August.

Romer, D. (1993). 'Openness and inflation: theory and evidence', *Quarterly Journal of Economics*, 108(4), 869–903.

Slaughter, M. (2001). 'International trade and labour demand elasticities', *Journal of International Economics*, 54, 27–62.

Terfous, N. (2006). *Globalization and the Labour Market in the Developed Countries*, Diagnostics prévisions et analyses economiques, Direction Générale du Trésor et de la Politique Economique No. 96 (January).

Van Welsum, D., and G. Vickery (2005). 'Potential off-shoring of ICT-intensive occupations', in *Enhancing the Performance of the Services Sector*, Paris: OECD, pp. 179–204.

Wood, A. (1994). 'How trade hurt unskilled workers', *Journal of Economic Perspectives*, 9(3), 57–80.

8   Monetary policy strategy in a global environment

Philippe Moutot and Giovanni Vitale

8.1   Introduction

Since the mid 1980s the world economy has gone through profound transformations of which the sources and effects are probably not yet completely understood. The process of continuous integration in trade, production and financial markets across countries and economic regions – which is what is generally defined as 'globalisation' – affects directly the conduct of monetary policy in a variety of respects. The aim of this chapter is to broaden the analysis of Chapter 2 (which examined macroeconomic impacts of trade globalisation) to also analyse the structural implications of financial globalisation for the domestic economies of developed countries, and to deduce from these implications lessons for the conduct of monetary policy and associated risks to price stability.

The most prominent stylised fact in the last twenty-five years is, from the point of view of the economic literature, that the level of inflation and its variability around this level has declined in both developed and, at some later stage, developing economies, leading several scholars and professionals to refer to this phenomenon as the 'Great Moderation'.[1] But other developments have gradually added up and also need to be taken into account. They include global imbalances that have appeared in the current accounts of some large countries as well as the recurrence of booms and busts with global consequences over the last decade and the more recent acceleration and fall of commodity prices, which has ended or, at least, interrupted the 'Great Moderation'.

The debate has thus long focused on three possible interpretations of the Great Moderation: structural change, higher ability of policy

We thank A. Dalamangas for helpful research assistance. The views expressed in this paper do not necessarily reflect the opinions of the ECB or of the Eurosystem. We thank participants at the International Conference of the Banque de France for comments on an early draft in 2007. All errors are ours.
[1] See among the others, McConnell and Perez-Quiros (2000) and Blanchard and Simon (2001).

235

makers and, more simply, good luck. Globalisation and its initial impact on import prices in particular may have played a role in the first and the last explanations either by changing the structure of the domestic economies involved in international trade or by exerting a somehow 'mechanical' downward pressure on inflation trends. This chapter investigates the wider implications of the associated changes in the adjustment mechanism of the national economies to exogenous shocks and monetary policy actions. We will argue that the three explanations above are interrelated and that, in the future, they may play out in many other ways than recently experienced. In particular, the recent increases in oil and other commodity prices constitute important, different and immediate tests of monetary policy in which some of the lessons above may have to be taken into account.

The chapter also refers to another less-studied stylised fact, the decrease of home bias over the same period, and to other associated characteristics of financial flows including the high recurrence of asset-price bubbles. Another feature of globalisation over the last ten years has been a simultaneous increase of pegs to the dollar and currency boards to the euro on the one hand, and of central banks targeting inflation, on the other. A related feature of globalisation is the change, in terms of relative size and financial power, of emerging countries and developed countries. While the US economy dwarfed both European and developing economies after the Second World War and until the 1990s, the end of the last century witnessed the emergence of large countries like India, China, Russia and Brazil. This decrease of the home bias, the diffusion of monetary policy strategies targeting inflation or pegging to a major currency and the new distribution of financial power not only change the impact of capital flows, but also affect the dynamics of exchange rates and more generally of international adjustments, including global imbalances and financial crises. These elements also have consequences for the conduct of monetary policy, its ability to anticipate and react to international crises, and the nature of international surveillance.

The chapter is organised as follows: the next section briefly reviews how trade globalisation might be influencing the euro area macroeconomy, building upon the arguments outlined in Chapter 2. Section 8.3 extends the discussion about the structural implications of globalisation to the financial sector. In particular, the section distinguishes between the eventual change in the 'home bias' and in the allocation of domestic savings and, more generally, the macroeconomic implications of the high level of integration of worldwide financial markets. Section 8.4 draws the main messages, including some implications for monetary policy and international policy cooperation. First, national monetary policy strategies must include the structural analysis of economic developments, in order to disentangle the possible shocks hitting the economy. In particular, the role of financial markets in the transmission of such shocks needs to be taken into account as their evolution and global integration is likely to play a significant role in the creation and distribution of liquidity across countries. The increased role of financial markets in the transmission mechanism provides further support to 'leaning against the wind' of possible asset-price bubbles. Second, the interdependence of financial markets across the globe strengthens the case for a new, more refined multilateral policy cooperation that integrates financial markets and international capital flows with economic developments and policy stances.

8.2   Globalisation, inflation and changes in the structure of the real economy

As outlined in Chapter 2, wages of unskilled workers in the industrialised countries have declined relative to the wage of skilled workers and the rate of profit of capital has increased. Moreover, due to the secular decline in transportation costs and communication, firms have also relocated the production of goods (and services) that have low-skilled labour content towards the newly emerging countries, while the production of goods (and services) with high-skilled labour content has shifted towards industrialised countries. As a result, in all major OECD economies import prices have declined relative to domestic producer prices in the last twenty years. It must be acknowledged that globalisation has led, however, not only to a decline in the relative price of imports of manufactured goods and services but also – especially in the last five years – to an increase in oil and commodity prices, largely due to higher global demand originating from China and other Asian countries, among others.

These developments have at least two impacts of relevance to central bankers. First, they undermine the use and indicator value of core inflation. Indeed, if the evolution of items included in such a concept becomes directly correlated with the evolution of items excluded, the notion of core inflation loses its meaning. Second, the increase in oil and commodity prices – including food – may lower the real income of lower-wage workers and increase their inflation perceptions, making the benefits of globalisation uneven, even when abstracting from production and competitiveness considerations. Moreover, by concentrating price increases on products frequently purchased, it may encourage a bias in perceptions that leads consumers to at least temporarily biased perceptions of their real income. To the extent that such perceptions may have an impact on the tendency to consume or save, on the support of the public for monetary policy and on the credibility of the central bank, this may also seriously affect the conduct of monetary policy. Furthermore, the acceleration in oil price increases in the beginning of 2008 – and its impact on headline price indexes in many economies – confirms some recent empirical evidence (Blanchard and Gali, 2007) on the crucial role played both by monetary policies focusing on the maintenance of price stability and by the flexibility of real wages in facilitating the absorption of the oil price shock. Central banks may therefore have to recall the lessons of the 1970s' oil price increases: the need to prevent second-round effects, the need for wages to quickly absorb the corresponding real income loss and the need for special communication in order to minimise gaps between perceptions of inflation and actual inflation.

The decline in global inflation may be related not only to the direct cyclical effect of globalisation on the relative price of imports – described in Chapter 2 – but also to a permanent effect that globalisation may have had on the structure of the real economy, in particular on the price and wage formation mechanisms, in the developed economies.

At first, globalisation may have permanently increased the level of output that an economy can produce, without generating inflationary pressures. The argument runs from the decline in the relative price of imported goods that increases the workers' real wages without increasing the nominal costs for firms. Hence, for any nominal wage, the labour supply in the economy would increase because workers would be willing to work more for the same nominal wage and because new workers would be willing to work for lower nominal wages. This process entails a rightward shift of the 'long-run' Phillips curve, which delivers both higher output growth and lower inflation. However, this approach does not take into account the effect of oil prices and commodities mentioned above. Also, the effect of oil and commodity prices on potential output may be significant in countries with low productivity growth. Moreover, the approach in the paragraph above may not give sufficient weight to considerations of competitiveness. In fact, it is most valid for countries which benefit from a sufficient level of product and services specialisation in order to employ mostly skilled workers. And even in that case, this does not take into account the adjustment dynamics necessary to make use of such skills in new fields when technology and telecommunications make it possible to use low-skilled workers for traditional products or services.

Indeed, in those countries that are endowed with potentially skilled workers the adjustment needed to compete with new emerging countries entails an increase in the import content of domestic production, including in those sectors which sell their products in the global marketplace. Hence, in developed countries the export sector has to go through a phase of significant transitional unemployment and lower consumption of workers. Thus, the economy may take quite some time to come back to medium-term potential output. The increase in firms' investment needed to maintain competitiveness is, in a first period, associated with diminishing production and only at a later stage do employment and consumption catch up. The example of Germany and more generally the euro area in this context is particularly notable.

Finally, the increase of oil and other commodity prices may, if it is substantial and permanent, have an impact on the production function of many economies. It may thus counterbalance the positive effect of cheaper prices for other imports, at least for countries which are not well enough specialised or not sufficiently energy efficient to take sufficient advantage of the latter. This may even lengthen the transitional process described above. In any case, the negative impact on the production function should reduce the output gap, thereby influencing inflation dynamics.

These adjustment dynamics have also consequences for monetary policy. First, indicators such as the 'output gap' and the 'NAIRU' (non-accelerating inflation rate of unemployment) may be biased to the extent that the usual statistical methods for their measurement are based on former and normally shorter cycles, which may result in a spurious amplification of both the decline and subsequent acceleration in trend dynamics. Second, the conduct of monetary policy may need to take into account the possibly prolonged adjustment in the export sector and maintain lower interest rates during the downturn but increase them in the recovery period at levels and speed that might be higher than normal. This may explain, along with more traditional arguments, the observation, since the start of this century, of a substantial deviation of observed policy rates in the major developed economies from the normative rate prescribed by standard Taylor Rules estimated on historical data.

A different structural explanation of the observed trend decline in inflation in the last twenty years focuses on the impact of globalisation on the adjustment mechanism to demand shocks. In particular, it is argued that globalisation has increased the incentives for firms to absorb changes in demand by adjusting employment rather than the price for the final products. In other words, the short-run Phillips curve, which maps excess demand over supply into inflation,[2] has flattened as a result of the increase in trade and production specialisation across countries.[3] As indicated in Chapter 2, the empirical evidence concerning the eventual flattening of the Phillips curve remains rather controversial. Overall, it seems to be true that the Phillips curve has flattened. Although this may give a sense of comfort to central bankers, they also need to be aware that such a Phillips curve may quickly see its slope change when the public learns about it. In this context, the consequences in terms of output of accepting an inflation creep and thereafter having to combat it – the so-called 'sacrifice ratio' – are also growing (Viñals, 2000).

However, the role of globalisation does not imply that global slack should be a major consideration, at least for large economies. Also, the impact of globalisation on import prices, which is a very relevant concern for small and medium-size economies, is less relevant for large economies. Moreover, the flattening of the Phillips curve is also the result of a combination of credibility and good luck. Indeed, globalisation may also have influenced the price-setting behaviour of firms, as mentioned by Benati (2007). Finally, even if the flattening of the yield curve is purely connected to the increased credibility of central banks, some stroke of 'bad luck' in the future cannot be excluded. Higher commodity prices, particularly if they affect the inflation perceptions of agents, could lead to a steepening of the Phillips curve.

8.3   The globalisation of financial markets

The progressive liberalisation of capital accounts that started in the 1980s in the developed economies and thereafter gradually involved also some of the more advanced emerging markets has, over the years, spurred the integration of world financial markets. The higher interdependence of financial markets and the accompanying financial innovation have changed the monetary transmission mechanism. It thereby poses new challenges to central banks that must interpret the developments in the domestic economy and, thus, assess their monetary policy stance.

Such challenges can be viewed as the results of an interaction among four main factors that characterise the latest developments in the

[2] And, in standard macroeconomic forward-looking models, inflation expectations.
[3] Gali and Monacelli (2005) model a small open economy trading with an infinite number of other foreign economies. In the Phillips curve of the model they show that the more open the economy is and the less substitutable domestic goods are with respect to foreign goods, the lower is the coefficient on the domestic output gap.

globalisation process of financial markets. First, the home bias of investors has decreased, although in unequal manners across main countries. Second, the weight of global financial transactions relative to trade and services transactions has increased, thus giving relatively more importance to financial determinants in driving the dynamics of exchange and interest rates, at least in the short to medium term. Third, such dynamics have been influenced by the diffusion across central banks of inflation targeting and currency board or pegging strategies. Fourth, the development of financial markets has spurred financial innovation and its diffusion, multiplying the techniques for the transfer of risks and thereby strengthening the channels of diffusion and transmission of financial shocks across sectors and countries.

In the following, we first analyse these stylised facts. Then we explain how their interaction may be at the source of a number of recent developments. We then describe how the assessment of global and national liquidity helps us eventually understand such mechanisms at both global and national levels. Finally, we describe how high volatility in global financial markets, eventually exacerbated by the bursting of asset-price bubbles, affects the transmission process of economic shocks and poses peculiar challenges to the conduct of monetary policy.

Four stylised facts of relevance to the functioning of global financial markets

The unequal reduction of the 'home bias'

Figure 8.1 shows that over the period 1985–2004 the sum of foreign assets and liabilities over GDP in industrialised countries and in the emerging and developing countries increased by a factor higher than 3 and 1.5, respectively.

The rapid increase in the cross-border investment flows fostered by the liberalisation of national financial markets, in combination with the decline in communication costs and vibrant financial innovation has certainly contributed to reducing the so-called 'home bias' of domestic investors over the last two decades.

However, the process has not been homogeneous across countries, leading to an increased heterogeneity of participants in international financial markets. For instance, in the USA the diversification of residents' investments into foreign assets peaked around the mid 1990s (Greenspan, 2003). In the rest of the industrialised countries and in those more advanced emerging economies that opened up to global capital markets the process started in the early 1990s and peaked around the beginning of the new decade when the correction in the US stock

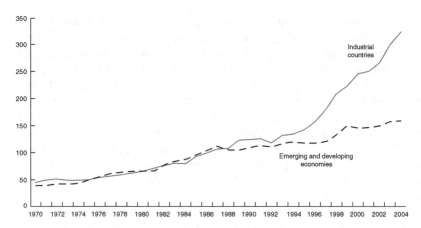

Figure 8.1 Sum of foreign assets and liabilities over GDP: industrial vs. emerging and developing countries
Source: Moutot and Vitale, 2009; Lane and Milesi-Ferretti, 2007.

market led to the reversal of the financial flows from the rest of world into the USA.[4] Therefore, it is fair to say that since the mid 1990s the decline in the 'home bias' at a global level has decelerated significantly (Greenspan, 2003).

However, important structural factors remain that justify the persistence of financial flows from emerging and newly industrialised countries towards countries with more developed and deep financial markets. First, private investors from emerging countries who do not benefit from sufficiently liquid and safe financial markets in their home country would find it convenient to invest their funds into lower-return foreign assets, either because they are less risky or because these assets would simply not be available in their home country. Second, official investors, like those Asian central banks of countries pegging their currency to the dollar, would also invest in developed countries' financial assets – and not necessarily in dollar denominated assets – as a result of having sufficient reserves to guarantee the stability of such pegs. In particular, countries with excess savings and still embryonic financial markets have accumulated large amounts of official reserves, which

---

[4] In the euro area, a further impulse to diversification for domestic investors was the introduction of the euro. In fact, the elimination of the intra-area exchange-rate risk spurred foreign investment in debt instruments across euro area countries. Foreign investment in equities has been less pronounced as national stock markets remain rather segmented.

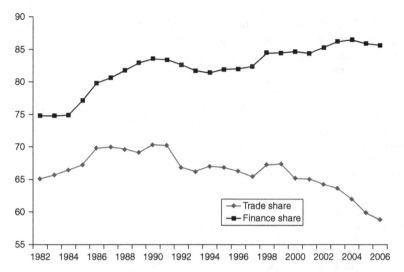

Figure 8.2 Share of advanced countries in world trade and cross-border financial positions
Source: Moutot and Vitale, 2009; Lane and Milesi-Ferretti, 2008.

are not necessarily managed in the same way as assets held by private investors. Hence, the relative size of players in global financial markets and their degree of risk aversion has become strongly heterogeneous, as shown by the emphasis given in the media as well as by OECD and IMF to sovereign wealth funds.

Financial versus trade and services transactions

Another stylised and related fact concerning global markets is that in developed economies, the size of financial transactions has grown a lot in comparison with the size of trade and services transactions (Figure 8.2).

This is the result of the continued deepening of developed financial markets and of the relentless financial innovation process as manifested by the significant growth in the size of their derivative markets. As a consequence, the role of global financial markets and their linkages in the transmission of economic shocks, both domestically and internationally, has increased substantially in the last decade and even exchange-rate movements across currencies with deep financial markets may now be driven more than in the past by global private and official portfolios reshuffling rather than current account positions (Brender and Pisani, 2007).

Table 8.1 *The evolution of monetary policy frameworks and exchange-rate regimes. A snapshot over the period 1991–2007*

Exchange-rate regime	Monetary policy framework				
	Exchange-rate anchor	Monetary target	Inflation targeting	IMF supported	Other
Other currency as legal tender	10(14)				
Currency board	13(8)				
Other fixed peg single currency	63(21)	2			
Other fixed peg composite	7(30)				
Peg with horizontal bands	5(7)		2		
Crawling pegs	6(13)	1			
Crawling bands	1(3)				
Managed floating	48	17	9	7	13
Independently floating	35(<2)	2	16		17
Fixed	105(96)				
Floating	83(<2)	19	25 {7}		17

Source: Moutot and Vitale (2009), IMF (2007), Pétursson (2000, 2004). Numbers in the table refer to April 2007; those in parentheses to 1991, in curly brackets to 1997.

The diffusion of inflation targeting and currency pegs in the context of central banking

Since the mid 1990s, the diffusion of currency boards and of inflation-targeting techniques across central banks has been fast (see Table 8.1).

In the early 1990s, currency boards were viewed as miracle solutions to create monetary stability at low cost in emerging economies. Therefore currency boards pegging to the dollar and to the euro have proliferated. However, it soon appeared that they were sometimes attracting capital inflows invested in real estate or in low-productivity projects financed in foreign currencies and thereby creating financial risks in case of appreciation of such currencies.

Then inflation targeting was successfully adopted by a number of central banks in developed and emerging countries. This monetary policy strategy, which is a practice recommended by the IMF, is hence now used by a majority of central banks. However, up to now, such inflation targeting has concentrated on the pursuit of price stability at horizons of two to three years, generally giving low weight to the need to monitor and possibly react to asset-price developments.

It is all the more true that the diffusion of inflation-targeting techniques has coincided with a debate on the need to 'lean against the wind' concerning asset-price bubbles, which until mid 2007 mostly tilted in the direction of 'inaction' under the influence of the Federal Reserve's, and particularly of A. Greenspan's, views. Indeed, it was believed that asset-price imbalances were impossible to identify at an early stage, that any action by the central bank would either be unsuccessful or harmful, and in the end would generate moral hazard.

However, as shown by Christiano *et al.* (2008) in a closed-economy context, the very application of inflation targeting in a context of a rising bubble might lead to a policy stance actually encouraging the growth of asset-price bubbles.[5] This may explain the fact that, as remarked by a number of observers, the occurrence of asset-price bubbles may have increased in a context of low inflation where inflation-targeting central banks are usually not monitoring money and credit closely enough.

Financial innovation and the transfer of risks

Lastly, over the last twenty years the integration of global financial markets has been accompanied by increasing financial development and liberalisation. In theory, financial innovation, by deepening and completing financial markets, is supportive of economic growth and improves the allocation of savings. New computing and information processing technologies have favoured the rise of new – often esoteric – financial instruments explicitly designed to unbundle and repackage the payoffs and the risks associated with primitive, more conventional, financial products and securities. Figure 8.3 below shows the rampant growth in the USA first and in the euro area after, of asset-backed securities (ABS) and mortgage-backed securities (MBS) issuances over the past ten years.[6]

This trend – originally aimed at a better sharing of risks across savers – was later extended to lending institutions in search of higher returns. That led to the exponential growth of credit derivatives, such as credit default swaps (CDS) and collateralised debt obligations (CDO).

---

[5] The logic of the argument relies on the stickiness of nominal wages, which do not increase sufficiently in response to an expected productivity shock, as it would if wages were flexible. Hence, the required increase in the real wage can only occur through a decline in the inflation rate. But this would call the inflation-targeting central bank to lower interest rates and then reinforce the stimulus effect arising on impact from the expected increase in productivity. Such a decline in the interest rate would also trigger a credit boom.

[6] The figure is based on a new data set developed at the European Central Bank (see Poloni and Reynaud, 2008). The European Securitazion Forum (ESF, 2008, Tables 2.1 and 2.2, page 5) calculates the amount outstanding at the end of the first quarter of 2008 of total ABS plus MBS in the USA at €6.3 trillion. Up to the same quarter, the total amount outstanding in Europe was €1.2 trillion. Data for the euro area are not available.

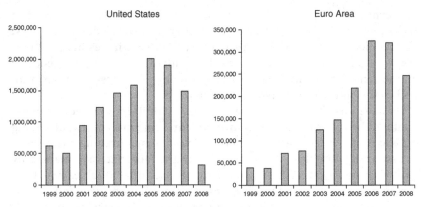

Figure 8.3 Net issuance of asset-backed and mortgage-backed securities: the euro area vs. the USA
Source: Moutot and Vitale, 2009; Poloni and Raynaud, 2008.

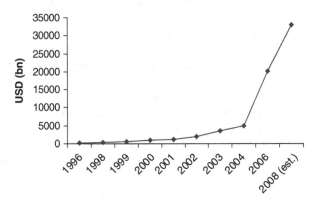

Figure 8.4 Global credit derivatives market
Source: Moutot and Vitale, 2009; British Bankers Association, 2006.

Figure 8.4 documents the sudden and sharp increase in CDS and CDO global issuance over the last three years. Their notional value in the first half of 2008 is estimated to have reached US$54 trillion.[7]

Together with many benefits like a better way for intermediaries to diversify risk, thereby reducing the transaction costs of investing and expanding access to capital, these developments went hand-in-hand with two side effects: a great increase in leverage and an unprecedented expansion of marketing for financial instruments.

---

[7] International Swap and Derivatives Association (2008). Notice that in Figure 8.4 the data for 2008 are estimates calculated in 2006.

The shift in banks' balance sheets away from holdings of relatively illiquid forms of assets (e.g. mortgage loans) to a business model whereby the banks originate an underlying loan which is then made tradable and negotiated in the open market (so-called 'originate-and-distribute model') has made it harder to draw clear distinctions between previously distinct categories of financial players. New investors – notably hedge funds – have been borne out of the need for market makers in previously unknown types of securities. But, more important perhaps, by allowing credit risk to be transferred across agents from different countries, it has also authorised the uncontrolled transfer of liquidity risks across countries and continents.

How these four factors have interacted over the recent past

The four stylised facts discussed above – and their interaction – provide one possible key for the interpretation of both the overall increase of inter-linkages across financial markets and the recent history of economic and financial tensions across large countries.

The empirical evidence about the inter-linkages in global financial markets

The liberalisation of cross-border capital flows and the vibrant developments in innovative financial markets in the last two decades combined with the increased readability of monetary policies aimed at price stability have facilitated and thereby increased the linkages between financial markets across the globe, thus making the adjustment mechanism of domestic economies – and the monetary policy transmission mechanism – more prone to being affected by developments in foreign economies. The sheer size of global capital cross-border flows certainly influences the price of assets in any economy by contributing to the determination of both the supply and demand and the premiums that investors require for holding certain assets (Bernanke, 2007). There is a flourishing literature that supports the view that the transmission of financial markets developments across the world has increased in recent years. Domestic markets increasingly react to economic news expected to change the path of policy rates in some 'centre' country, which is typically the United States.

Ehrmann *et al.* (2005) underline the importance of international spillovers, both within asset classes and across financial markets.[8]

---

[8] The authors argue that an important share of the behaviour of financial markets is explained by foreign asset prices. On average, about 26 per cent of movements in European financial assets are attributable to developments in US financial markets, while about 8 per cent of US financial market shifts are caused by European

Although the strongest international transmission of shocks takes place within asset classes, they find evidence that international cross-market spillovers are significant, both statistically and economically. For instance, shocks to US short-term interest rates exert a substantial influence on euro area bond yields and equity markets, and in fact, over the period 1989–2004, they explain as much as 10 per cent of overall euro area bond market movements. But the transmission of shocks also runs in the opposite direction as, in particular, short-term interest rates of the euro area have a significant impact on US bond and equity markets. Furthermore, they show that in almost all cases the direct transmission of financial shocks within asset classes is magnified substantially, mostly by more than 50 per cent, via indirect spillovers through other asset prices. In a more recent contribution, Ehrman and Fratscher (2006) focus on the link between US monetary policy and the stock market in foreign countries and they show that US monetary policy shocks have significant and in some cases sizable effects on foreign stock prices. Moreover, they provide evidence supportive of the fact that US monetary policy shocks affect foreign stock markets through foreign short-term interest rates and exchange-rate changes. Finally, they show that sensitivity to US monetary policy shocks is higher in those countries that are more integrated globally – rather than only with the USA – in real and financial terms. This latter result suggests that domestic financial conditions in any country do not necessarily depend simply on the financial conditions in the US market, which is the most developed and liquid in the world, but also on some second-round effects that are due to the complex web constituting the global financial and real linkages.[9]

The stylised facts also help explaining recent financial tensions at the global level

The above-mentioned four stylised facts can help explain some of the recent economic developments that have occurred both in single countries and at a global level. First, as explained above, the decrease in the

developments. The larger importance of US markets is found particularly for equity markets; for instance, movements in US stock prices trigger corresponding change in the euro area, with more than 50 per cent of the US market developments being reflected in euro area stock prices. By contrast, European equities have an insignificant impact on their American counterparts.

[9] In a more recent contribution, Bayoumi and Swinston (2007) analyse the transmission of movements between the real bond yields and inflation expectations across a number of countries. Based on high-frequency data of inflation-indexed bonds they find that the causation in real bond yields goes univocally from the USA to the other countries in the panel. The spillover in inflation expectations appears to be less important and the direction of causation is less clear.

home bias in principle implies that domestic investors are able to reduce the risk of their portfolio without reneging on expected returns.[10] Hence, the propagation of shocks hitting the economy through the financial system is likely to be smoother than it would be in the case of lower country diversification. Also, the stability of the financial system itself is in principle greater when financial shocks occur or the risk attitude among investors changes. However, many elements may also make the benefits of the decrease volatile and actually generate costs. First, such benefits should be contrasted with the cost of the speculative bubbles which are inherent to the functioning of capital markets. A case in point is the burst of the 2001 bubble in the US stock market which coincided with a slowdown of growth in many countries. Another is the Asian crisis in 1998, which did not only affect regional stock markets but also local bond, debt and exchange-rate markets. The size of the costs for local economies led a number of affected countries in the region to switch to economic and financial policies aimed at accumulating substantial foreign exchange reserves. As for the current financial turmoil, which started as a localised real-estate crisis, it affects the USA, the euro area and other European countries as a result of the recently developed risk transfer techniques, not only through the dynamics of their respective exchange rates, but also through its impacts on the money, bond and stock markets in both economic areas.

Second, the growing importance of international financial transactions over the last twenty-five years may imply that investors' behaviour and portfolio reshufflings could affect asset and foreign exchange markets in a novel way. Instead of reflecting fundamentals and their prospects, global asset and foreign exchange markets may in some instances be less volatile than normally expected over extended periods and thereafter evolve in a disorderly manner. This implies that several regimes of financial and foreign exchange market volatility may successively prevail. Figure 8.5 shows the standard deviation of asset and foreign exchange prices in selected markets.[11] In both the US and the euro area stock markets the evidence of a 'regime shift' occurring around the mid 1980s is quite evident. By contrast, frequent switches in volatility regimes are apparent in the exchange rate graphs.

---

[10] The seminal contribution is Markowitz (1952), which shows how the variance of a portfolio with the same mean return decreases when the correlation of the assets composing the portfolio declines. Grubel (1968) and Solnik (1974) are the first papers to illustrate how investing in foreign assets represents a possible diversification strategy that actually lowers the variance of a portfolio.

[11] The standard deviation plotted in the charts is computed over a 30-day moving window.

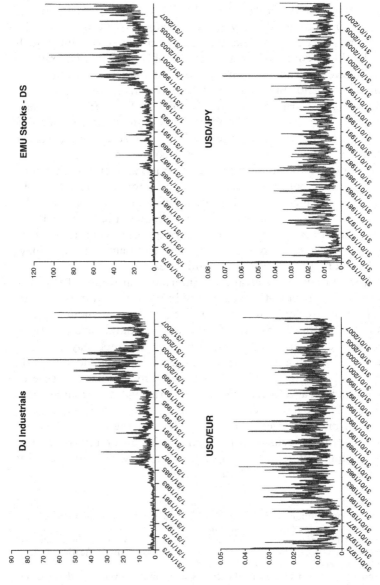

Figure 8.5 The volatility of the US and the euro area stock markets and of the USD/EUR and USD/JPY exchange rates

Source: Moutot and Vitale, 2009; Financial Thomson Datastream and authors' calculations.

Indeed, if exchange rates are driven less by current account deficits or surpluses and more by capital flows and financial developments, the definition of their equilibrium levels becomes less precise. In particular, regimes of low exchange-rate and financial market volatility and regimes of high volatility can be at the same time more durable and alternate more swiftly. On the one hand, low exchange-rate volatility seems to further encourage the decrease in 'home bias' (ECB, 2006) and therefore the seeming disconnection between traditional fundamentals and exchange rates, prolonging low volatility periods. The period 2004–2007 offered an example of such a regime between large currencies, with low volatility of exchange rates prevailing despite strong current account imbalances, even in cases of large and non-fundamentally based exchange-rate movements (euro/yen). At the same time, switches to high volatility regimes happen whenever unexpected financial developments lead to financial instability, itself resulting in exchange-rate instability and a pause or a reversal in the decrease of the home bias. The periods between the US stock market crash and 2004 and also the developments since late 2007 offer such an example.

Third, speculative bubbles and strong financial flows accompanied by low exchange-rate volatility may develop, amplify and make large current account disequilibria – or 'global imbalances' – more persistent than usually expected. The US example is well known. The low exchange-rate volatility combined with the desire of foreign governments in Asia and OPEC to invest their reserves in dollars has led to an extremely low yield curve, especially at its long end. This has allowed an easy financing of a real-estate boom, leading in turn to an increase in US households' wealth that fostered private consumption growth and households' leverage at the cost of a continuous decrease in savings.

These developments are not dissimilar in their fundamental characteristics to what had already happened in the second half of the 1990s, when the high-tech bubble in the USA was substantially financed by speculative investment flows originating in Europe, where financial institutions and private investors used the opportunities of low interest rates to borrow in euro and invest in the technological sector of the US stock market. In other words, the issue of global imbalances appears as the outcome of a situation with the following characteristics: the combination of countries with excess savings and a country with low savings but an attractive financial centre leads to the development of an asset-price movement. The latter allows for an increase of consumers' wealth, which in turn justifies and perpetuates the lower savings – and the increasing leverage – of the low-savings country.

Fourth, those countries experiencing low inflation and low exchange-rate volatility are also more likely to be originators of capital flows that may ultimately fuel an asset-price bubble in the destination country. As an example, the US stock market bubble that developed in the second half of the 1990s was partly financed, close to its apex, by Europe-based investors who were driven by the expectation of a protracted period of productivity growth in the USA. At the time, the continuous depreciation of the euro versus the dollar provided further incentives for capital to flow from Europe into the USA. Moreover, in the euro area interest rates were low and inflation developments were moderate and smooth, while US interest rates were relatively higher despite subdued price developments. Low inflation volatility periods may also facilitate large capital movements through so-called 'carry trades', which may ultimately lead to large deviations of exchange rates from equilibrium. A recent and much-discussed example is the carry trade organised by global financial investors by borrowing in Japanese yen and investing the proceedings in many other countries that were either following a successful inflation targeting strategy or with a currency board or a peg to a major currency. Once again, the low inflation and interest rate environment in Japan – and the expectation of its durability – fostered large capital outflows from Japan into high-yielding markets until the eruption of the financial crisis in June 2007 and the consequent increase in the volatility of asset prices. The apparently durable profitability of such carry-trade activities combined with a sustained depreciation of the yen over protracted periods, has been a source of interrogation which only stopped when the financial crisis erupted and reversed the depreciation of the yen.

These events suggest that the initial success of monetary policy or exchange-rate regimes like inflation targeting and currency pegs could have contributed to the development of large capital flows from one country to another. For example, the spreading of inflation-targeting strategies across central banks in both developed and developing economies may have increased the recent intensity of carry trades. Indeed, if a central bank targeting inflation in a country with low interest rates does not lean against excess credit creation, the corresponding liquidity, if not used to finance local assets, may fund carry trades toward other higher inflation or higher expected return countries. This may reflect underdeveloped financial markets or the lack of equilibrating investment opportunities in the source country. If the recipient country is a credible inflation fighter, its bilateral exchange rate will tend to appreciate because the capital inflows will increase its asset prices. As a consequence, wealth effects will increase consumption growth while inflation remains subdued, at least for some time. In such circumstances, investors in the originating country will see their expectation of higher returns validated and may be encouraged to continue pouring capital into the high-yielding assets. This is probably the story one can tell for the developments observed from 2005 until mid 2007 between the yen and the New Zealand and Australian dollar – as well as many Eastern European currencies – but this also characterises the dynamics of the euro/dollar exchange rate between 1999 and 2001.[12]

Finally, past and more recent financial crisis episodes show a common element: the bursting of the asset-price bubble breaks down the optimistic and self-fulfilling investors' expectations and capital flows unravel. It is at this point in time that many factors, including the nature of the actual investors – i.e. households, financial institutions, pension and trust funds – or the positions taken on derivative markets by operators to cover and transfer risks, affect the way the capital inflow reversal impacts economic developments and the transmission of monetary policy in both the country receiving and in the one originating the capital flows. As apparent in the recent financial turmoil, the uncertainty about the identity of economic agents participating in the sharing of risk may also create a risk of liquidity in many markets. Hence, it is increasingly likely that asset-price bubbles will have an international impact and make it increasingly difficult to gauge in real time the location of such impact. Under such circumstances the time needed to identify such risks may be part of the crisis dynamics itself.

The bursting of a bubble may not be the end of the story, however, as the way it is managed by monetary and fiscal authorities may itself give rise to other bubbles. In the US case, the decision to keep interest rates low for a long period after 2001 may have encouraged the subsequent real-estate bubble. In the Japanese case, one might argue that once the balance sheets of banks had been repaired, the lack of sufficient measures to curtail the growing size of the public debt convinced Japanese private agents to search for higher returns abroad. Indeed, their substantial savings might have been accompanied by a reluctance to invest in a country where the prospect of increasing tax rates is a natural consequence of the level of public debt. This also leads to delays in the increase of interest rates by a central bank concentrating on low forecasts of inflation, thereby encouraging and facilitating the development of carry trades.

---

[12] For an exhaustive discussion of the recent and past carry trade episodes involving the yen, see Winters (2008).

Globalisation and its reflection through monetary aggregates

Overall, not only the faster transmission of shocks across asset classes and across countries but also the dynamics of asset-price developments, including boom-bust movements, the associated flows of capital and of boom–bust movements need to be understood in order to explain the monetary and financial impact of globalisation, including global imbalances. This implies that beyond the real economy developments described in Section 8.2, monetary policy assessments now need to take into account the evolutions implied by the interplay of the four above-mentioned stylised facts. This is somewhat facilitated by making recourse to the concept of global liquidity. However, another useful approach is to develop the analysis of monetary aggregates and financial flows to complement the usual economic analysis. Such considerations also helps take into account the specific phenomena underlying the successive developments of risk-taking and risk-averse attitudes among economic agents.

Global liquidity may help reflect the impact of foreign-originated shocks

The globalisation of financial markets increases the importance of foreign developments in the domestic monetary policy transmission mechanism. In the three years before August 2007, the composition of cross-border capital flows changed significantly from equity and foreign direct investments into more liquid assets, thus creating a sizeable amount of 'global' liquidity that could move quite freely across financial markets.[13] Consequently, one of the most debated issues at the level of world central banks at the moment is the implication of 'global' liquidity for the conduct of monetary policy.

Research conducted at the ECB (Rüffer and Stracca, 2006) seems to suggest that global excess liquidity affects economic conditions in the euro area in a way that accords with the theoretical predictions, i.e. an expansion (contraction) of global excess liquidity increases (reduces) the inflationary pressures in the euro area. Furthermore, this research also shows that domestic liquidity conditions are important indicators for inflationary pressures in the other G7 economies. Hence, combining these results, it could be argued that the research supports the argument that the euro area domestic inflation is affected by 'global' inflation.

[13] Coincidentally, over the same period the daily correlation between changes in the ten-year swap rates in the United States and Germany increased to 0.65 from less than 0.2 over the period 1990–2003 – see Bernanke (2007). The same picture emerges for the correlations between interest rate pairs with other G7 countries.

This is a result that other authors obtain (e.g. Ciccarelli and Mojon, 2005) in different contexts and thus seems to be rather robust to modelling and methodological differences. However, in the last analysis, domestic inflation always remains a phenomenon controllable by domestic monetary policy as explained in the next section. Hence, while useful to gauge global inflationary risks, it remains unclear whether and how such information can be used in the context of domestic monetary assessments.

Another 'global' channel of transmission from liquidity conditions to inflation involves the overshooting of commodity prices following an expansion of money supply. Browne and Cronin (2007) use a co-integrating VAR model on US data to show that while both commodity and consumer prices are proportional to the money supply in the long run, commodity prices initially overshoot their new equilibrium values in response to a money-supply shock, and the deviation of commodity prices from their equilibrium values has explanatory power for subsequent consumer price inflation changes. However, this approach does not take into account the money supply of countries other than the USA, or assumes that such supplies would be strongly correlated with the US data, which may be true over some periods but not for others.

Also, the concept of global liquidity, while helpful at a global level does not reflect the tensions generated by cross-border flows, which it internalises. Although it can be useful in order to understand global trends, possibly complementing the notion of 'global slack', for instance concerning commodity prices, it does not help to identify the individual roles of national or regional monetary policies. However, this increasing importance of capital flows creates practical difficulties for central bankers, be they pure inflation targeters or interested in monetary analysis and/or financial flows. In the first case, as argued before, the inclusion of asset prices, financial sectors and capital flows in models of the economy would be highly desirable, but is not yet easy to achieve. In the case of central bankers also interested in monetary and/or financial flows analysis, international capital flows tend to make the link between money and prices unstable in the short to medium term, making the direct interpretation of monetary aggregates more difficult, but also more promising.

The role of monetary analysis in identifying the impact of capital flows on price stability and asset prices

Monetary aggregates and their counterparts at the national or regional level, as they reflect international capital flows, may also be used to yield essential information on their impact and on the risks they create for the evolution of asset prices. The analysis of monetary aggregates and their counterparts, i.e. loans to the private sector and net external assets, allows the central bank not only to gauge medium- to long-term inflationary risks by correcting monetary aggregates from estimated portfolio shifts but also to form scenarios about plausible use of the corresponding liquidity. The identification of underlying trends combined with the estimation of the likely impact of the various scenarios concerning capital flows on the domestic economy allows the evolution of prices and of the associated risks to be measured better. Thus, they are helpful in supporting a 'risk-management' approach to price stability by monetary authorities.

In this context, a direct approach to taking into account asset-price movements and inflationary pressures simultaneously has recently been proposed. As shown by De Santis *et al.* (2008), asset prices in the USA and the euro area interact with money in the euro area and influence the relationship between inflation and monetary aggregates.[14] In particular, the interplay of Tobin's q in the two areas reflects well the shape of financial flows observed in the balance of payments of the euro area. Such inclusion of asset prices within money demand functions explains and deals with the instability of traditional money demand equations apparent after 2001 in the euro area. It also shows that the correction of monetary aggregates by ECB staff to measure the underlying trend of money demand, called 'portfolio shifts', was justified. It demonstrates that money and asset prices both in the euro area and the USA interact. Hence, monetary aggregates have the potential to help point at the risks created by asset-price developments induced by capital flows.

For instance, the central bank will tend to interpret the moderate growth of both money and credit as a signal that money growth is likely to be driven by domestic money demand, thus posing fewer risks to price stability. Further, if money growth is low but credit dynamics are more buoyant, it is likely that net external assets of non-monetary and financial institutions are growing and that the domestic economy is financing investment abroad. In these circumstances, the central bank may have to form an opinion about the likely developments of the economies where domestic capital flows are directed. In case it views the foreign investment dynamics as led by an asset-price bubble, it may warn investors and communicate its concerns. At the same time, those capital outflows may signal a fundamental disequilibrium that may lie, for instance, in the domestic fiscal policy that is expected to constrain

---

[14] The policy-regime choice in one country, thus, while in appearance justifiable as stability oriented, in fact only transfers possible imbalances abroad through the financial channel and threatens the stability of the recipient country's financial system.

the evolution of inflation, or in the level of national productivity and consequently in the external value of the domestic currency.

In other circumstances, it is money that grows fast while credit dynamics are subdued. In this case, money growth is led by the repatriation of foreign investments, whose proceeds are normally deposited with local financial institutions and result in an increase of domestic money. Typically these repatriation flows do not pose significant risks to price stability as they represent portfolio reallocation of wealth and they are unlikely to translate into excess demand. However, the central bank should monitor credit developments as the boost in domestic liquidity may lead financial institutions to relax credit conditions and eventually trigger an unsustainable loan binge.

The most complicated combination, however, may be the one where money and credit both grow quickly. In this case, capital flows do not matter much. The central bank must be able to assess if these developments are due to fundamental factors, like a more-or-less sustainable increase in productivity growth or, for instance a positive shock in real-estate prices. In the first case, higher credit growth may be compatible with a higher desire of households to smooth their income over time. By borrowing more today, households increase the entire profile of their consumption path and they are able to do so because their expected real income is higher, due to the increase in productivity growth. In the second case, credit growth may be driven by the increase in household wealth, eventually exacerbated by the characteristics of a domestic financial system that allows households to increase their leverage significantly. In these circumstances, central banks need to elaborate on possible scenarios and take into account the whole transmission mechanism, in order to assess properly the nature of the shock underlying the money and credit dynamics and also the eventual risks to price stability that those shocks would create.

What is rarely done, however, because of the use of monetary analysis at national rather than international level, is to use it to better understand and perhaps identify the impact of national policies in initiating cross-border capital flows, leading to asset-price movements abroad, and affecting global liquidity. Indeed, the bursting of an asset-price bubble in one country, such as Japan, may have global consequences if the fight of its monetary authorities against subsequent deflationary trends thereafter leads to a durable facilitation of carry trades toward other zones. In particular, the deterioration of its fiscal position, if lasting, may be seen as providing a guarantee that interest rates will remain low for a prolonged period and encourage outflows of an excess liquidity created to fight against deflation. This encourages inflows in economies offering higher interest rates, for instance if their peg to another major currency guarantees high rates with limited foreign exchange risk in a period of low global volatility. In a similar way, the bursting of the high-tech bubble in the USA led to substantial capital inflows in the euro area and to money hoarding, explaining substantial growth rates of monetary aggregates without corresponding price pressures.

The emergence of new financial market products and players and the 'behavioural' or 'risk taking' channel of monetary policy

The emergence of new categories of investors and financial intermediaries, whose behaviour and incentives may be quite different from the traditional categories of market players like the banks has probably modified the way shocks propagate across financial markets and monetary policy impulses are transmitted to the rest of the economy (Rajan, 2006a). The same is true with the generalisation of credit derivatives which, due to their 'off-balance-sheet' status, often make the international propagation of their effects difficult to follow.

First of all, the proliferation of financial intermediaries whose main value added is in securitising and making liquid – i.e. tradable in the market place – assets that until a few years ago would have been highly illiquid and remained on the originators' balance sheet has increased the ability of the financial system to multiply liquidity. To be sure, this is by no means a problematic development per se, but rather one of the desirable outcomes that macroeconomic stability – which mostly has to be ascribed to the increased quality of monetary and fiscal policy in many countries over the last twenty-five years – is supposed to deliver. In a stable macroeconomic environment that is vastly less risky and friendlier to businesses than it used to be in the not-so-distant past, higher expected profits – and lower risks around those profit expectations – ought to induce greater risk taking, and low short-term volatility to encourage the creation of market liquidity by financial institutions. Figure 8.6 draws from balance-sheet data of both the US financial and non-financial corporate sectors to show how both sectors of the US economy actively manage their own balance sheet.[15] Security dealers and brokers – which include the once well-known large US investment banks – in particular, tend to create liquidity during periods of asset-price booms and drain liquidity during periods of asset-prices decline.

[15] That is to say that leverage is pro-cyclical. When asset price increases, the equity capital of the firm increases, thus reducing its leverage, which is defined as the ratio of assets over equity. If firms tend to target a constant, or even increasing, leverage ratio they must take up new debt and purchase new assets.

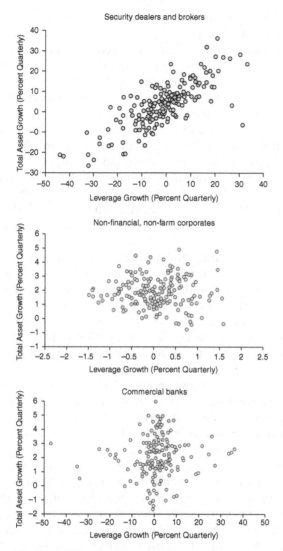

Figure 8.6 Total assets and 'leverage growth'
Source: Moutot and Vitale, 2009; Adrian and Shin, 2008.

Such behaviour tends to impart 'bubbly' dynamics to asset prices, thus feeding its own collapse. The beneficial effects of 'liquefying' specific assets, like mortgage loans, becomes sclerotic once the unsustainable dynamics in the price of the underlying assets – which in this case are the house prices – reverts, and financial institutions engage in massive de-leveraging, causing a drainage of market liquidity which hits the global financial system at its heart.

Furthermore, behavioural shifts have occurred – like they always did on occasion of past episodes of asset-price bubbles – that are associated with new products and increased incentives of financial markets' players to pursue risky investment strategies. Risk shifting, illiquidity seeking, tail-risk seeking and, of course, herding (Rajan, 2006b) may affect the way central banks influence the economy through the conventional channels of transmission. In other words, the classic channels – interest rate, balance sheet, bank lending and liquidity channels – might be affected in such a way as to influence the effectiveness of monetary policy to an extent that was unknown before. This is what some authors prefer to introduce as a supplementary channel which they call a 'behavioural' or 'risk-taking' channel for the transmission of monetary policy.

In an era when banks dominated financial systems, incentives for bank officials were clear. Their salary would rarely depend on the bank's short-term investment returns and they thus had little interest in seeking extra returns that, being more risky, could have jeopardised the bank's balance sheet. For their part, shareholders were happy to enjoy the steady rent arising from the limited competition in the market for funds and the system was able to deliver stable but inefficiently conservative financial intermediation flows. In the modern, deregulated and competitive environment, investment managers in investment banks or in other financial intermediaries have, at least up to now, worked with an incentive structure commensurate to the new context. As the penalty of bad investment performance in the new environment was believed to be less drastic than a bank run, investment managers may have perceived that there is more upside than downside to adding risk in order to generate extra returns immediately affecting their own salaries. In such an environment, what really mattered for many investment managers was to perform better than their peers, or at least, not worse. And this generates two perverse consequences (Rajan, 2006a). First, investment managers try to boost returns by investing in assets that have risk characteristics easily concealed from investors, namely that perform extremely badly in case of extreme events but offer generous returns the rest of the time. The finance literature calls these 'tail risks'. The second perverse consequence is the incentive for investment managers to herd with competitor managers, because this behaviour provides them with the insurance that they will not underperform their peers. It is easy to appreciate how both behaviours tend to reinforce each other in periods of asset-price increases to provide the impetus for an upward spiral, which feeds itself and is prone to develop into a credit bubble.

The combination of financial innovation and behavioural shifts of market participants increases the vulnerability of the international financial system to sudden gyrations in markets' risk perceptions and tolerance. The explosive dynamics imparted by the ability of financial institutions to pack and sell risk to credit growth becomes an equally powerful implosive force when risky events materialise and hit financial institutions' balance sheets. Furthermore, if the losses are realised on off-balance-sheet positions, by definition there is no market that can offer actual prices due to the absence of market makers and clearing houses. In such contexts, liquidity crises can easily erupt as most participants have difficulty assessing both the soundness of their own balance sheets and those of their counterparts.

One clear example of such perverse dynamics is the ongoing financial turmoil that originated in the US sub-prime mortgage market. Over the period 2002–2005 the combination of rising house prices and very low interest rates contributed to increase both households' demand for mortgage credit and the risk appetite of financial institutions in search of higher returns. Thanks to financial innovation, primary mortgage lenders securitised their loans, thus in practice separating out their lending business from the risks implied by holding mortgage loans on their own balance sheets. Through mortgage-backed derivatives mortgage lenders could lock in their return on the mortgage while the buyers of the mortgage risks, mostly hedge funds and non-bank institutions, would obtain the extra return they were seeking. In the absence of market players with a higher tolerance for risk, these dynamics would not have developed. In normal times, these are beneficial dynamics because they help allocate capital more efficiently to those agents that can bear the particular risk/return profiles of their investments and results in a higher provision of funds to those who may need it.

However, after the significant decline in house prices and the tightening of monetary policy that started in 2006, the defaults on mortgage loans and home foreclosures in the USA increased, until the market for mortgage-backed securities came to a sudden standstill in August 2007. Credit and liquidity risk worldwide increased sharply and the turmoil spread very quickly from the USA into global financial markets and from mortgage markets to other asset classes including money markets. In these circumstances, financial institutions around the globe could no longer sell the risk in the market and were forced to retain a significant amount of non-performing mortgage loans on their balance sheet. Hence, such financial institutions had to cut their exposures to other investments in order to repair their balance sheets and the global credit flows dried up sharply.

These developments show that in some circumstances the presence of high-risk investors with relatively short-term investment horizons can instil perverse dynamics and foster asset-price bubbles, eventually leading to an increase of leverage in the economy much above a sustainable level. Beyond logical considerations concerning the reforms of the regulatory framework that should be aimed at avoiding *ex ante* any unsustainable credit creation dynamics, the changes in the financial markets' microstructure and the ability to engineer and supply more innovative and complicated products thus have a few important implications for monetary policy.

First, central banks have to make sure to avoid the risk of becoming, paradoxically, victims of their own success in achieving macroeconomic stability and earning high credibility. Periods of low macroeconomic volatility may well be those periods when market dynamics 'take a life of their own' and depart from any rational considerations of possible risks. This implies that central banks have a duty to base their analysis, recommendation and policy decisions on a firm focus on fundamental trends in the economy.

In particular, central banks should be very cautious when communicating to the markets and the public in general in order to avoid fostering unsustainable expectations among market participants. In some circumstances, the unfounded expectations of a certain future policy course may have an amplifying effect on asset prices and thus may contribute to the build-up of those financial imbalances which would quickly and expensively unwind once expectations change.

Third, central banks should devote maximum effort to understanding the extent to which the transmission channel of monetary policy in a stable macroeconomic environment may be affected by both a high degree of integration of global financial markets and an ever-developing market microstructure. For example, globalisation and the perverse behaviours spurred by financial innovation may have combined in the last two years to make the long end of the yield curve less responsive to the monetary policy tightening – especially in the United States, but also in the euro area – than it was expected to be on the basis of historical experience. It is very likely, in fact, that global savings were flowing into the United States, attracted by the unsustainable low-risk–return profile offered by new financial products and by the mirage that the credit risk premium had almost disappeared.

Fourth, central banks need liquidity policies well adapted to the occurrence and development across time of deep financial scares.

Ex ante, a liquidity management framework that allows a wide range of high-quality collateral and a large number of possible counterparties is helpful in maintaining market access of illiquid but solvent institutions. Moreover, international cooperation in order to allow the dispersion of liquidity in foreign currencies across domestic banks is also needed.

8.4   Conclusion

Globalisation, which initially seemed to be characterised by its downward impact on prices and inflation, is now increasingly recognised as a complex factor with multiple influences. While its potential for generating upward pressures on inflation is fully recognised, its other effects, including the rapid transmission of financial shocks, are also apparent. This has generated questions of many types: has the ability of national central banks to control inflation at national level been impaired? Conversely, can the propagation of financial scares be controlled or prevented? In particular, which techniques should be adopted or developed by central bankers to facilitate such control? More generally, what role might international cooperation play in such fields?

Globalisation does not weaken the case for a domestically conducted monetary policy aimed at price stability over the medium term. In cases of capital and/or goods markets integration, higher openness does not impair the ability of domestic monetary policy to control inflation. Inflation is always in the end a monetary phenomenon, i.e. a phenomenon that the central bank can control.[16] However, globalisation is most likely to have an impact on the determination of the domestic real interest rate, especially at long horizons (Rogoff, 2006) through both goods and asset-price international arbitrage. Moreover, recent developments such as the crises in government-sponsored enterprises and the bankruptcy of several investment banks in the USA make clear that propagation risks have enormously increased as a result of financial integration, and have altered the functioning of the monetary policy transmission mechanism.

Hence, simple rules and concepts like 'output gap' or 'core inflation' need to be supplemented by new and eventually more sophisticated

---

[16] Woodford (2007) uses an open-economy structural model to show that neither a high degree of financial market integration nor a higher role of a 'global' measure of economic activity slack on the dynamics of domestic supply are likely to weaken the ability of national central banks to control the dynamics of domestic inflation. Taylor (2008) argues that monetary policy cooperation does not deliver additional gains as compared to domestic monetary policy. Central banks are better off when they act on their own to the extent they incorporate in their decisions the expected actions of the other central banks.

tools. In particular, structural models incorporating adjustable production functions, variable exchange-rate pass-through, a link between the domestic and the international business cycle and financial variables may be very useful in identifying possible shocks hitting the economy and also in devising the right response to them.

8.4.1   *Financial integration, asset prices and monetary policy*

Global financial integration provides the channel for foreign-originated shocks to spill over into other markets and eventually foster asset-price dynamics that are not necessarily consistent with the maintenance of domestic price stability. Empirical evidence confirms that capital flows across countries can influence domestic asset-price movements and portfolio allocation. Thus, the higher probability of asset-price bubbles – and their possible collapse – may have pernicious consequences for macroeconomic and financial stability.

One lesson that can be drawn from the financial turmoil that started in mid 2007 is that central banks cannot benignly neglect asset-price developments and, eventually, step in once the bubble bursts, because this behaviour encourages moral hazard and inflicts costs and welfare losses that the central bank cannot avoid completely. Rather, central banks need to learn how to 'lean against the wind' efficiently (Loisel *et al.*, 2007), despite the uncertainty concerning the ability to identify bubbles and influence asset-price dynamics.

To be sure, asset prices should not be targets of monetary policy. Rather, central banks should develop a broad range of models and indicators in order to ensure that the fundamental analysis of asset-price developments is as robust as possible. The generalised persistence of unexplained paths for the residuals across statistical and econometric models and the eventual instability in their parameters may well flash a warning light that a bubble is in the making.

The ECB two-pillar strategy provides one possible framework that allows monetary policy makers in Europe to take into account asset-price dynamics in their assessment of the risks to price stability.

The systematic monitoring and analysis of monetary aggregates helps in identifying and distinguishing between underlying trends and the more volatile components of asset prices. In combination with the analysis of financial market microstructure – including the functioning of continuously new and more complicated financial products – this systematic monitoring naturally leads to constructing 'risk scenarios' concerning the likely developments in some part of the economy or of financial markets. In this way the policy maker can assess the relative probabilities of a larger number of uncertain future developments and, thus, make a more robust assessment of its own monetary policy stance.

On the basis of the 'risk scenario' analysis, central banks could consider the possibility of adjusting their monetary policy stance in response to excessive asset-price movements, when there is a high probability that capital flows and credit dynamics are driven by self-fulfilling expectations of continuously increasing asset prices or unrealistic expectations about the developments in fundamentals. It is important, however, that such action is not perceived as targeting asset prices. In fact, its goal should be to avoid increasing disequilibria of such prices rather than supporting them at any equilibrium level.[17]

In this interpretation, 'leaning against the wind' would naturally call for closer cooperation between central banks and supervisory authorities in order to provide monetary authorities with a thorough analysis of the risks embedded in the financial system, which is constantly evolving both in terms of products and of the characteristics of its players.

8.4.2 Globalisation and international policy cooperation

The higher integration of financial markets and the role of new countries in the global exchange of capital challenge also international fora to strive for better analysis and understanding of the ongoing changes in the international financial system. Since the 1980s, many systemic crises have occurred that had different explanations and developed in different ways. Each of these crisis episodes led international institutions to learn from their mistakes and implement monitoring and cooperation frameworks that would have reduced the risks of a similar crisis. The G7 has been instrumental in shaping the international financial architecture as it reacted to the need to better involve emerging market economies. In particular, since the creation of the Group of Twenty (G20) forum of finance ministers and central bank governors in 1999, emerging market countries have been involved in global economic and financial stability issues like exchange-rate regimes, prudent

[17] Ultimately, this approach would not differ in substance from the approach that central banks already adopt when exchange-rate dynamics depart from their estimated 'fundamental' value. In normal times, the central banks of large economic areas do not intervene in the foreign exchange markets to avoid creating conflicts with their primary objective of domestic price stability. However, occasionally these central banks may find it optimal to intervene in a coordinated manner with a view to 'throw sand in the wheels' of speculators, once their internal analyses show that actual exchange-rate developments are not compatible with any of the models that are supposed to explain exchange-rate behaviour.

debt management, domestic financial deepening and international codes and standards. The G20 has also played an important role in forging consensus on reforms of the Bretton Woods institutions and has been constructively involved in helping shape mechanisms of crisis prevention and resolution.

However, the development and the integration of global financial markets poses new challenges to policy makers and suggests that international cooperation needs to take new forms in order to address such challenges.[18] The multilateral consultation procedures inaugurated and sponsored by the IMF in 2006 on global imbalances may prove to be the right forum for this purpose, under the condition that the analysis is broadened in order to fully incorporate the interrelated dynamics of global financial markets. In particular, the multilateral consultation procedure should take a global perspective and assess the risk to monetary and financial stability by taking into account both the possible existence, assessment and the prospective impact of asset-price disequilibria and their international channels of transmission. In particular, a multilateral exercise that focuses also on capital flows and their nature could help in assessing asset-price developments and eventually help central banks to set monetary policy in a manner that incorporates the risk of a bubble building up and eventually bursting in the medium term.

Finally, a better cooperation in terms of liquidity provision is also needed. A first example of successful cooperation comes from the auctions of US dollar liquidity jointly organised by the Federal Reserve, the ECB and the BNS since the start of the turmoil in mid 2007. Its generalisation might be envisaged to deal with other crises in the future. Moreover, international institutions must better understand the dynamics of liquidity crises and be able to advise countries on their best strategies.

REFERENCES

Adrian, T., and H. S. Shin (2008). *Liquidity and Leverage*, FRB New York staff report No. 328 (May), Federal Reserve Bank New York.

Bayoumi, T., and A. Swinston (2007). *The Ties that Bind: Measuring International Bond Spillovers Using Inflation-Indexed Bond Yields*, IMF working paper No. 128 (June).

---

[18] Here, international 'cooperation' indicates a more-or-less formal framework which facilitates the exchange of information among policy makers and the sharing of views about the nature and the consequences of particular international policy considerations. The term 'cooperation' does not signify any act of various policy authorities that would imply a common decision to have an immediate consequence on their respective policy instruments.

Benati, L. (2007). 'The time-varying Phillips correlation', *Journal of Money, Credit and Banking*, 39(5), 1275–83.

Bernanke, B. S. (2007). 'Globalisation and monetary policy', remarks at the Fourth Economic Summit, Stanford Institute for Economic Policy Research, Stanford, California, March.

Blanchard, J. O., and J. Gali (2007). *The Macroeconomic Effects of Oil Price Shocks: Why Are the 2000s So Different from the 1970s?*, NBER working paper series No. 13368 (September).

Blanchard, J. O., and J. Simon (2001). 'The long and large decline in U.S. output volatility', *Brookings Papers on Economic Activity*, 1, 135–64.

Brender, A., and F. Pisani (2007). *Global Imbalances. Is the World Economy Really at Risk?*, Dexia SA, Belgium British Bankers Association (2006). Credit Derivatives report.

Browne, F., and D. Cronin (2007). *Commodity Prices, Money and Inflation*, ECB working paper No. 738 (March).

Ciccarelli, M., and B. Mojon (2005). *Global Inflation*, ECB working paper No. 537 (October).

Christiano, L., C. Ilut, R. Motto, and M. Rostagno (2008). *Monetary Policy and Stock Market Boom-Bust Cycles*, ECB working papers No. 955 (October).

De Santis, R., C. A. Favero, and B. Roffia (2008). *Euro Area Money Demand and International Portfolio Allocation: a Contribution to Assessing Risks to Price Stability*, ECB working paper No. 926 (August).

ECB (2006). 'Effects of the rising trade integration of low-cost countries on euro area import prices', *ECB Monthly Bulletin*, August 2006, Box 6, 56–7.

Ehrmann, M., and M. Fratzscher (2006). *Global Financial Transmission of Monetary Policy Shocks*, ECB working paper No. 616 (April).

Ehrmann, M., M. Fratzscher, and R. Rigobon (2005). *Stocks, Bonds, Money Markets, and Exchange Rates: Measuring International Financial Transmission*, NBER working paper No.11166 (March).

ESF (2008). *ESF Securitazion Data Report*, 1Q:2008.

Gali, J., and T. Monacelli (2005). 'Monetary policy and exchange rate volatility in a small open economy', *Review of Economic Studies*, 72(3), 707–34.

Greenspan, A. (2003). 'Global finance: is it slowing?', speech delivered (via satellite) at the International Symposium on *Monetary Policy, Economic Cycle, and Financial Dynamics* hosted by the Banque de France, Paris, March.

Grubel, H. G. (1968). 'Internationally diversified portfolios', *American Economic Review*, 58, 1299–314.

IMF (2007). *Annual Report on Exchange Agreement and Exchange Restrictions*, Washington, DC: IMF.

International Swap and Derivatives Association (2008). *Summaries of Market Survey Results*, 1H2008 (at www.isda.org/).

Lane, P. R., and G. M. Milesi-Ferretti (2007). 'The external wealth of nations mark II: revised and extended estimates of foreign assets and liabilities, 1970–2004', *Journal of International Economics*, 73(2), 223–50.

(2008). 'The drivers of financial globalisation', *American Economic Review*, 98(2), 327–32.

Loisel, O., A. Pommeret, and F. Portier (2007). 'Monetary policy and herd behaviour in new-tech investment', paper presented at the conference *Banking and Asset Markets: Developments, Risks and Policy Issues*, hosted by CEPR-Fondation Banque de France, 29–30 November, Paris.

Markowitz, H. (1952). 'Portfolio selection', *Journal of Finance*, 7(1), 77–91.

McConnell, M., and G. Perez-Quiros (2000). 'Output fluctuations in the United States: what has changed since the early 1980s?', *American Economic Review*, 90, 1464–76.

Moutot, P., and G. Vitale (2009). *Monetary Policy Strategy in a Global Environment*, ECB occasional paper No. 106.

Pétursson, T. G. (2000). 'Exchange rate or inflation targeting in monetary policy?', *Monetary Bulletin*, Central Bank of Iceland, 2(1), February, 36–45.

(2004). 'Formulation of inflation targeting around the world', in *Monetary Bulletin, Central Bank of Iceland*, 6(1), March, 57–84.

Poloni, P., and J. Reynaud (2008). 'How to measure credit risk transfer in the EU', paper presented at the Fourth IFC Conference on *Measuring Financial Innovation and Its Impact*, Basel, 26–27 August.

Rajan, R. G. (2006a). 'Has finance made the world riskier?', *European Financial Management*, 12(4), 499–533.

(2006b). 'Monetary policy and incentives', address at the conference on *Central Banks in the 21st Century* hosted by the Central Bank of Spain, 8 June, Madrid.

Rogoff, K. (2006). 'Impact of globalisation on monetary policy', paper presented at the Symposium on *The New Economic Geography: Effects and Policy Implications*, Jackson Hole, August.

Rüffer, R., and L. Stracca (2006). *What is Global Excess Liquidity and Does It Matter?*, ECB working paper No. 696 (November).

Solnik, B. H. (1974). 'Why not diversify internationally rather than domestically?', *Financial Analyst Journal*, 30, 91–135.

Taylor, John B. (2008). 'The impact of globalisation on monetary policy', paper presented at the Symposium on *Globalisation, Inflation and Monetary Policy*, hosted by the Banque de France, March, Paris.

Viñals, J. (2000). 'Monetary policy issues in a low inflation environment', paper presented for the first Central Banking Conference on *Why price stability?* hosted by the European Central Bank, 2–3 November, Frankfurt.

Winters, C. (2008). *The Carry Trade, Portfolio Diversification and the Adjustment of the Japanese Yen*, Bank of Canada discussion papers No.2/2008.

Woodford, M. (2007). 'Globalisation and monetary policy', paper prepared for the NBER conference on the *International Dimensions of Monetary Policy*, 11–13 June, Girona, Spain.

9   Monetary policy in a global economy: past and future research challenges

John B. Taylor

In these brief remarks I want to discuss the role of economic research in dealing with the enormous economic policy challenges of globalisation. I believe we can learn much by reviewing how researchers in the past dealt with difficult policy problems and how they successfully solved them.

Let me start out by recalling the challenges that policy makers, and especially central bankers, faced in the wake of the demise of the Bretton Woods system in the 1970s. High and volatile inflation, frequent recessions and very volatile output were plaguing the USA and most other industrial countries. For example, US inflation hit 12 per cent in 1975, fell to 5 per cent in 1977 and then increased to 15 per cent in 1979. The standard deviation of real GDP growth was large at 2.8 per cent in the United States and 2.7 per cent on average in the G7. Many observers were criticising the performance of policy makers.

However, research in monetary economics rose to the challenge, forcefully arguing that inflation stabilisation should be the paramount concern of monetary policy and deriving optimal monetary policy rules in models putting rational expectations and the Lucas critique at their core for the first time, but without assuming away real effects of money.

The consequences of this dramatic shift in the theory apparently led to shifts in the practice of monetary policy; the resulting change in economic performance was momentous. Inflation decreased and became a lot more stable and the standard deviation of real GDP growth was cut in half in G7 countries. The US economy experienced only two recessions in the twenty-five years from 1982 to 2007. And those two were short and mild by historical comparison. Although it is difficult to prove that this 'Great Moderation' was due to better monetary policy, I think the temporal correlation is striking and strongly suggestive of a causal link.

Written version of keynote address presented at the Conference on Globalisation and the Macroeconomy, European Central Bank, 24 July 2007.

Similar daunting challenges were posed for economic policy making by the emergence of financial and currency crises in emerging market economies starting around 1995 with the Mexican financial crisis. Soon there were crises in much of Latin America, in South East Asia and in Russia. Once again researchers in many quarters focused on the problem, and their research diagnosis can be summarised as follows: exchange-rate pegs were inconsistent with macropolicies in many emerging market countries; there was too much currency mismatch as a result of government and private sector borrowing in foreign currencies; foreign exchange reserves were too low; and the responses by the official sector, largely the IMF, were too unpredictable and actually may have created rather than contained contagion of crises from one country to another. Fortunately this research was applied, and we saw better policy making, apparently underpinned by these research insights. The IMF introduced a new exceptional access framework (EAF) which provided guidance or rules for when it would intervene. And countries increased their foreign exchange reserves, moved to more flexible exchange rates, and reduced the currency mismatch.

As with the example of the Great Moderation, this change in policy led to a momentous improvement in performance. The crises in the emerging markets ended in 2002, completing what we therefore might call the eight-year financial crisis in emerging markets. Risk spreads on emerging market debt came down sharply.

Researchers and policy makers can congratulate themselves on these achievements, but it is important that they learn from the connection between the research and the policy, and not become complacent in preventing a return to the bad old recession-prone and crisis-prone world. Although some of the challenges may appear to be even more daunting than these past challenges, research can be quite valuable in helping to address them successfully. You can see this by examining a couple of possible upcoming challenges: the role of exchange rates and international coordination in the design of policy rules, and the development of sound principles for currency intervention, diplomacy and the assignment of exchange-rate policy responsibilities within governments.[1]

Concerning the role of international coordination in the design of monetary policy rules, there are several changes, both theoretical and empirical, that could potentially lead to different recommendations. Flatter Phillips curves and reduced exchange-rate pass-through could

---

[1] Note: these examples are given from the vantage point of July 2007 and thus before the flare-up of the financial crisis in August 2007 when many more challenges started arising.

indicate the need to revise current policy practice, for instance by paying more attention to exchange-rate developments. However, the answer from research on this issue has been mixed so far. For instance, Chapter 5 in this volume by Kumhof, Laxton and Naknoi argues that central banks should pay attention to the real exchange rate when setting interest rates. In contrast, ECB research has reached a quite different conclusion on the need for monetary policy coordination.[2]

In any case, exchange rates do appear in many estimated policy rules. A more important but closely related empirical finding is that interest-rate decisions at one central bank influence interest-rate decisions at other central banks. A likely reason for central banks to follow each other in this way is to prevent exchange-rate fluctuations. This finding has very important policy implications. For example, if you include the US federal funds rate in a regression explaining the ECB interest rate, it has a significant effect in the 2000–2006 period. This means that if the policy rate is too low in the United States – as it appears to have been during the 2002–2004 period – then the policy rate in Europe will also be too low. Thus policy errors can spill over to other countries; a poor local crisis can be turned into a global crisis. This is obviously a potential problem worth pursuing by researchers.

A second issue revolves around the development of principles for currency intervention and currency diplomacy. Whether or not the exchange rate appears in policy rules, there is still the open question of whether intervention could and should be used as an independent policy instrument. In my view, the G7 countries are right in avoiding interventions in currency markets in recent years, both actual and verbal, as their efficacy is questionable. The fact that Japan stopped intervening in March 2004 is a big and welcome break with the past.

However, other countries, especially China, have continued to intervene, leading to very large increases in foreign exchange reserves in recent years. This requires that countries develop an exchange-rate diplomacy strategy as they engage with China. Such a strategy must be multilateral and involve all the interested parties, as forcefully shown by the example of how the G7 coordinated their response to dealing with the Chinese yuan undervaluation. This strategy has led to a 9.4 per cent appreciation against the US dollar since the summer of 2005.

In this light, the 'assignment problem' becomes particularly relevant, namely deciding whether the finance ministry or the central

---

[2] See Günter Coenen, Giovanni Lombardo, Frank Smets and Roland Straub (2007) *International Transmission and Monetary Policy Cooperation*, ECB working paper No. 858.

bank should be ultimately in charge of the currency. Despite the fact that a case in favour of the latter could be made given the close link between the exchange rate and the interest rate, the main monetary policy instrument, I believe there are distinct advantages in assigning currency responsibilities to finance ministries. For example, the close interactions with diplomatic responsibilities linked to other non-monetary policies, like trade and fiscal policy, argue for a role for finance ministries concerning the exchange-rate regime of the country or of other countries.

In conclusion, I want to stress the key lesson to be learnt from the experience with past challenges. The focus of monetary and financial research on practical policy objectives was essential for the research to help monetary policy meet past challenges of globalisation. This helped to increase price and output stability. Research also helped to halt the emerging market financial crises and contagion of the 1990s. If this proactive focus on practical issues is maintained, there is no reason to believe that monetary theory and research cannot help us meet the current challenges we are facing and future challenges of globalisation as well.

Index

Printed in the United States
by Baker & Taylor Publisher Services